The Undaunted Psychologist

ADVENTURES IN RESEARCH

The Undaunted Psychologist

ADVENTURES IN RESEARCH

❖

EDITED BY

Gary G. Brannigan
Matthew R. Merrens

Temple University Press
Philadelphia

Temple University Press, Philadelphia 19122

ISBN 1-56639-015-X

Library of Congress Cataloging-in-Publication Data

The Undaunted psychologist: adventures in research / edited by
Gary G. Brannigan and Matthew R. Merrens.
    p.   cm.
  ISBN 1-56639-015-X (cloth)
  1. Psychology—Research—Case studies.   I. Brannigan, Gary.
II. Merrens, Matthew R.
BF76.5.U45   1993   92-16793
150'.72—dc20

About the Editors

❖

Gary G. Brannigan (Ph.D., University of Delaware) is Professor of Psychology at SUNY—Plattsburgh and a Fellow of the Society for Personality Assessment. His research is primarily on psychological assessment and therapy with children. He has served as director of the Psychological Services Clinic at SUNY—Plattsburgh and is currently a consultant to the Early Education Program. He is also serving on the editorial boards of three journals. Dr. Brannigan has published numerous articles, chapters, and books, including (with A. Tolor) *Research and Clinical Applications of the Bender Gestalt Test* and (with N. Brunner) *The Modified Version of the Bender Gestalt Test.* He is an avid sports fan who has coached and coordinated youth baseball and basketball. He also enjoys music, art, and collectibles, such as toy trains and baseball cards.

Matthew R. Merrens (Ph.D., University of Montana) is currently Chair and Associate Professor of Psychology at SUNY—Plattsburgh. He has published in the areas of personality assessment and behavior modification. He has served as coordinator of a large, innovative introductory psychology course and has written several general psychology handbooks. Dr. Merrens was a recipient of the State University Chancellor's Award for Excellence in Teaching. He and his family enjoy biking, hiking in the Adirondacks, and swimming with their golden retriever, Kodiak, in Lake Champlain.

To my wife, Linda, and my sons, Marc and Michael
GGB

For Roberta, Jennifer, Ed, Peg, Rebecca, and Daryl
MRM

Contents

———— ❖ ————

Preface

———— ❖ ————

The impetus for this book came from our frustration with current textbooks that, albeit unintentionally, lead students to believe that research is a dry, humorless activity, devoid of adventure and fun. It is our desire to show students what psychological research is like, and to share with them the excitement and challenges that are characteristic of the process.

This volume recounts the research adventures of fifteen psychologists. We asked the contributors to tell how they encountered research situations that were especially interesting, unique and/or problematic, and that demanded some creative form of resolution or understanding. In addition to relating their struggles with research questions, contributors were asked to write in a personal, narrative style that would provide genuine insight into the psychological research process. Further, we asked them to communicate in a manner that would be understandable and enjoyable for a nonprofessional audience. Their stories reflect a wide range of research topics that correspond to the essential chapters in most introductory psychology textbooks: development, biopsychology, sensation and perception, learning, memory, language, intelligence, motivation, consciousness, personality, psychopathology, psychotherapy, and social psychology.

While this book is targeted for the initiate to the study of psychological science, there are lessons to be learned for all of us. As Robert Baker noted in his book *Psychology in the Wry*, "if we are to succeed in establishing a true science of human behavior, we must first take a long, hard, critical look at our own behavior."

Gary G. Brannigan
Matthew R. Merrens

Acknowledgments

◆

This book reflects the efforts of fifteen "undaunted" researchers who took the time to write chapters so that students of all ages can understand and appreciate the process of psychological science. We wish to express our appreciation and thanks for the quality of their work.

The reviewers of this book deserve high praise for their many helpful remarks and recommendations that further served to make each chapter more understandable for our readers. We thank Charles Blaich, Wabash College; Eugene Doughtie, University of Houston; Mary Alice Gordon, Southern Methodist University; Rosemary Hornack, Meredith College; Karl Scheibe, Wesleyan University; Benjamin Wallace, Cleveland State University; Paul Wellman, Texas A & M University; Drew Westen, Harvard Medical School; and Jeremy Wolfe, Massachusetts Institute of Technology.

We are very grateful to the State University of New York—Plattsburgh, for providing an ongoing scholarly and supportive atmosphere in which the development of teaching and instructional materials is highly valued. We also appreciate the recommendations and suggestions provided by our colleagues, specifically Philip DeVita, Jeanne Ryan, Naomi McCormick, and Leon Harris.

We also wish to recognize the psychology students at Plattsburgh who served as readers. Their advice and counsel were invaluable and certainly helped to make this book more readable and student-focused.

This book would never be more than a pile of handwritten scratchings on legal pads were it not for the unwavering dedication of our secretary, Judy Dashnaw. Judy was not only instrumental in word processing the text, but also contributed her vast editorial background in making this project a reality.

Last, we would like to thank our wives, Linda Brannigan and Roberta Merrens, for their reading and rereading of drafts, their editorial advice, and most of all their wisdom and support.

Gary G. Brannigan
Matthew R. Merrens

Introduction

❖

The stories in this book are about people. They are also about ideas. But, most important, the stories tell how people get ideas and what they do with those ideas.

The people in the stories are scientists. They are scientists engaged in the study of behavior—psychology.

During the course of their lives these psychologists have developed a curiosity about the world and a desire to understand what is going on around them. This orientation is not generally learned from textbooks, but rather from people, as the following story about Richard Feynman the Nobel prize–winning scientist reveals.

We used to go to the Catskill Mountains, a place where people from New York City would go in the summer. The fathers would all return to New York to work during the week, and come back only for the weekend. On weekends, my father would take me for walks in the woods and he'd tell me about interesting things that were going on in the woods. When the other mothers saw this, they . . . wanted my father to take all the kids, but he didn't want to because he had a special relationship with me. So it ended up that the other fathers had to take their children for walks the next weekend.

The next Monday, when the fathers were all back at work, we kids were playing in a field. One kid says to me, "See that bird? What kind of bird is that?"

I said, "I haven't the slightest idea what kind of a bird it is."

He says, "It's a brown-throated thrush. Your father doesn't teach you anything!"

But it was the opposite. He had already taught me: "See that bird?" [my father] says. "It's a Spencer's warbler." (I knew he didn't know the real name.) "Well, in Italian, it's a *Chutto Lapittida*. In Portuguese, it's a *Bom da Peida*. In Chinese, it's a

Chung-long-tah, and in Japanese, it's a *Katano Tekeda.* You can know the name of that bird in all the languages of the world, but when you're finished, you'll know absolutely nothing whatever about the bird. You'll only know about humans in different places, and what they call the bird. So let's look at the bird and see what it's *doing*—that's what counts." (I learned very early the difference between knowing the name of something and knowing something.) He said, "For example, look: the bird pecks at its feathers all the time. See it walking around, pecking at its feathers?"

"Yeah."

He says, "Why do you think birds peck at their feathers?"

I said, "Well, maybe they mess up their feathers when they fly, so they're pecking them in order to straighten them out."

"All right," he says. "If that were the case, then they would peck a lot just after they've been flying. Then, after they've been on the ground a while, they wouldn't peck so much any more—you know what I mean?"

"Yeah."

He says, "Let's look and see if they peck more just after they land."

It wasn't hard to tell: there was not much difference between the birds that had been walking around a bit and those that had just landed. So I said, "I give up. Why does a bird peck at its feathers?"

"Because there are lice bothering it," he says. "The lice eat flakes of protein that come off its feathers."

He continued, "Each louse has some waxy stuff on its legs, and little mites eat that. The mites don't digest it perfectly, so they emit from their rear ends a sugar-like material, in which bacteria grow."

Finally he says, "So you see, everywhere there's a source of food, there's *some* form of life that finds it."

Now, I knew that it may not have been exactly a louse, that it might not be exactly true that the louse's legs have mites. That story was probably incorrect in *detail,* but what he was telling me was right in *principle.*

That's the way I was educated by my father, with those kinds of examples and discussions: no pressure—just lovely, interesting discussions. It has motivated me for the rest of my life, and makes me interested in *all* the sciences. (It just happens I do physics better.)

I've been caught, so to speak—like someone who was given something wonderful when he was a child, and he's always looking for it again. I'm always looking, like a child, for the wonders I know I'm going to find—maybe not every time, but every once in a while.

Most of us have not been fortunate enough to have a parent who was truly capable of teaching us about the wonders of the world. But this does not mean that we cannot learn.

As Richard Feynman learned from his father and as apprentices learn from artisans, we can learn about psychology by sharing the research experiences of fifteen eminent psychologists. We will see that for these psychologists, all the world is truly a stage. They conduct their work in such diverse settings as drugstores, courthouses, street corners, and hospitals, and in such exotic locations as the beaches of Walney Island, England, and the mountains of Africa. They represent many areas of psychology and will show us how neurosurgery is conducted and brain function examined, how personality-assessment instruments are devised, how psychotherapeutic techniques are developed, how military personnel are trained, how premature infants are helped to thrive, and much, much more. Enjoy the adventures!

The Undaunted Psychologist

ADVENTURES IN RESEARCH

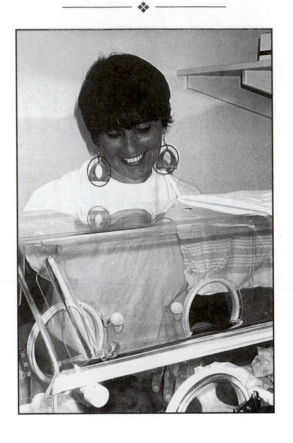

*T*IFFANY **M.** FIELD *(Ph.D., University of Massachusetts) is currently Professor of Psychology, Pediatrics, and Psychiatry at the University of Miami Medical School. She has published widely in the fields of infants born at risk, effects of maternal depression, and, more generally, the social and emotional development of children. She has edited a number of volumes in these areas along with a series titled* Stress and Coping, *and has just written a book titled* Infancy. *She has a Research Scientist Award from the National Institute of Mental Health, and so she is free to conduct research full-time. When she is not busy directing the Touch Research Institute and a related nursery school, she spends time in jazz ballet with her teenage daughter or snorkeling in some exotic waters with her significant other.*

1

The Therapeutic Effects of Touch

❖

I t seems to me that researchers study the things they do for a few very simple reasons. First, they are interested in the question. By definition, researchers are very curious creatures. If they were not researchers they would probably be detectives. Second, their research follows personal concerns. If you conducted a survey among researchers you would find that nine out of ten are personally or socially concerned about the subject they are studying. Thus, the phrase "research is me-search" appropriately describes this phenomenon. Finally, the zeitgeist, or the social, political, and, most particularly, the economic climate, dictates much of what we study. Currently, for example, AIDS and cocaine research occupy more medical researchers' time than any other topics. It is not just coincidental that these areas also receive the lion's share of research spending in several of the National Institutes of Health, the government agencies that provide the largest amount of grant monies. There is, thus, a bandwagon phenomenon of researchers switching areas of interest as the problems and the available monies of the times shift. Researchers are not the only professionals whose specialties are guided by economics. But, they did not become researchers for economic reasons, since they are not paid for their investigatory work in the same sense that lawyers are paid for their investigations. Most will tell you (I am beginning to sound like a social psychologist) that they came to be researchers because research is fun, interesting, challenging, and affords them a relatively independent lifestyle. Instead of punching a time clock, we work 16 hours a day, 7 days a week, and we never retire. These general remarks (based on an informal survey of 13 of my colleagues) helped me (and perhaps the other 13) understand the various and sundry routes my research has taken.

3

RESEARCH AS ME-SEARCH

I will tell you only the details that seem to fit with the general puzzle. When I was growing up, I wanted to be three different people: Albert Schweitzer, Margaret Mead, and Eleanor Roosevelt. I decided to write to them to find out which one of them I "really wanted to be." They all wrote back. Eleanor Roosevelt said that it was "not much fun being the first lady," and Margaret Mead wrote that she was "very lonely in the field." Albert Schweitzer was the only one who didn't complain. So, I turned to medicine. I tried medicine long enough to learn how to massage patients. (Back in the 1960s that was actually part of the curriculum.) Not liking the responsibility of dying patients, I moved to occupational therapy, working mostly with quadriplegic and paraplegic patients. Finding that depressing, I switched to psychiatry. Following training in psychotherapy, I spent much of my time conducting group therapy with adolescent and adult psychiatric patients. Unhappy with the fact that we did not know what we were doing, why we were doing what we were doing, or whether or not what we were doing was really working with these patients, I left on a two-year sailing trip. Sailing was a soul-searching activity that ultimately returned me to graduate school to become a researcher. Never did I think that those early experiences with massage and adolescent psychiatric patients would emerge later in my research career.

While I was a graduate student (a fairly old one, since I had already worked some 10 years), I became pregnant. However, I lost my first baby during delivery to postmaturity syndrome. This is a syndrome that results from the placenta's efficiency peaking just prior to term age (40 weeks gestation) due to gradual calcification of the placental tissue. Nutrients and oxygen cannot be as efficiently transported to the fetus, and the fetus goes into distress. Because of wide individual variability in the calcification process, some women can carry a baby two to four weeks beyond due date, while others experience a stillbirth. Instead of suing my obstetrician-gynecologist, who should have referred me to a surgeon for a caesarean section when my labor did not progress, I conducted my first research on postmaturity syndrome, published the paper, and sent it to the obstetrician-gynecologist to enlighten him about the origin of his error.

Following a stillbirth, most mothers (and fathers) are advised to have another child immediately. My second child was born prematurely by design (and by caesarean section) in order to avoid another potential stillbirth. With a grant from the state of Massachusetts I proceeded to conduct a longitudinal study of postterm babies with postmaturity syndrome and preterm babies with respiratory-distress syndrome. My daughter is now 15 years old (going on 27) and I have been studying premature infants for the same 15 years.

REDUCING STRESS IN PRETERM INFANTS

A tour through any neonatal intensive-care unit will strike you with how stressful life must be for these little creatures who are born too soon and too small. Outside the womb they are bombarded with excessive light and sound. Unfortunately, the sound levels inside their incubators approximate the decibel level of a diesel bus departing from a busy street corner. Light, too, is a problem that contributes to visual defects. Mostly, although paradoxically, they suffer the greatest pain from the very procedures that are essential to sustaining their lives. As Jerold Lucey (a famous neonatologist) has noted, "The prematurely born infant emerges into a hectic, cold, noisy and bright environment filled with mysterious equipment and peopled by masked strangers who try to help. Almost everything done to or for the infant is painful, and that pain can certainly be felt, although it cannot be communicated. The infant who must be tube-fed cannot cry and is not fed by mouth for weeks. His or her feet are slashed periodically for blood samples. The infant's respirator roars away night and day keeping his or her lungs inflated and sustaining life—but at what price?"

After observing these stressed-out preemies for a number of years, my colleagues and I began to explore various ways to reduce this stress. Our first consideration was how we could intervene in a cost-effective manner, since we had no money. For example, we thought of ways of adapting procedures that were already in place and of using volunteer sources of labor. Our second consideration was how we might exploit the coping skills of the newborn. Since we knew that the fetus could suck his or her thumb rather vigorously, we thought that the newborn might use sucking as a way of alleviating stress and calming himself or herself. So, the first way we attempted to reduce stress involved the very simple procedure of giving the infant a pacifier. We assumed that if infants were sucking on pacifiers they would probably cry less, because sucking and crying are somewhat incompatible. Thus, we gave pacifiers to babies when they were receiving such invasive procedures as heelsticks. Heelsticks are just what they sound like, heel punctures to draw blood to monitor various chemicals. In a simple study, we gave one group of preemies pacifiers during heelsticks, while another group of babies did not receive pacifiers during this procedure. As we had predicted, the group that received the pacifiers cried less, showed slower respiration, and slower heart rate, suggesting that they were less physiologically disorganized by the heelstick procedure because they were sucking on a pacifier.

In another study we gave pacifiers to babies who were being tube fed. Babies are often tube-fed when they are premature because people think that they are not sufficiently developed to suck and swallow without choking. Thus they are fed through a tube that is often passed through the nose or through the throat region. This, too, can be a stressful procedure and one we thought could be alleviated by sucking. In this study there were additional side benefits for those infants who received the pacifier during tube feeding. The pacifier infants were weaned from tube feeding sooner, they were easier to bottle feed, they gained more weight per day and they were discharged several days earlier, for a hospital-cost savings of approximately $4,000/per child. The last finding, the cost savings, was the most applauded result and the one we assumed would convince the neonatology community that all babies should receive pacifiers during these procedures. However, in many nurseries the pacifier was simply taped to a blanket roll, often out of reach of the infant. In addition, most of the neonatology community remained unimpressed by our findings because there was no obvious underlying mechanism for why sucking on a nipple during a tube feeding should lead to significant weight gain. This was disappointing to us because we felt that the weight gain and the hospital-cost savings in themselves warranted the adoption of this soothing procedure. Nevertheless, we persevered and assessed a number of potential mechanisms, including the possibility that the infants were saving energy (calories) by being less active. However, all our attempts to resolve this issue proved futile and we became extremely frustrated. Fortunately, in another laboratory, neonatalogist Judy Bernbaum conducted the study that offered an underlying mechanism. She simply included carmine dye in the formula so that the transit time of the fluid could be traced as it went through the digestive system. She was able to show that preemies who were given the opportunity to suck on a pacifier showed more rapid transit time of the formula (and the carmine dye). Identifying the underlying mechanism for the sucking–weight-gain relationship significantly contributed to a more widespread adoption of this procedure. The preemie had demonstrated how his or her own sucking activity could reduce stress.

MASSAGING PRETERM INFANTS

Meantime, in a neonatal intensive-care unit in another part of the country, a research nurse named Susan Jay was showing that nursing personnel could also reduce stress by "laying hands" on the infant. She simply laid her hands on the abdomen of each infant for 12 minutes a day for 12 days and was able to document a decreased need for oxygen as well as reduction in several stress behaviors such as clenched fists, grimacing, and startles. We decided to take this procedure a step further and provide the infants with a body massage. We called this treatment tactile-kinesthetic stimulation for fear that a term such as massage might be dismissed as something that occurred only in California. We were also very conscientious about demonstrating that this was a safe procedure. Jerold Lucey (the neonatologist who noted the horrible plight of the preemie) had published a paper with his colleagues suggesting that any handling was disorganizing for the preemie. They used a measure called $TcPO_2$ (oxygen tension) to show that even simple handling decreased the levels of oxygen in the blood. This led to a universally accepted practice called "minimal touch," meaning, just as it sounds, that preemies should be touched only at a minimum, and only during limited times. Unfortunately, people generalized this to mean that even "tender loving touch" might be disorganizing.

Lucey, in his talks, mentioned anecdotal data showing that "tender loving touch" actually increased instead of decreased blood-oxygen levels, but, as he said, he was leaving the collection of those data to our team. So, one of the first things we did was measure blood oxygen or $TcPO_2$ level changes during massage in comparison with changes in oxygen tension following an invasive procedure (e.g., the heelstick). Fortunately, it turned out that the change in $TcPO_2$ accompanying massage was negligible, while the decrease following the heelstick was significant.

Feeling safe to proceed, we then randomly assigned some babies to a group that would receive massage and others to a group that would not receive massage. The massage group received 45 minutes of massage a day for a 10-day period in 15-minute sessions at the beginning of each of three consecutive hours. The massage was administered in three 5-minute segments: the first, stroking in the prone position; the second, passive movements of the limbs in a supine position; and the third a repeat of the first. The massage strokes were carefully timed so that they would be the same for all infants. For the massage part of the procedure we stroked the head, the neck, the shoulders, the arms, the backs, and the legs. The infants did not appear to enjoy being massaged on the chest or abdomen region, probably because they had learned a conditioned association between being touched in those parts and invasive procedures, which typically occur in those regions. Another important factor was applying pressure. The massage for babies should be comparable to a Swedish massage for adults in which some pressure is applied for each stroke. This was particularly important because we noted that in some studies where babies had been massaged there was no weight gain while in other studies there was weight gain. It appeared that in those studies where no weight gain occurred, the stroking was very light (probably because the investigators considered, rightly so, that preemies are fragile). Light stroking, however, appears to be aversive to preemies, as if they experience it as a tickle stimulus. Thus, pressure is extremely important.

Following the 10-day period we noted significantly fewer stress

behaviors in the massaged babies, including less mouthing, facial grimacing, and fist clenching. We also noted that they scored better on the
Brazelton Newborn Behavior Assessment Scale, including better scores
on the habituation (a primitive form of learning), orientation (responses
to social stimulation), motor behaviors, and range of state behaviors (the
infant's ability to calm itself). The infants also gained 47 percent more
weight than those infants who did not receive massage, even though
they did not consume any more formula. Thus, the obvious explanation
for greater weight gain, i.e., greater formula intake, was eliminated as a
possible explanation from the start. The second possible explanation, i.e.,
saving calories by being less active, was also eliminated. The infants,
instead of being sleepy and more restful (as typically occurs to adults following massage), were awake more often and were more active (based
on our time-lapse–videotape sleep observations).

We looked in the literature for other possible explanations and stumbled upon some rat research suggesting that if you exercise a rat, the rat
will gain weight even though it is not consuming more food. Thus, for
the moment we speculated that our massage was causing an increase in
weight gain by an increase in metabolic efficiency. This interpretation,
however, was a significant leap from these data. Surprisingly, our follow-up assessment at eight months of age indicated that these infants
still had a weight advantage and, perhaps more surprising, they were
showing an advantage on infant mental and motor skills. Of course we
would not suggest that these data at eight months are a direct result of
the massage per se. Instead, we would speculate that the infants, by
virtue of becoming more like "Gerber babies," were more fun for their
parents, and their parents in turn probably played with them more and
provided more stimulation, which more directly contributed to their better development.

Fortunately, serendipity had come our way early in the course of our
studies. Dr. Saul Schanberg (a pediatrician/pharmacologist/animal
researcher) and I happened to be on the National Institute of Mental
Health small-grant study section. This study section met so frequently
that we became a rather intimate group of collaborators. Saul had been
studying the mother rat and her rat pups in an early-separation
paradigm (where pups are separated from their mothers), attempting to
determine why the mother is critical to growth function in the offspring.
One of his pet variables was ODC (ornithine decarboxylase), which is a
fancy label for an element in protein synthesis. In his studies he demonstrated that the simple removal of the mother from the rat pups led to
dramatic decreases in ODC in the heart, liver, and brain—in fact, in all
parts of the brain (cerebellum, brain stem, and cortex)—and that the rat
pups failed to thrive. The question then became "What is it that the
mother provides that is missing when she is removed from the rat
pups?" Well, as is so often the case, a young graduate student discovered

the answer. In his position as the animal caregiver, he was forced to be nocturnal with the nocturnal rats and sufficiently entertain himself to remain awake. This student observed, like other rat researchers before him, that mother rats do lots of things for their pups, such as carry them around, pinch their tails and tongue-lick them (they in fact tongue-lick their pups to induce elimination). As in a "Eureka, I got it" experience, he hastened to buy a paintbrush, dip it in water, and rigorously stroke the rat pups in a simulation of tongue-licking. This stimulation effectively returned the ODC levels to normal in the brain, heart, and liver. The other maternal behaviors did not serve the same function.

Schanberg and his colleagues tried several types of stimulation to show that it was only the specific effects of rigorous tongue-licking (or paintbrush-licking) that specifically led to a return to normal functioning. He showed, for example, that vestibular (spinning) stimulation did not have the same effect, nor did kinesthetic (moving the limbs) stimulation. In the case of vestibular stimulation, he spun rat pups around on a merry-go-round–like apparatus, and, in the case of kinesthetic stimulation, he passively moved the rat paws just as we had passively moved the baby's lower and upper limbs in flexion and extension during our massage treatment. By measuring levels of ODC, growth-hormone levels and cortisol levels, he was able to show that only the heavy stroking (tongue-licking, massage-like stimulation) was able to return the levels to normal.

These data inspired us to replicate our study with preemies, but this time we took under-the-skin measures such as the growth-hormone and cortisol levels that had been measured by Schanberg and his associates. In this replication we were able to document, once again, that the massaged babies gained more weight, performed better on the Brazelton Newborn Scale, and were discharged earlier at a significant hospital-cost savings. One new finding in this study was that they engaged in less-active sleep, again as evidenced on the time-lapse videotapes. This was interesting to us because a group of investigators had by now demonstrated that the only variable at the newborn stage that predicted 12-year IQ was active sleep (a less-mature form of sleep, unlike deep or quiet sleep); more active sleep at the newborn period was related to lower IQ scores. In our study, the massage group engaged in less active sleep (another finding in a positive direction). When we examined the levels of cortisol and growth hormone we noted no differences between the treatment and the control groups. Surprisingly though, the massage group showed higher levels of catecholamine activity, and the increased release of gastrointestinal hormones (e.g., gastrin and insulin) that contribute to food absorption. It became conceivable to us that the same kind of mechanism was underlying our repeated observations of massage leading to weight gain, and that this may be the missing puzzle piece we've been looking for.

In the interim, we have begun to massage other groups of babies. Terrible epidemics are evident in neonatal intensive-care units around the world, including cocaine exposure during pregnancy and AIDS in infants. Thus we have extended our massage treatment to cocaine babies with very much the same effects.

In the case of the AIDS infant, of course, the important question is whether massage can alter immune function. Data from the laboratory of Chris Coe suggest that the immune function in monkeys can be facilitated by tactile stimulation. In addition, we now have data showing that massage increases serotonin levels and natural killer-cell activity in HIV-positive men, which suggests that the immune system is positively affected by massage.

Just as preemies are rarely touched, child and adolescent psychiatric patients are almost never touched during their often lengthy stays on psychiatric units. Just as the preemie's agenda in the hospital is to gain weight, the child and adolescent psychiatric patients' agenda is to get their anxiety levels under control and to return to normal function. Data on relaxation therapy suggest that child and adolescent psychiatric patients can be helped to relax and reduce their anxiety levels. Massage is considered a form of relaxation therapy. Thus, as we tried massage with this population, we anticipated significant reductions in anxiety. We found that simply giving a 30-minute back massage led to decreases in self-reported anxiety, as well as self-reported depression. In addition, the child and adolescent psychiatric patients showed an immediate increase in pleasant emotions and a decrease in behavioral anxiety and fidgeting. As might be expected, they also showed a decrease in activity level, along with a decrease in pulse and cortisol levels. These data are perhaps not surprising given that there is a significant reduction in activity necessitated by lying still for the massage. These children and adolescents were receiving back massages, which meant that they were lying on their stomachs and necessarily inactive. However, comparisons between day 1 and day 5 of the massage period (they had received 30-minute massages daily for a 5-day period) suggested that there are even long-term effects associated with daily massage. First, there was a significant decrease in self-reported anxiety and depression levels between day 1 and day 5 of the massage period. The nurses also noted an increase in positive affect and a decrease in anxiety level and fidgeting across the 5-day period. These observations were confirmed by a watch that measured activity, which also showed a decrease in activity over the 5-day period. Sleep was also affected. The amount of nighttime sleep increased from 80 to 91 percent (of the time in bed) and, conversely, the period of time spent awake decreased significantly. Finally, we noted decreases in urinary cortisol levels and urinary norepinephrine levels (indices of stress). Thus it would appear that massage is a very effective form of treatment for reducing anxiety levels in child and adolescent psychiatric patients.

That brings us up to date on our massage story. Even though touch is the first sensory system to develop, and the skin is the largest sense organ, we know considerably less about touch than about the other senses. We know even less about the therapeutic effects of touch from therapies like massage. So, we are hopeful that these little pieces will help to solve the mystery of touch.

In the meantime we have persuaded Johnson & Johnson to give us funds to start the first touch-research institute in the world. We will be exploring ways to get touch back into the school system. We will also be investigating the effects of massage on a number of different groups of sick children, including those with diabetes, AIDS, and cancer, as well as neglected and abused children. To raise money for this institute, we will need to write grants to federal, state, and private funding groups and give a lot of show-and-tell sessions to corporations like Johnson & Johnson to convince them that their philanthropic efforts will help the health and development of children. I guess this qualifies us as undaunted psychologists.

Acknowledgment

This research was supported by NIMH Research Scientist Award #MH00331 and NIMH Basic Research grant #MH40779 to Tiffany Field. Correspondence and requests for reprints should be sent to Tiffany Field, The Touch Research Institute, University of Miami Medical School, P.O. Box 016820, Miami, FL 33101.

SUGGESTED READINGS

FIELD, T. (1990). *Infancy*. Cambridge, MA: Harvard.
——— & BRAZELTON, T. B. (EDS.) (1990). *Advances in touch*. Skillman, NJ: Johnson & Johnson.
MONTAGU, A. (1986). *Touching: The human significance of the skin*. New York: Harper & Row.

WILLIAM A. FISHER *(Ph.D., Purdue University) is Professor of Psychology and has a cross-appointment in the Department of Obstetrics and Gynecology at the University of Western Ontario in London, Canada. Dr. Fisher is on the Editorial Board of the* Journal of Sex Research, *a Fellow of the Society for the Scientific Study of Sex, and on the Board of Directors of the Planned Parenthood Federation of Canada. He has more than 50 publications in the area of human sexuality, including his book* Adolescents, Sex, and Contraception *(co-edited with D. Byrne), and has received several awards for excellence in university teaching. Dr. Fisher and his wife share a two-career, three-child family, and passions for travel, hiking, and folk music.*

2

Confessions of a Sexual Scientist

———— ❖ ————

When I am introduced to an audience as a sexual scientist, I am generally expected to justify why a nice professional like me is in a field like this. When I am speaking to fellow psychologists, I usually stress that the psychological study of human sexuality is core social psychology (sex is after all perhaps the ultimate interpersonal behavior), core developmental psychology (sexual behavior develops predictably across the life span), core biopsychology (where would we be, sexually speaking, without testosterone?), and so on. When I am speaking to an audience of laypersons, I generally emphasize that the psychological study of sexuality is a socially significant activity because we must gain leverage over disturbing problems such as AIDS infection, teenage pregnancy, sexual violence, sexual dysfunction, and the like. But when I am speaking with an audience of friends, I emphasize that even if the psychological study of human sexuality were not a core psychological concern, and even if it were not a socially beneficial activity, I would be active in the field anyway, because sexual science is *fun*. Like no other area in psychology, I have discovered in sexual science an outlet for my passion for generating ideas to help us understand and improve a category of behavior that is both socially significant and poorly understood. So, I admit it; I am a sexual scientist. I have spent my career trying to learn enough to help reduce unwanted pregnancy, sexually transmitted disease, and sexual assault, and heaven forbid, to help promote rewarding sexual function. Here is my confession.

Sexual science began with a strong moral position. Hundreds of years ago, in 1758, Simon Andre Tissot, the right-thinking Swiss physician, broke the news to the world about the link between masturbation and insanity. Sylvester Graham, in the 1830s, popularized a nutritional system for the prevention of wet dreams, degeneracy, and disease, based upon consumption of the Graham Cracker and other whole-wheat products. John Harvey Kellogg of Battle Creek, Michigan, invented the Corn Flake in 1878 as an integral part of his program of health promotion via proper nutrition, exercise, and sexual abstinence. Richard von Krafft-Ebing, one of the most noted psychiatrists of his time, published *Psychopathia sexualis* in 1882 to illuminate the link between sexual behavior and moral degeneracy.

When sexual science began to be more objective than moralizing, it accomplished its greatest work, but its pioneers paid a considerable price. Alfred C. Kinsey, an Indiana University biology professor, began innocently enough to co-teach a noncredit course on marriage in 1938. As a result of this involvement, Kinsey found out how little was known about sexual behavior, and following his instincts as a natural scientist, began collecting the lifetime sexual histories of hundreds and ultimately thousands of individuals. Kinsey published *Sexual Behavior in the Human Male* in 1948, and *Sexual Behavior in the Human Female* in 1953. These volumes provided objective evidence concerning the statistical commonness of sexual fantasy, masturbation, premarital and extramarital intercourse, and same-sex sexual contacts, without a whisper of condemnation for these acts; and not-so-incidentally, the books enraged individuals and groups everywhere. Kinsey was thoroughly investigated; his financial backers were threatened with a McCarthy-era congressional investigation, and they withdrew their support. He died not long after publication of the female volume while honoring a speaking engagement that his doctor had ordered him to cancel.

At about the time of Kinsey's problems in the mid-1950s, William Masters began his legendary research on the physiology of the sexually responding human being. Masters was forbidden from borrowing books by his own university library; petitions from students and faculty sought to have his medical school sexuality course canceled; his equipment was sabotaged; and major journals categorically refused to publish his work.

Still, however, sexual scientists were courageous enough, or twisted enough (choose one), to continue with their work, and they even succeeded in subverting a major governmental effort to relabel sex as sin. In 1968, the U.S. President's Commission on Obscenity and Pornography was appointed to study the negative effects of pornography and to suggest means for regulating this plague, and sexual scientists willingly accepted government funding for sex research and produced volume after volume of work on pornography. These investigators—many psychologists among them—could not find evidence to incriminate smut, and they in fact concluded that pornography effects were minimal and benign. Fortunately, Richard Milhous Nixon and Spiro Agnew, America's moral leaders at the time, took every opportunity to condemn this research publicly, shortly before each was forced to resign from public office because of circumstances that were more than a little bit questionable.

So it goes with sexual science. In the view of many, it involves amoral investigators observing immoral behavior. How, then, did *I* become involved in this tawdry enterprise? I've asked myself this question a thousand times, mostly between the hours of 2 A.M. and 4 A.M., as an alternative to sleep. Partly, I suppose it was the times: I am a child of the 1960s, and all children of the sixties took a secret pledge to question authority forever. Partly, it is my personality: I find it incredibly exciting to study socially significant problems and to try to devise solutions to them. Sexual science is laden with opportunities for such work. Mainly, though, it was accident: I brought my willingness to question authority, my passion for discovery, and my social conscience to the graduate program in social psychology at Purdue University, and there I met Donn Byrne, one of the world's foremost sexual scientists. Donn had been a pioneer in the study of interpersonal attraction, and in the mid-1970s was beginning to study sexual behavior, which he correctly recognized as perhaps the ultimate form of interpersonal attraction. Donn was tolerant enough to take me on as his graduate student, generous enough to share his thoughts with me, and curious enough to confront the many interesting and unanswered questions that one quickly encounters in this field. My descent had begun.

Graduate training at Purdue followed an apprenticeship model: we were treated like junior faculty, and expected to produce psychological science on a corresponding level. This was a brilliant strategy for graduate training—we were performing the literature reviews, the research design, execution, and analysis, and the writing, submission, and publication of manuscripts that we would be expected to do as professionals—and it was also a terrifying experience to have to perform at this level from day one. The strategy worked, however, and Donn created an extremely strong cadre of graduate students who thought like scientists, produced like scientists, and stimulated one another immensely. In my own case, Donn initially slid an imposing stack of IBM cards across his desk to me, explained that they contained the data from a study of men's and women's reactions to pornography, and suggested that I might like to work on the analysis of these data if I had the time. Of course I was interested, even though the prospect of learning enough statistics and computer skills to do so made me twist and squirm for weeks afterwards.

When the data from this study were analyzed, I was faced with a chance finding that was completely paradoxical, that I could not understand, and that has dominated my thinking and my research ever since. Our findings showed that the men and women who had the most negative feelings about the sexual movies also had, or planned to have, the *most* children. How could people who are uncomfortable about sex end up with lots of children? I puzzled over this finding for some time, but hampered as I was by the burden of a higher education, I could make no sense of this result. Eventually, Donn thought through a totally novel and very powerful explanation. According to his theory, having children is "easy" insofar as it requires only occasional intercourse and a little luck. Not having children, however, is much more complicated: one must anticipate having intercourse in advance, acquire information about birth control, talk with a partner about it, acquire contraception from a doctor, clinic, or pharmacy, and actually use it consistently and correctly. In Donn's view, men and women with negative or ambivalent feelings about sex feel just relaxed enough to have intercourse, but are too anxious to plan for contraception in advance by engaging in the complex series of behaviors required to practice birth control. Hence, persons who have negative feelings about sex may well end up, paradoxically, with the most children. In contrast, persons who feel more comfortable with sexuality should be relaxed enough to have intercourse, and relaxed enough to negotiate the rather complicated script of contraceptive behaviors as well, and they should end up with fewer and better planned offspring. Beyond a certain theoretical elegance, these ideas seemed to have considerable social significance as well. Given that something like 1,000,000 American teenagers become pregnant every year, anything that would help us understand sex without contraception could help guide effective sex-education programs to reduce the scope of this problem.

At this stage of the game, we had moved from a chance observation (persons with negative feelings about sex have many children) to the statement of a mini-theory (persons with negative feelings about sex are least able to think about intercourse in advance, to learn about birth control, to talk with their partner about it, and to acquire a form of it and use it consistently and correctly). Now it was time to conduct research to test the truth value of this theory, to undertake what I like to think of as the "put-up-or-shut-up" activity that separates psychological science from armchair speculation.

We cast about, initially, for ways to test the proposition that sex-related emotions determine the performance of contraceptive behavior. In one early study, we tried to get a very close, "real life" look at how sex-related feelings might affect performance of a specific contraceptive behavior. Jeffrey Fisher (my fellow graduate student and half of the world's most-accomplished team of brother sexual scientists), Donn Byrne, and I began what has since become known—if you move in the right circles—as "The Famous Rubber Study." Jeff reasoned that people's emotional responses to "early" phases of the contraceptive behavior sequence (such as acquiring contraceptive devices) would determine whether they continued with the process and performed the all-important "later" phases (such as actually using contraceptives and doing so consistently). Hence, we decided to examine emotional responses to the purchase of contraceptives, and associated evaluations that might inhibit or facilitate further contraceptive behavior. We approached the owner of a campus drugstore, and to our considerable surprise, he agreed to let us study undergraduate men's emotional and evaluative responses to condom purchasing in his store. (The drugstore owner, it turned out, was interested in condom purchasing, because condoms were the most frequently stolen item in his store. He told us that it was not uncommon to see on his security camera a man wearing a $400 suit stealing 75 cents worth of condoms.)

Working through our psychology department subject pool, we recruited 40 male freshmen, who reported to the drugstore every half hour or so, one by one, in the early morning before many customers had arrived. As in almost all of our research, our subjects were informed of the procedures involved in this experiment in advance, they were volunteers, and they were aware that they could omit answers to any questions they chose, or leave the experiment at any time. The freshmen were told that they were participating in a study of male purchasing behavior, and that they would purchase a male-related product—either acne cream, a "jock-strap itch" medication, or a 3-pack of lubricated condoms. Each subject participated in a rigged drawing, held behind the drugstore magazine rack, to determine which product he would purchase. All of the men, of course, received instructions to purchase a 3-pack of lubricated condoms, and each was given enough money to do so. The students then dutifully made their way to the pharmacist's counter at the back of the drugstore, haltingly requested a 3-pack of lubricated condoms, paid for their purchase, and brought the condoms back to us. Following this, the students retreated to the drugstore storeroom, completed a couple of brief questionnaires concerning their feelings while making their purchases, and indicated their evaluations of condom use and related issues.

When we finished running the last freshman through the infamous rubber study, we headed back to the university and began to analyze our data. We divided our sample into men who had very negative emotional responses to the condom purchase and men who had less-negative emotional responses to the situation, and compared their evaluations of contraceptive purchasing. We found that men who had very negative emotional responses to buying condoms also evaluated condoms in general, and condoms in use, quite negatively. They believed that condoms were unreliable; they thought that the pharmacist was thinking all kinds of negative thoughts about them; and they even evaluated the drugstore negatively. Apparently, these young men felt quite uncomfortable buying condoms, and they generated evaluations of condoms and of the condom-purchase situation that "justified" or explained why they felt about it the way they did. These negative emotional and evaluative reactions, of course, could later get in the way of using condoms (they were, after all, evaluated negatively in general, in use, and in terms of reliability) or of ever purchasing them again ("the pharmacist thought I was terrible," and "the drugstore was not a pleasant place to shop anyway"). All of these findings pointed to the need to reengineer the condom-purchase situation—through point-of-purchase displays, reassuring statements by the pharmacist, and other modifications that normalize condom-purchasing—so as to make it a more emotionally pleasant situation that would produce more-positive contraceptive evaluations and increase the likelihood of future condom purchasing and use.

Beyond the formal data analysis, the informal observations we made in our field research setting—the local drugstore—were in many ways as valuable as the more quantitative observations we had recorded. For example, we noticed that the freshmen males were physically very nervous and their voices quivered, and this made real for us the anxiety that can sometimes be associated with basic and necessary contraceptive purchases. We also noticed that the clerks who took our subjects' money never made eye contact with them, and never actually touched their hands when giving change. This suggested to us that staff training in this area could possibly serve to normalize condom purchasing, to reduce purchasers' anxiety, to increase sales of a very necessary commodity, and to increase goodwill toward the drugstore.

We learned another lesson in the drugstore as well: Murphy's Law definitely applies outside the comfortable confines of a lab. Since we were starving students at the time of this research, we could afford to buy only a single 3-pack of "research condoms." Consequently, we had the druggist give the same packet of condoms to each subject; we retrieved them from the subject after his experimental participation, and recycled them again and again and again. All went well until very early one morning. When I arrived at the drugstore to begin to set up for the day's research activity, a young male was speaking with the pharmacist, but as he was not a subject, I paid no attention to him. As he left the store, the pharmacist came out from behind his counter, sauntered up to me, and remarked, "That young man was easily the most anxious subject in your entire study." At this point, *I* became nervous, and let the pharmacist know that the young man in question had *not* been a subject in our study. "Oh my God!" said the pharmacist. "That explains why he asked for a dozen condoms! And I only gave him that same old tired 3-pack. . . ." With this realization, the pharmacist was out the door like a shot, running after the hapless customer, and shouting "Hey, mister!! Stop!!!" It was too late: the customer—terribly nervous to begin with—literally jumped into his car, spun his wheels, left twin skid marks, and was out of the parking lot in a flash.

At this early point in our research, the data were providing bits and pieces of support for the notion that people's feelings about sex determine their ability to perform important contraceptive behaviors. It was apparent, however, that if we were ever going to conduct systematic research on the link between feelings about sex and contraceptive behavior, we would need to devise a good measure of people's more or less stable feelings about sexuality, and then study the relationship between such feelings and a diversity of contraceptive acts. We began to take the view that individuals' feelings about sex were really one of their enduring personality traits—like IQ or authoritarianism or whatever—and to assume that people possessed stable tendencies to react to most sexual matters with relatively negative to relatively positive emotions. We christened this new dimension of personality "erotophobia-erotophilia" (after considering and rejecting a "prude–pornophile" split), and set about constructing a measure of individual differences in erotophobia-erotophilia, or negative-to-positive emotional response to sex.

The first step in producing a measure of a personality trait is to create items that seem logically to measure the trait in question. IQ-test items should appear to measure mental sharpness, authoritarianism scale items should measure political beliefs, and the like. In line with this approach, we wrote descriptions of hypothetical sexual situations, and asked respondents to tell us what their emotional reactions to these situations might be. In this way, we hoped to get a sample of people's negative-to-positive emotional response to sexuality, which is exactly what we wished to measure. Leonard White, my fellow graduate student, drinking buddy, and co-dragon slayer in the grad school wars, took the lead and wrote 53 items that described hypothetical sexual situations and asked subjects about their emotional responses to them. For example, one of the items included the following hypothetical sexual situation: "Swimming in the nude with a member of the opposite sex would be an exciting experience." Subjects were asked to indicate their agreement or disagreement with the emotional reaction (excitement) that was indicated.

Once items that *appear* to measure the personality trait under study have been written, it is necessary to demonstrate with data that the items actually *do* assess what the wise researcher thinks they do. To validate our measure of erotophobia-erotophilia, we administered the items to a large group of undergraduate men and women, together with a measure of the tendency to respond to questionnaire items in a socially desirable but not necessarily truthful way. We also showed the undergraduate men and women a series of explicit erotic slides, and asked for their emotional reactions to these slides.

To use our data to decide whether the erotophobia-erotophilia items indeed measured negative-to-positive emotional responses to sexuality, we established three criteria. First, subjects' responses to the item had to be correlated with their emotional responses to the erotic slides. If a subject responded to an erotophobia-erotophilia item in an emotionally positive fashion, his or her emotional responses to the erotic slides ought to be positive as well. Second, subjects' responses to the item had to be unrelated to their tendencies to answer questions in a socially desirable but not necessarily truthful fashion. We wanted an accurate measure of erotophobia-erotophilia, not a measure of self-promotion. Third, the item had to "work." It had to be related to emotional responses to erotica and to be unrelated to social desirability for both male and female subjects. Fortune was kind to us, and it emerged that 21 of our erotophobia-erotophilia items met our criteria as valid measures of emotional response to sexuality. We christened our 21-item measure of erotophobia-erotophilia as the "Sexual Opinion Survey," mostly because the initials "S.O.S." held a strong fascination for us as graduate students.

Armed with a technique for measuring individuals' levels of eroto-phobia-erotophilia, we began a program of research to examine the relationship of negative-to-positive feelings about sex and the five critical contraceptive behaviors that had been identified earlier. Essentially, we wanted to find out whether erotophobic persons were comfortable enough to have intercourse, but were too uncomfortable with the topic to learn about contraception, anticipate intercourse in advance, discuss contraception with their partners, acquire it publicly, and use it consistently.

An early study in our program concerned itself with the link between erotophobia-erotophilia and the ability to learn contraceptive and related sexual information. If erotophobic individuals are too uncomfortable to learn what they need to know about contraception, they will not be in good shape when it comes to practicing birth control. To examine this issue, I adopted a truly simple (and some would say truly sneaky) approach. One midwinter week, I gave my undergraduate human sexuality class its annual bonecrusher midterm on a variety of sexual and contraceptive topics. After returning students' exams, I innocently asked them to complete the Sexual Opinion Survey and to indicate their human sexuality midterm mark and their last year's grade point average in general. When the results were in, it turned out that erotophobic students scored nearly a full letter grade lower on the human sexuality midterm than did erotophilic students. We were also able to demonstrate that erotophobes' and erotophiles' grade-point averages in other courses during the past year had been equivalent. Erotophobia is not stupidity, but rather sexual anxiety that interferes quite specifically with sexual but not with other types of learning. We would love to know whether erotophobic persons attended fewer classes, studied less efficiently, or had recall problems. That would be a terrific topic for future research—but at some point along the line negative feelings about sex seem to get in the way of learning the kind of information that is necessary for the practice of contraception.

Emboldened by our success in linking erotophobia-erotophilia with the learning of necessary sexual information, we moved on to the second item on our research agenda. Is erotophobia-erotophilia related to the ability to anticipate sexual intercourse—and the need for contraception—in advance? In our view, erotophobic persons should be unwilling to anticipate sexual intercourse, and the need for contraception, in advance, because this might seem to erotophobes to involve "planning sin" and should be emotionally costly for them. In contrast, erotophilic persons should have little difficulty planning intercourse, and contraception, in advance; according to our theory, they should actually look forward to it. To study the question of erotophobes' and erotophiles' ability to anticipate intercourse—and by extension to anticipate the need for contraception—we studied a sample of male undergraduates. Well over one hundred freshmen came to our lab, and each one completed the Sexual

Opinion Survey, and told us whether or not they expected to have sexual intercourse during the coming month. Approximately one month later, we brought these undergraduate men back to our laboratory, and asked each whether he had had sexual intercourse during the preceding month, and if so, whether he or his partner had used contraception to prevent pregnancy. Our results showed that relatively few erotophobic men expected to have sexual intercourse during the coming month, while erotophilic men had fairly substantial expectations of sexual good fortune during this time. Our follow-up results showed later that erotophobic men had substantially *underestimated* their likelihood of having sexual intercourse during the month under study, and this was problematic from the standpoint of contraception. Quite a number of erotophobic men had unexpected—and contraceptively unprotected—sexual intercourse. In contrast, erotophilic men suffered from what might be called (with apologies to Charles Dickens) "great expectations." Erotophilic men *overestimated* their likelihood of having intercourse, but more of their intercourse was contraceptively protected, because they were more likely to obtain contraceptives in advance of expected (vs. unexpected) intercourse.

We were on a roll. Erotophobia seemed to interfere with learning about sex and contraception, and with anticipating intercourse (and the need for contraception). Our next study dealt with the relationship of erotophobia-erotophilia and the public acquisition of contraception. As those of you who have sweated out a clinic visit for contraception may know, the public acquisition of birth control can be somewhat like a public announcement of what you and a partner intend to do with your genitals in the near future. We reasoned that erotophobic persons would find the public acquisition of contraception to be particularly difficult and would avoid this crucial behavior. Erotophilic persons, in contrast, have more positive feelings about sex and ought to have an easier time with the public acquisition of contraception.

Our study of the relationship of erotophobia-erotophilia and the public acquisition of contraception took place, ironically enough, at Indiana University, home of the Kinsey Institute for Sex Research, and home at the time as well to a considerable number of unplanned pregnancies among Indiana University undergraduates. We were able to identify two groups of women at the school—those who were sexually active but were inconsistent users of contraception, and those who were sexually active inconsistent users of contraception who had just broken out of their risky pattern by making a visit to the campus contraception clinic. Women in each group were asked to complete the Sexual Opinion Survey measure of erotophobia-erotophilia. Our results showed, as expected, that the women who were sexually active, inconsistent contraceptors were moderately erotophobic: relaxed enough about sex to have intercourse, but too up-tight to publicly acquire contraceptives at the clinic. The women who were sexually active, inconsistent contraceptors who had finally made their way to the contraception clinic, in contrast, were significantly more erotophilic: they were relaxed enough about sex to "do it," and relaxed enough eventually to negotiate the public acquisition of needed contraceptives. Once again, negative feelings about sex appeared to interfere with a critical contraceptive behavior.

The next stage of the contraceptive process involves a novel form of oral sex: talking about sex and contraception prior to having intercourse. Studying the relationship between erotophobia-erotophilia and ability to engage in presex discussion of contraception presented a real challenge to us. I personally favored waiting patiently in the local lover's lane, hidden behind a bush, equipped with tape recorder, flashlight, and questionnaires, but neither the university ethics committee, the granting agency, my mentor, nor my wife could be persuaded that this was a smart idea. Hence, we created a laboratory method for studying the link between feelings about sex and ability to communicate about sexual topics, and conducted research that has since become known as the infamous "Talking Dirty Study." We brought undergraduate men and women into our laboratory, had them complete the Sexual Opinion Survey measure of erotophobia-erotophilia, and asked each one to deliver a prewritten speech, on either a sexual or a neutral topic, into a menacing video camera with a red light on top, supposedly being videotaped for later presentation to an audience. The first thing we noticed was that, even though subjects were delivering prewritten speeches, many could not pronounce basic sexual vocabulary items that appeared in the sexual speech. Here for the first time we learned of a number of new sexual-anatomical structures, including the "virginia," "the scotrum," and "the testicules." The second thing we learned was that erotophobic subjects had a terrible time delivering the sexual message, compared to erotophilic subjects: they experienced strongly negative emotional reactions when delivering the sexual message; they believed that the audience would evaluate them, and the content of their speech, quite negatively, and they refused to sign a release form that was represented as giving us permission to utilize their videotaped speeches in future research. The third thing we learned, yet again, was that erotophobia-erotophilia was related to reactions to sexual situations, but was not related to reactions to neutral situations. Erotophobic and erotophilic subjects differed markedly in their responses to delivering the sexual speech, but they didn't differ a bit in their reactions to delivering the neutral message. To the extent that we can extrapolate beyond these laboratory findings, our results suggest that erotophobic emotions may interfere with yet another critical contraceptive behavior—presex discussion of contraception.

There remained one outstanding issue to study in the contraceptive-behavior sequence research, however, and that involved investigating the link between erotophobia-erotophilia and consistency of contraceptive use. Since erotophobic people seemed to have difficulty with each of the preliminaries—anticipating intercourse, learning about, discussing, and acquiring contraception—it seemed likely to us that erotophobic persons would have difficulty with the consistent use of contraception as well. To test this relationship, we divided a sample of university women into three groups: some of these women were sexually inactive, some were sexually active but inconsistent users of contraception, and some were sexually active and consistent users of contraception. We compared these women's levels of erotophobia-erotophilia, as measured on the Sexual Opinion Survey. As expected, it turned out that the sexually inactive women were highly erotophobic—too uncomfortable with sex to have intercourse, and in no danger of unplanned pregnancy. The sexually active women who were inconsistent contraceptors were moderately erotophobic—just comfortable enough to have intercourse, too uncomfortable to prepare for contraception with any consistency in advance. Finally, the sexually active women who were consistent contraceptors were the most erotophilic women in the study—relaxed enough about sex to have intercourse, *and* relaxed enough about sex to prepare for contraception consistently in advance.

Our research thus far had been satisfying from both the standpoint of theoretical understanding and the potential for solving social problems. With respect to theory, we had shown that people develop enduring tendencies to respond to sexuality with a range of negative-to-positive emotions, and we had demonstrated that feelings about sex may generalize and determine people's inclination to perform a variety of sex-related contraceptive acts. With respect to social problem-solving applications, we had succeeded in demonstrating that contraception involves performance of a relatively complicated sequence of behavioral acts; that prevailing negative feelings about sex interfere with the performance of these acts; and that the key to improving contraceptive behavior likely lay in teaching people to perform the specific series of acts that are involved in contraceptive behavior, and in relaxing negative feelings that people may have about performing these acts.

At this point in my career, I had completed my Ph.D., and actually found paid employment at a major university. Coincidentally, the university was experiencing a significant problem with unplanned pregnancies among its undergraduate students. Given my work in this area, the authorities at my university did the most frightening thing that can ever happen to a researcher who has suggested the problem-solving possibilities of his or her research. They took me seriously, and began to devise a campus-wide pregnancy-prevention program based upon our group's contraceptive research over the years. What is worse, the university authorities asked me to consult on this project, just to be sure that if a debacle occurred, there would be someone without tenure to blame. To make a long story short, we created a student-written, student-produced video, in which individuals much like those in the target audience modeled each stage of the contraceptive-behavior sequence (anticipating intercourse, learning about contraception, discussing it with partners, acquiring it, etc.) in such familiar campus surroundings as the campus bar, the local drugstore, and the university health clinic. We modeled for students the entire contraceptive-behavior sequence in the settings in which students would have to carry it out, and we presented it with a great deal of anxiety-diffusing humor, including a reptilelike male who bad-mouths condoms and then slinks out to buy some on the sly, and a spermicide foam fight between the male and female protagonists, which was my personal favorite. We created a student-written booklet as well, which walked the reader, with humor, through the entire sequence of contraceptive behaviors, and was intended to provide a print back-up to the video, that could sit on students' bookshelves till needed. The entire idea behind this educational program, of course, was to teach—by showing models—the specific sequence of behaviors involved in effective contraception, and also to relieve anxieties about executing this sequence of behaviors, by showing socially similar others walking through the sequence unharmed, mirthful, and sexually fulfilled.

Our video *Can We Talk?* has been shown to thousands of students each year, in student dormitories, in university classes, and at an annual health fair. Every incoming student at our university receives the booklet as well. To supplement these interventions, we saw to it that condom machines were installed opposite each university bar and on each university dormitory floor. In addition, student health service personnel lecture to numerous dormitory floors and other student groups, communicating about the behavioral script of necessary contraceptive behavior, and by their presence and their statements normalizing these behaviors and reducing apprehension about enacting them.

I regarded the educational package we had created as a great start, but I had a nasty need to know whether all of our research-based interventions would actually work. Consequently, I hatched a really sneaky idea for evaluating the success or failure of the intervention. I arranged to obtain information from the student health service concerning the number of positive pregnancy tests performed there each year; I arranged as well to get pregnancy-rate information concerning other groups of similar-aged women who did not receive this educational program. We were prepared to believe that initially there might actually be an apparent *increase* in the number of positive pregnancy tests performed at the student health service, since we had worked hard in our intervention to make the service seem to be an accessible and user-friendly source of help for sex-related problems. Eventually, however, if the program was working, the number of positive pregnancy tests should drop at our university, and be relatively unchanged in the "untreated" comparison groups. So, we sat back and waited anxiously for the pregnancy-test data to come in. The first year figures showed that there had been a 27.7 percent drop in our campus pregnancy rate, compared with a 5.9 percent drop in the comparison group! Then, we waited again for succeeding years' data, since it was critical to demonstrate continued change across time. The second-year figures came in: they showed an additional 11 percent drop in our campus pregnancy rate, and a 1.2 percent *increase* in the comparison-group pregnancy rate! At the time of this writing, we have a total of five post-intervention years of pregnancy-rate data. The pregnancy rate at our campus dropped precipitously—nearly 40 percent—during the first two years of the intervention, and it has stayed down since. No parallel changes were observed in the comparison group, whose pregnancy rate stayed fairly stable. We are, of course, delighted to have moved from a chance observation early in graduate school, through the conduct of a conceptually based series of related studies, through the implementation of an apparently successful intervention based upon this research. We regard these intervention findings as merely suggestive, at this point, because we don't know precisely which intervention elements produced the observed change, and because we need to replicate these results in further, experimental research.

Then a curious and exciting event occurred. My wife and I decided to have a thoroughly planned child, the first of three who have kept us sleepless, incoherent, but happy during much of the past decade. As it happened, one of my students was pregnant at the same time, and it occurred to her that wives' and husbands' feelings about sexuality might influence their sex-related behavior during pregnancy and the postpartum period. As an alternative to divorce or a contract killing, we chose to study not my wife's pregnancy, but the pregnancy experiences of 50 couples who were enrolled in a local childbirth-education class. We obtained the voluntary participation of these couples, and asked them to complete the Sexual Opinion Survey to measure their erotophobia-erotophilia, and to respond to a questionnaire concerning their sexual functioning and satisfaction during pregnancy. We then proceeded to leave the couples strictly alone until three months after the birth of their child, at which time we intruded again and asked them to tell us about their experiences during delivery and during the postpartum period. Our findings were both fascinating and consistent with theory. Erotophobic wives and/or husbands reported less sexual activity and satisfaction during their pregnancies, and erotophobic women reported a much later resumption of sexual intercourse after the birth of their babies. What was more, erotophobic women were much less likely than erotophilic women to breast-feed their infants; presumably, erotophobic women's negative feelings about sex made it uncomfortable for them to engage in the small amount of breast and nipple manipulation that is involved in breastfeeding. Erotophobic men, for their part, were significantly less likely than erotophilic men to actually attend the birth of their child. Possibly, the sexual aspects of actually observing childbirth were too much for erotophobic men to deal with. Later, we examined the link between erotophobia-erotophilia and other sexual-health behaviors. We have learned, for example, that erotophobic women are relatively unlikely to self-examine their breasts for signs of cancer or to get annual pelvic exams and Pap smears. Overall, our research is beginning to suggest that erotophobia-erotophilia travels with individuals across their lifespans. Erotophobia seems to interfere with sexual adjustment during adolescence and young adulthood—in terms of contraceptive behavior—and erotophobia seems to interfere with sexual adjustment later in life as well, in terms of sexual accommodations during pregnancy, breastfeeding, sexual health care, and the like.

After years of studying the effects of laypersons' erotophobia-erotophilia, I became aware of the obvious fact that professionals may also be erotophobic or erotophilic, and that their feelings about sex are likely to affect their professional behavior in relation to sexuality. The suspicion that, say, erotophobic teachers and erotophobic doctors might find it difficult to deliver sexuality education or sex-related medical services appealed to me as an interesting idea, and also resonated strongly with that part of my personality that remains forever fixated in the 1960s "question authority" phase of development. These ideas quickly stimulated a series of studies that have become as popular as a lead condom, as far as teachers and physicians are concerned.

Our first study was undertaken to examine possible links between health-education teachers' erotophobia-erotophilia and their sex-education teaching activity. Given the sometimes arbitrary nature of some school administrators, it was recognized that a significant number of erotophobic health educators end up teaching sex education to unsuspecting primary- and secondary-school students. Erotophobic sex-education teachers, it was speculated, should be too uncomfortable to teach about many sensitive—but still important—sexual topics. Therefore, erotophobic teachers ought to believe that many sensitive and important sex-education topics are in fact unimportant, and should fail to teach these topics. Bill Yarber, a colleague who was at Purdue, began an ambitious pair of studies of this subject, using hundreds of practicing sex educators in Indiana's primary and secondary schools as his subjects. Each of the sex-education teachers completed the Sexual Opinion Survey and a number of other background measures. They also rated the importance of teaching about a variety of "controversial" sex-education topics, and indicated whether or not they actually taught about these sensitive but important issues. When the results were tabulated, it was quite clear that erotophobic sex educators rated many "controversial" sex-education topics (such as where to get and how to use birth control) as relatively unimportant, and they were significantly less likely to teach about these topics and others such as abortion, sexual alternatives to intercourse, and the like. Moreover, it turned out that teachers' erotophobia-erotophilia was the single best predictor of whether or not they actually taught about these sensitive but important sex-education issues. Teachers' feelings about sex more powerfully affected their sex education practices than did their educational background (B.A. or M.A.), years of teaching experience, married versus single status, number of children, religion, etc.

I followed up this research with a study of medical students' feelings about sex and their amount of medical-sexual knowledge. My research group gained access to the entire third-year medical-school class at a nameless medical school in a galaxy far, far away. The medical students each completed the Sexual Opinion Survey, and a detailed test of their medically related sexual knowledge. Next, the medical school threw a voluntary three-session refresher course in medical sexology, which focused on bolstering students' knowledge and comfort around medical-sexual issues, and we lurked in the background, carefully recording which students attended. Finally, we retested the entire third-year class with respect to their medical-sexual knowledge. Our results showed exactly what we had expected (and feared): erotophobic medical students knew significantly less about medical-sexual issues than did erotophilic medical students; they systematically avoided taking the voluntary refresher course in sexual medicine; and those few erotophobic medical students who did take the refresher course showed no pre- to post-test improvement in medical-sexual knowledge.

From the standpoint of theory, these results excited us: erotophobia-erotophilia determined the sex-related behavior of professionals, just as would be expected. From the standpoint of society, however, we were depressed: teachers' and future physicians' emotions appear to override their training and interfere with sex-related professional functioning. With these results as a guide, however, we were able to make some concrete—and, we hope, effective—suggestions for the selection and training of teachers, physicians, and others who may be involved in providing sex-related services. First, it seems possible to use measures of erotophobia-erotophilia to identify professionals who are comfortable enough with sexuality to acquire skills and to deliver services in this area. Second, our results underscore the need to train professionals to try to disconnect their personal feelings about sexuality from their professional functioning in this area. Third, our investigations suggest that it is critical to educate professionals with considerable attention to relaxing their negative feelings about sexuality, as well as to providing specific professionally relevant information and skills. Many of these suggestions are in fact being incorporated into professional education curricula, and it will be critical—and exciting—to conduct research to monitor the success or failure of these modifications.

Throughout the years, our thinking about the psychological factors that govern sexual behavior has evolved and this thinking has exerted an influence on our research. Fairly early on, Donn Byrne presented the *Sexual Behavior Sequence* as a comprehensive theory for understanding human sexual behavior, and it goes well beyond the initial "mini theory" concerning erotophobia-erotophilia. The Sexual Behavior Sequence proposes that individuals' emotions *and* information *and* fantasy jointly determine their sexual behavior, and that the positive or negative outcome of individuals' sexual behavior will feed back into the system and affect individuals' future sexual feelings, cognitions, imagery, and behavior. There is a developmental aspect to the Sexual Behavior Sequence: it is proposed that we learn feelings about sexuality very early in life, and these feelings likely determine the nature of information about sexuality that we acquire later, and the kind of sexual imagery that we absorb later and that provides the scripts that guide our sexual activity. There is also an interpersonal aspect to the Sexual Behavior Sequence: it is argued that people are most likely to form sexually and romantically compatible relationships if they are similar in their feelings, thoughts, and fantasies about sex, and it has been speculated that successful relationships are characterized by increasing convergence across time in partners' sexual emotions, cognitions, and fantasy. Unsuccessful relationships, it is speculated, are marked by initial dissimilarity in partners' sexual feelings, thoughts, and fantasies, and by increasing divergence in these factors across time. Many of these propositions remain to be tested, and they are mentioned here as an explicit invitation to research involvement.

Let me close this chapter with a mid-career reflection on my involvement with sexual science. My work on the psychology of sexual behavior has provided me with deep feelings of discovery and accomplishment, and I believe that it has made some small contribution to human welfare as well. Let me encourage you to study sexual science, to conduct sexual science, and to experience for yourself many of these same rewards.

SUGGESTED READINGS

Byrne, D. (1977). Social psychology and the study of sexual behavior. *Personality and Social Psychology Bulletin, 1,* 3–30.

———— & FISHER, W. A. (ED.). (1983). *Adolescents, sex, and contraception.* Hillsdale, NJ: Erlbaum.

FISHER, W. A. (1986). A psychological approach to human sexuality: The Sexual Behavior Sequence. In D. Byrne & K. Kelley (Eds.), *Alternative approaches to the study of sexual behavior* (pp. 131–171). Hillsdale, NJ: Erlbaum.

———— BYRNE, D., WHITE, L. A., & KELLEY, K. (1988). Erotophobia-erotophilia as a dimension of personality. *Journal of Sex Research, 25,* 123–151.

———— & GRAY, J. (1988). Erotophobic-erotophilia and sexual behavior during pregnancy and postpartum. *Journal of Sex Research, 25,* 379–396.

ROBERT L. ISAACSON *(Ph.D., University of Michigan) is currently a Distinguished Professor in the Psychology Department, State University of New York at Binghamton. His major research interests are reflected in his numerous research articles on the limbic system of the brain, as well as in four books he co-edited (with Karl Pribram),* The Hippocampus, Volumes 1–4, *and two editions of* The Limbic System. *He also edited (with Karl Jensen) books on food-related toxicities:* The Vulnerable Brain and Environmental Risks, Volume 1: Malnutrition and Hazard Assessment; *and* Volume 2: Toxins in Food. *When not in the office or laboratory, he can be found on a nearby golf course or tennis court—except when there is snow on the ground. Then, look for ski tracks.*

Toward an Understanding of the Limbic System

❖

It is hard to imagine a more fascinating or more interesting life than struggling to find out how the brain works. All of my days in the laboratory have
been "fun." But my research and study of the brain is motivated by far more
than the joy it provides. I believe that learning some of the secrets of the nervous
system will be of value to mankind. This is not an abstract motive. Retarded children are very real, as are people with other brain disorders, such as multiple scle-
rosis, Alzheimer's disease, depression, and schizophrenia. My ultimate goal is to
better understand the human condition and to help provide information on
which effective therapies and treatments for the neurologically impaired can be
based.

Laboratory research often progresses slowly and methodically. Each experiment builds on the results of previous experiments. One of the most important
things I do is to decide on the next project to be undertaken. I assess the many
possibilities and try to determine which is most likely to lead to the most important information. Such decisions are not easy. They must be based on extensive
knowledge of the research literature and comprehensive understanding of the
most recently collected data. Therefore, the life of the neuroscientist is one of
study as well as action. The library is as important to me as the laboratory.

EARLY INFLUENCES

All of my training in psychology was at the University of Michigan. As an undergraduate, I fulfilled both prelaw and premed requirements, leaving my future
options open. Since I had gone through college under the NROTC Holloway program, I was commissioned at the time of graduation. I served in the Navy for
three years at the time of the Korean War and, during that time, I developed a

friendship with a lieutenant commander. We were both assigned to the battleship *Missouri* during the Korean War and spent a year together on the ship. My friend had just completed two years at Oxford as a Rhodes Scholar. He spoke at least 11 languages fluently, not to mention Latin and Greek. He often entertained the officers in the ward room by engaging the head of the Navy Chaplain Corp in religious arguments, arguments conducted in English, Latin, and Greek. His knowledge of literature, history, and political science was so great that my curiosity about the world was sparked and never stilled. I decided to pursue a career in which the search for knowledge would not only be tolerated but rewarded. Psychology seemed the natural path to this goal. All in all, I spent a lot of time in Ann Arbor, going from freshman to professor in 22 years—with three years out for the Navy.

During my graduate-school days I had the good fortune to work with several noted researchers, representing a variety of areas of psychology. But one of the most important events of my career occurred as a first-year graduate student when I was assigned to help the motivation–personality theorist John Atkinson in his motivation course and its associated laboratory. This laboratory collected information about the behavioral consequences of different degrees of motivation to succeed, to avoid failure, to seek power, as evaluated by projective tests designed by David McClelland, Atkinson, and others. "Jack" Atkinson taught me to respect all of the information generated in our experiments, to trust data, to believe that subjects—animal and human—always give us important information. This is a hard job. It takes a great deal of thought and creativity to divine the messages that are hidden in the data that are complex and sometimes "unexpected." Since we trusted the data, we spent hours examining all of the intercorrelations among them, tried new interpretations of what we had found, and continually developed new ways to explain what we had found. This method of extensively analyzing the data and searching for new ways of considering them has proven to be invaluable in all of my later research. It is essential for finding out what the information from an experiment means.

There were other influences as well. For example, Charles J. (Jim) Smith and Robert McCleary were hired, and shortly thereafter James Olds came aboard. At that time, Jim Olds was coming from his postdoctoral work at McGill University where he first had been exposed to physiological psychology. He had previously obtained his Ph.D. in social psychology from Harvard. But, under the influence of Donald Hebb at McGill, he became enamoured with the biological side of our field, just as I had. While working at McGill, he and Peter Milner discovered that there were localized places in the brain which, when electrically stimulated, produced rewarding effects. These places are sometimes called the "pleasure centers" of the brain. This discovery was hailed, at the time, as a major breakthrough in the understanding of brain function. After his two years at McGill, Jim elaborated upon this research while at the Brain Research Institute at UCLA before coming to Michigan. Bob McCleary joined the faculty after obtaining his M.D. and Ph.D. degrees from the Johns Hopkins University. He came to Michigan from a year or so in the medical branch of the Air Force. One of his jobs there was to evaluate the emotional effects on troops at different distances from an atomic explosion. This may have been what interested him in the study of emotion and the role of certain limbic-system regions in behavior. However, I worked with him in studying how learning processed on one side of the brain was passed over to the other side. Our experimental subjects were very large goldfish. Jim Smith joined the Michigan Psychology Department directly after obtaining his Ph.D. from McGill. He had (and has) an encyclopedic knowledge in almost all domains of psychobiology and assumed an informal role as advocate and advisor for many students in psychobiology. These people provided the foundation for the growth of physiological psychology at the University. Their ideas, skills, and research enthusiasm motivated me to pursue this relatively new domain coupling biology and behavior.

Given the presence of such wonderful teachers and researchers, it now seems odd that none of them became my mentor. As it turned out, my dissertation was chaired by an expert in the field of learning, Edward Walker.

It was my dissertation research, however, that eventually led me to my life's work: the study of the limbic system. The limbic system is a term that came into common usage in the 1950s, although it had first been introduced into the scientific literature in 1878 by the French anatomist, Paul Broca. He used the term to designate that portion of the brain surrounding the core of the forebrain and brain stem, lying just below the outer surface of the brain that is called the neocortex. The most prominent structures in the limbic system are the hippocampus, the amygdala, and the septal area.

MY RESEARCH BEGINS

For my doctoral dissertation, I chose to study the electrical activity of the dog brain as it learned a simple conditioning task. I chose this study after reading reports of an unusual form of amnesia that resulted from the destruction of the temporal lobes in patients with intractable epilepsy, patients for whom no medication was effective and whose disease was so intense that it was life threatening. (Note: Inside the temporal lobes are the portions of the limbic system called the hippocampus and amygdala.) The amnesia was for recent events; that is, from the time of surgery up until almost the present minute. Typically, patients could remember things that were going on for several minutes, keeping in mind the names of people with whom they were talking and following the general course of the conversation. However, once their attention was diverted or the flow of conversation interrupted, memories were gone. Usually, this amnesia was studied in patients with one temporal lobe removed, but in the initial reports the patients had both temporal lobes removed. In some instances the temporal lobe was not removed but the central portions destroyed, including the amygdala and a good portion of the hippocampus. Most of the reports of the amnestic consequences of the temporal-lobe surgery were made by Brenda Milner in conjunction with the neurosurgeons William Scoville or Wilder Penfield.

The relationship between the temporal lobe (and the embedded hippocampus) with memory was further strengthened by the book *Speech and Brain Mechanisms,* by Penfield and Lamar Roberts (1959). The book reports a number of investigations conducted during surgery on the human brain by Penfield. With the informed consent of the patient, regions of the brain were electrically stimulated during the course of the operation. (During such operations, the patient is awake and can talk with the surgeons and others in the operating room. A local anesthetic is applied to the scalp and the skull. The brain, itself, is "silent" with regard to pain. The brain tissue does not have receptors for pain and, therefore, the procedure is without pain to the patient.) In some cases the stimulation of regions in the temporal lobe evoked memories and presensations associated with memories. From these descriptions of memory-like events that could be evoked from electrical stimulation of the human brain, many people thought that the temporal lobe, or more likely, the hippocampus within it, acted like a tape recorder, constantly monitoring the environment and storing the information in permanent form. When I mentioned these ideas about the temporal lobe to Lamar Roberts, he turned to me and slowly said, "I see you didn't read the book, either." He had me. I had relied on the descriptions of others about his book. He went on to explain that the memory-related phenomena that are reported from stimulation of the brain occurred only in patients with temporal-lobe epilepsy. Patients with epilepsy originating in other brain areas or with tumors or trauma, when undergoing neurosurgery reported no memory-related events when the temporal lobes were stimulated. Thus he regarded the occurrences in the temporal lobe patients to be exceptional and not representative of the conditions in persons without this form of disease. Still, the idea lingers that the temporal lobe is involved in human memory and this idea can still be found in many books, probably written by people who, like me, had not read his book.

My research required the implantation of many fine wires into the temporal lobes of dogs. The surgery, under sterile conditions, was tedious and done in much the same way that electrodes were implanted into the temporal lobes of people to determine the locus of epileptic foci. The dogs were given general anesthesia and their heads were held in stereotaxic instruments (i.e., instruments that allow the scientist to map brain regions in three dimensions) to ensure greater precision in the placement of the electrodes. Each operation lasted 8 to 12 hours. After the dogs recovered from surgery, and all did, they were trained to lift a foreleg in response to one tone and not to lift it when a different tone was presented.

Looking back on this early study, it is remarkable how naive I was. I had assumed that if the hippocampus was truly an important neural component in the brain's mechanisms underlying learning and memory, its patterns of electrical activities ought to reflect this function in an apparent fashion—perhaps in the same way exposure to visual stimulation disrupts the relatively slow, synchronous rhythms (alpha rhythms) of the visual cortex. The results were somewhat disappointing since the training experience and the retention testing failed to reveal any remarkable changes in the electrical rhythms of the hippocampus during learning. Only a few changes were observed, particularly just before the animal made a response, whether it was right or wrong.

About this time, I met Dr. Cornell Guirgea, a neurosurgeon from Romania, and he suggested that we study the effects of lesions in the hippocampus formation of some of these dogs. From our original collaborative work came the observation that animals without a hippocampus could learn and remember and, indeed, often did so more readily than intact animals.

I decided to systematically study this phenomenon, i.e., the very rapid learning in animals with complete hippocampal lesions, using rats in active avoidance tasks. In the first experiment, Robert Y. Moore, an intern at the University of Michigan Hospital; Robert Douglas, an undergraduate honors student; and I performed the operations with clean surgical technique. Each rat was anesthetized and the lesions were made while the animal was held in a stereotaxic instrument. After suitable openings were made in the skull, the dura was opened, and we removed the cortex overlying the hippocampus and the hippocampus by aspiration (a lesioning technique involving the removal of tissue by a suction device). Gel foam was inserted into the wounds, the temporal muscles were replaced over the skull, and the scalp was closed. We allowed the rats several days to recover from surgery before training was begun. A control group underwent the same procedures except for the removal of the hippocampus.

We trained the animals on a shuttle-box avoidance problem for five consecutive days. This task simply requires the animal to cross to the side of the box opposite to the one it was on, within five seconds after the onset of a buzzer. If the animal fails to cross in time, it receives a shock from the grid floor. The shock and the buzzer terminate when the animal crosses to the other side. If the animal crosses before the shock, the buzzer terminates as the animal crosses the center of the box and the rat is not shocked. This counts as an avoidance response.

The animals with hippocampal lesions reached our learning criterion

(9 avoidance responses in 10 trials) more rapidly than the control animals. While we successfully replicated my findings with dogs using a simple active avoidance task, we wondered if all avoidance learning would be facilitated by such lesions. The answer was "no." For example, in one experiment, we trained rats (lesioned and controls) to enter a small compartment while hungry, for a food reward. After 35 trials, spread over four days of training, they were given one shock while they were eating in this compartment. The intensity of the shock was sufficient to drive the animals out of the compartment. We resumed training following the shock trial.

The results were quite dramatic. Every one of the animals with hippocampal lesions reentered the compartment on the very next trial following the shock, whereas not one of the control animals entered the compartment on even the second or third postshock trial. Thus, here and in subsequent research we found that lesioned animals were drastically impaired in passive avoidance tasks, ones in which a response had to be withheld to avoid punishment. These results led in turn to the question of whether or not the lesioned animals simply could not inhibit learned responses. The answer here, once again, was "no." The animals with hippocampal lesions had difficulty in withholding responses only in certain situations. In some of our experiments, whether or not they were impaired depended on the time allowed between responses or tests. For example, we trained deprived animals in operant-conditioning boxes to press a bar for reward. After several days of training, during which they received a reward each time they pressed the bar, the animals were required to wait a specific period of time between responses (bar presses). If the animals pressed the bar too soon, the reward was not given and a new period of waiting began. We found that rats (and cats) with hippocampal destruction could wait for 10 to 15 seconds in between bar presses if this wait permitted a food reward to be given. But, if they were required to wait 20 or more seconds, their efficiency of performance declined and they began to exhibit signs of frenzy; they began to push the bar just about as fast as they could instead of waiting for the correct amount of time to elapse before pushing the bar again. Studies by other researchers in similar situations found that any time the conditions of reward became "unpredictable" or in some way "uncertain," the lesioned animals appeared to suffer a panic attack and respond vigorously without apparent concern for their lack of rewards. Apparently, when the waiting time between responses exceeds 20 seconds for rats (and cats), this amounts to uncertainty for them.

The results of each experiment led to new hypotheses and new experiments. At this time it is safe to say that I've been directly involved with some 150 or more experiments, following up our original studies. In these studies many different types of training and testing models have been used, selected on the basis of particular goals generated by preceding experiments. From this research, some interesting patterns emerged. For example, a former student of mine, David Olton, coined the term "cognitive load" to indicate how demanding a task may be for the animal or person to learn and/or retain. It was his view that damage to the hippocampus will be most apparent in tasks with substantial "cognitive loads," a position I would endorse. With easy loads, even severe damage to the brain may go unnoticed. Further, brain-damaged animals may perform even better than normal ones because they may be less interested in exploring their environments and less prone to interference from even subtle alterations in the environment. However, as the load increases and thus taps deeply or widely into the full range of cognitive or memorial capabilities of the animals, we see greater and greater disturbance of behavior.

Over the years my personal interests became more and more focused on alleviating the effects of hippocampal damage. In my early research, I was unable to alter all of the behavioral changes produced by this type of lesion at the same time. As one example, the administration of an antipsychotic drug (haloperidol) will reduce or eliminate the hyperactivity and overresponsiveness of animals with hippocampal lesions when they are required to wait 20 seconds for their rewards. But their performance is still inefficient—they manage to get only a few rewards. With hippocampal damage the coordination among the many systems and levels of systems of the brain is impaired. The animals can perform well enough in uncomplicated, well-defined situations, but when too much is demanded of them, they fail. Failure can drive them to frenzied activity resembling panic attacks in people.

We did not give up, however, the search for ways to adjust the remaining systems of the brain so as to compensate the lesioned animals for the loss of the hippocampus. There are now possibilities for effective interventions. Recently, Drs. Donna Maier, Jeanne Ryan, and I found that drugs affecting the release of the neurotransmitter norepinephrine in the brain and the hormones of the adrenal gland may increase the abilities of animals with hippocampal damage to deal with heavy cognitive load tasks. Extensions of these studies could lead to methods of improving the abilities of people with debilitating memory problems.

PULLING IT ALL TOGETHER

The limbic system does not do its work independently of other "systems" of the brain. Therefore, no reasonable theory of the activity of the limbic system can be developed until a more general framework for the brain's activities has been achieved. While this accomplishment is not likely in the foreseeable future, researchers seek a theoretical structure for understanding the diverse facts of nature and science. We need some conceptual framework for thinking about the brain and its parts and, therefore, various theories have been offered in the past, including ones based on telephone switchboards, computers, and holograms. All are only metaphors taken from other contexts and applied to brain activities. There is nothing wrong with metaphors as long as they are not confused with facts.

The theoretical approach that seems to offer a general and stimulating perspective for understanding brain function comes from a remarkable physician and scientist, Paul MacLean. He suggests that the brains of currently living mammals, including humans, have components that represent three major types of systems:

1. A protoreptilian (or R-Complex) brain
2. An old (early-developing) mammalian brain
3. A new mammalian brain

An illustration of these "three brains" in one is shown in Figure 3-1. The R-Complex is thought to represent the fundamental core of the nervous system, consisting of systems in the upper spinal cord and parts of the midbrain, the diencephalon, and the basal ganglia. The older mammalian brain is, in essence, the limbic system. The new mammalian brain refers to the expansion of neocortical tissue, so prominent in primates and in certain other species including sea mammals.

The R-Complex is involved with the capabilities for "ancestral learning and ancestral memories"; it plays a crucial role in the establishment of home territories, the finding of shelter and food, breeding, social dominance, and other primal behavior patterns. The "limbic" brain is nature's tentative first step toward self-awareness and, in the human, for the awareness of individuality. This intermediate brain receives information from the peripheral nervous system, as well as chemical signals communicated throughout the blood, as to the internal conditions of the body. In the limbic system, information about internal states is mixed with information from the outside world. The mixing of these two kinds of information provides the basis for self-awareness. Furthermore, the elaboration of information arising from inside the person or animal is thought to provide a necessary component of, or context for, memories. All memories depend on a mixture of information from the inner and outer worlds. This mixing of the two kinds of information makes it significant for the individual. The hippocampus is thought to be an especially good place for such mixtures to occur. It receives "internal information" via the septal area and "external information" from sensory systems projecting to nearby neocortical areas. It should be noted that all sensory systems send their information more or less directly to both neocortical regions and to R-Complex systems. The limbic system receives its information "second hand" but from both of these primary targets.

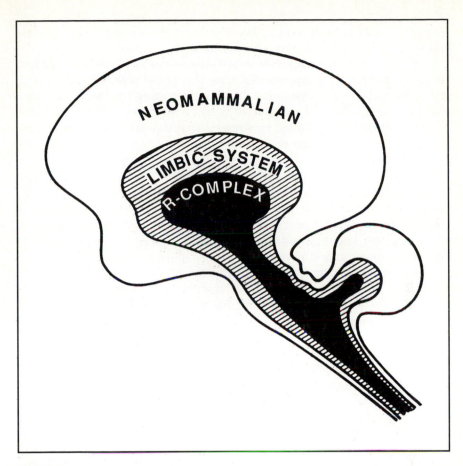

FIGURE 3.1
A model of the triune brain drawn as conceptualized by MacLean.

The neocortex is "mother of invention and father of abstract thought," according to MacLean, responsible for the cold (nonemotional) analysis of the external environment. It operates "unhindered by signals and noise generated in the internal world." It is thought to have a predilection for dividing things into smaller and smaller units, to perform abstractions, and to allow the development of reading, writing, and arithmetic.

My thoughts about the function of the "three brains in one" agree fairly well with MacLean's analyses. *But, I also think the limbic system is a strong regulator of the R-Complex.* I believe that it is able to override the inherited and learned responses collected in the R-Complex. One of the more interesting questions in neuroscience has been how this regulation is achieved. Understanding these mechanisms is the target of many neuroanatomists as they investigate connections between the limbic system and specific regions of the core of the brain.

The limbic system represents an advance in neural organization because it provides the animals that have this tissue with better means of coping with the environment. It does so by providing the means to better integrate the activities of the internal world with changes in the environmental contingencies. It must be stressed that the old mammalian brain is not homogeneous. Parts of the limbic system are concerned with primal activities related to feeding, fighting, fleeing, and sex; others are related to emotions and feelings; and still others combine messages from the external world with those predicted by systems of the neocortex. Disruption of the usual activities of the limbic system by epileptic episodes can produce a host of experiences and feelings; among the most interesting are knowing fundamental truths, feelings of depersonalization, hallucinations, and paranoia.

Another important aspect of the limbic system and its components is the ability to regulate and, indeed, interrupt the activities of the R-Complex. On the basis of behavioral analysis, this regulation seems to be inhibitory in nature. Experimental stimulation of the limbic system often produces a suppression of ongoing behaviors, and lesions made within it often seem to "release" various activities—animals fail to stop responding when it is to their benefit to do so; they persevere in previously acquired behaviors. Things once learned tend to resist change.

The circumstances under which the hippocampus acts to regulate the activities of other brain regions seem to be conditions of uncertainty, those instances in which what is supposed to happen doesn't. Life becomes uncertain when old patterns of responding fail to produce the anticipated rewards, when old habits fail to pay off. When these things happen, the normal animal or person stops ongoing activities in order to reassess the situation. With animals that have sustained large lesions of the hippocampus, this doesn't happen. The old, established patterns of behavior continue. One function of the hippocampus can be seen as a mechanism that suppresses the activity in the R-Complex when the unexpected happens. This suppression prevents the animal from continuing in its old ways of responding or from overreacting if the R-Complex loses all regulation.

The limbic system, through its suppression of the R-Complex patterns of behavior, makes it possible to form rapid and, at times, useful temporary associations. The limbic system makes possible the suppression of the traditional ways of responding in order to allow behavioral modifications based on information from the internal environment as directed by the neocortical tissue. Both the limbic system and the neocortex become elaborated in mammals and usually work in concert.

These observations would be compatible with the view that the limbic system is responsible for the suppression of previously learned behavioral sequences. Therefore, it can be viewed as the mechanism that is directed toward the elimination of influences from the past, that is, from the stored memories of the reptilian brain. The limbic brain, in collaboration with the neocortical system, provides the basis of forgetting chronic memories, the deeply embedded images of the R-Complex, and thus opens the way for new, temporary associations.

SUMMING UP

Many researchers have examined the evolution of the primate brain. Most tend to emphasize the development of the neocortex, but this cannot be, by itself, the hallmark of human development. Several land and sea mammalian species have more neocortex, both absolutely and relatively. It seems to me that if there is a special character to the human primate, it is the parallel development of the neocortex and the limbic system. Nonhuman primates have well-developed neocortical regions but little in the way of limbic development. Looking at the position of the human on both cortical and limbic factors provides an interesting observation: what makes the human brain unique is a high level of development on both factors. That is, not only do people differ from other primates in their ability to look into themselves to generate feelings about others, but the feelings themselves may be more intense or elaborate as well.

If we ask the question of what a human is, the answer seems to be an organism in which the three major brain systems act together and in harmony. We need to know the world, to appreciate and sympathize with others, and to be able to use abstractions to help realize our individual potential without reducing that of others. When brain regions become impaired and no longer serve us properly, a variety of symptoms result, but it is impossible to make statements about the region responsible for a particular change, except in trivial instances. It is harmony of the systems working together that is of critical importance. To understand the brain, we must someday learn the secrets of its composition.

These, then, are my working ideas about how the brain, especially the limbic system, is put together. It is written in broad strokes and there are many details that we need to fill in to complete the entire picture. But, at least it is a beginning.

Acknowledgments

Undertaking so many experiments on the effects of hippocampal damage, both behavioral and biochemical, has required the collaboration of many graduate students over the years. I wish I could name them all here, but there are just too many. They know who they are, however, and how much I treasure my association with them.

SUGGESTED READINGS

ISAACSON, R.L. (1972). Hippocampal destruction in man and other animals. *Neuropsychologia, 10*, 47–64.

———— (1982). *The limbic system* (2nd ed). New York: Plenum.

MACLEAN, P. D. (1990). *The triune brain in evolution: Role in paleocerebral functions.* New York: Plenum.

MISHKIN, M., & APPENZELLER, T. (1987). The anatomy of memory. *Scientific American, 256*, 80–89.

OLTON, D. S. (1989). Dimensional mnemonics. In G. H. Bower (Ed.) *The psychology of learning and motivation* (pp. 1–23). San Diego, CA: Academic.

PENFIELD, W., & MILNER, B. (1958). Memory deficit produced by bilateral lesions in the hippocampal zone. *Archives of Neurology and Psychiatry, 79*, 475–497.

———— & ROBERTS, L. (1959). *Speech and brain mechanisms.* Princeton, NJ: Princeton Univ. Press.

SCOVILLE, W. B., & MILNER, B. (1957). Amnesia after bilateral mesial temporal lobe excision: An introduction to case H. M. *Neuropsychologia, 6*, 211–213.

MARVIN ZUCKERMAN *(Ph.D., New York University) is currently Professor of Psychology at the University of Delaware. He has published widely in the fields of personality assessment, sensation seeking trait, and biological approaches to personality. While he has constructed many tests, the two most known and used are the Multiple Affect Adjective Check List (with B. Lubin) and the Sensation Seeking Scale. His books include:* Emotions and Anxiety; Sensation Seeking: Beyond the Optimal Level of Arousal; Biological Bases of Sensation Seeking, Impulsivity, and Anxiety; *and* Psychobiology of Personality. *His interest in the phenomena influenced by sensation seeking has led to the study of sports and vocations; social, sexual, and marital relationships; tastes in art, the media, fantasy and humor; habits of smoking, drinking, drug use, and eating. With the exceptions of sports and drug use his recreational activities cover the same areas.*

4

Out of Sensory Deprivation and into Sensation Seeking: A Personal and Scientific Journey

❖

I have often been asked why I study sensation seeking, as if there must be some motivational factor related to my personal needs. This is strange because no one assumes that someone who studies anxiety is anxious, or that someone who studies schizophrenia is schizophrenic. The selection of an area of interest is usually a mixture of pragmatic and personal factors with an element of serendipity and pure chance.

The interaction between one's unique constellation of genes and environment is mysterious. In the Minnesota study of twins separated at birth and adopted into different families, there were two men who, after they were reunited as adults, found that they had both become firemen. While this might be a coincidence, the odds are approximately 340,000 to one against it, and such coincidences happened only among identical twins and never in fraternal twins. Perhaps if I had an identical twin somewhere he would have ended up as a psychologist studying a topic like sensation seeking. At least I am sure that he would not be a conservative accountant living in the suburbs of Milwaukee.

There is little need to dwell on my family background since behavior genetics research suggests the surprising conclusion that shared family environment has little to do with personality. On my father's side my great grandfather was a rabbi, my grandfather was a teacher, and my father was a mechanical engineer who came to this country to get a secular college education, something impossible for Jews in czarist Russia. My mother's father was a quiet intellectual who left Russia to escape family pressures to become a rabbi like his father, as well as the czar's military draft. In the United States he was forced to earn his living as a small businessman in order to support his family. My maternal grandmother waited on the customers while he sat in the back room drinking tea from a glass, in the Russian manner. He ran for alderman in Cincinnati on the Socialist ticket. He lost, of course, and retreated to his backroom study. Both grandmothers and my mother lived the traditional Jewish role for women. Their values centered around their families, keeping them well loved and well fed, too much so of the latter. Neither of my parents seems to have been much of a sensation seeker, although there are some hints that my father was not always a model husband, especially during times when my mother took me to spend our summers at the family home in Cincinnati. My mother's sensation seeking outlets centered largely around games of mah jong and bridge for low stakes. Apart from love, somewhat contingent on good grades, my father gave me two important values: education and doing work you love even if you never become rich at it.

Until my mid-teens, personal sensation seeking partly focused on football, but mainly was fantasy derived from the novels of Dumas (e.g., *The Three Musketeers*) and series like *The Boy Pioneers* or pulps like *Flying Aces*. Later, I began to enjoy the fiction of Hemingway, Dos Passos, and Thomas Wolfe and my tastes in magazines shifted to science fiction.

The first portent of a career in psychology occurred when I was about 15 and became interested in a book on graphology. Perhaps this foreshadowed my interest in personality assessment, although at the time it was just fun to analyze the personalities of friends and family through their handwriting. Nasty questions of reliability and validity never disturbed my early practice of character analysis.

At sixteen I went to the University of Kentucky where I discovered the disinhibitory joys of drinking, sex, and hitchhiking around the country. Toward the end of my liberated year in Kentucky, in a more introspective and mildly depressed frame of mind, I read Freud's *The Interpretation of Dreams* and *The Psychopathology of Everyday Life*. I promptly "lost" the book on a train, but was not repressed enough to prevent my obtaining another copy. I wrote a term paper, "Sexual Symbolism in Dreams," for an English course. My instructor insisted that it was not a "proper" subject, but I went over his head to the chair of the department. The instructor was not pleased and retaliated with a grade of C. During the writing, my own dreams proved to be a rich source of material, redolent with symbolic and not so symbolic sex (my first serious love affair had just ended). I found myself interpreting my dreams while I was still dreaming them. I decided to be a psychoanalyst and interpret other people's fantasies and dreams rather than translate my own into fiction or poetry.

The next year the Second World War ended and with it my fantasies of military glory. But at 18 I was drafted into the Army, which still needed men to replace those being demobilized. Several months of tough basic training in the swamps of Louisiana followed by a long dreary year of garrison duty killed any residual desire for a military career. It is fortunate that I did not have to actually fight in a war since I would have undoubtedly been killed. I was officially declared "killed" twice during one day of intensive "combat" maneuvers. Some of us were not born to be warriors.

After the Army I returned to college at New York University and shortly thereafter, I married, at the wrong age, to the wrong woman. That marriage lasted an unhappy 12 years and produced two great children and eventually three beautiful and brilliant grandchildren. I have no regrets. Who am I to question the mysterious outcomes of assortative mating?

I began New York University in a premed program with the goal of psychiatry and eventually psychoanalysis. But a solitary C in a crucial chemistry course ended my medical career. Fortunately, N.Y.U. had recently started a graduate program in clinical psychology and this seemed to be a more direct path to what I wanted despite the restrictions then on clinical practice and psychoanalytic training. Besides, I loved psychology courses, even the experimental ones, hated chemistry, and avoided biology altogether, except for what I learned in physiological psychology. In view of my current interests in the psychobiology of personality, I wish I had loved chemistry and biology more, but like most students then and even today, I did not see the connection.

I began to realize that there was another psychology outside the Freudian mode. Freud's emphasis on the primacy of sexual motivation is quite attractive to adolescents and young single adults (what else is there?), but the ideas of psychosexual stages of personality and the Oedipus complex required a great deal of credulity. Scientific training in psychology made me realize that what the psychoanalysts preached was not "science," and the methods used to develop their theories were about as scientific as astrology.

Learning theories seemed more palatable. But even these theories, derived largely from studies of harried, fearful, and starving white rats, seemed to have little to do with problems of personality and psychopathology. I was interested in studies showing that male rats would cross an electrified grid for access to females in heat. Now that was science; "libido" quantified and defined in terms of number of grid crossings or level of shock endurance! But there was one finding that mystified me—sometimes rats would cross the shock grid just to see what was on the other side. Given the choice of different paths to the same goal they would alternate paths rather than use the same one all the time. Harry Harlow reported that monkeys confined in sterile cages would work at lever pressing for long periods just to obtain glimpses of the world outside. Something that had little to do with the conventional primary drives (hunger, thirst, sex, and pain avoidance) was at work even in the normally cautious rat. The learning theory answer was an "exploratory drive," but the biological sources of the drive were a mystery.

I became interested in the "New Look" in perceptual research. Some audacious researchers were suggesting that personality needs and values might influence how we perceive the world, particularly in difficult viewing conditions like very brief stimulus exposures. For my dissertation, I decided to study the perception of aggressive and neutral words following a frustrating failure experience by subjects who were high or low in aggressiveness trait. Aggressiveness was measured by the Rosenzweig Picture Frustration Test, which requires subjects to give their imagined responses to a series of everyday stresses portrayed in the form of cartoons. My results were rather disappointing in that the stress induced by failure-frustration interfered with recognition of words, but the effects were not influenced by the content of the words or levels of subjects' aggressiveness trait. In retrospect, I suspect that my failure to find a personality-situation interaction owed as much to the use of a poorly validated projective test to assess the aggression trait as to the experimental design and the hypothesis. This experience taught me a lesson. If you want to define a personality trait with a test, you should use one with demonstrated validity or else develop your own. Subsequently, I did research on personality assessment which showed that projective tests were not useful in measuring traits like aggression, hostility, anxiety, depression, or dependency. But right after my dissertation research I felt depressed and doubted the usefulness of laboratory research in the study of personality.

My preclinical and postdoctoral work offered little intellectual satisfaction. Colleagues at the state hospitals where I worked were an odd mixture of older institutional types with vague organic theories, who were quick on the "shock" button, and young psychoanalysts with elaborate theories about why patients said what they did or did what they didn't talk about at all. There was a psychiatric director who was a classic manic-depressive. You did not see much of him during the depressive phase, but when in the manic phase he would dramatically expound on a grand theory of psychiatry. The theory started at the atomic level and extended to the universe, with people bobbing around in atomic harmony somewhere in between. The main point of the theory was motion. It was a symptom of my growing discontent with the Freudian paradigm that his theory began to sound just as plausible as those offered by the more sober psychoanalytic types.

My lack of faith in psychoanalytic theories interfered with my enjoyment of clinical work. Even if my therapy patients got better I never understood why. I once treated a depressed middle-aged man who wanted to talk only about his wife's extravagant spending habits, not about their relationship or his childhood. I finally gave up and helped him work out a reasonable budget for his wife. He showed a dramatic improvement and profusely thanked me for his "cure." In contrast, other patients developed remarkable insights but failed to get better. I think therapists either must have a great deal of faith in the theoretical context that they work in, or else not worry about theory at all.

I credit my born-again scientific interest to Arnold Buss. I moved to Carter Memorial Hospital in Indianapolis where Arny was the chief psychologist. Arny is an intellectually provocative and skeptical person with a high level of activity and enthusiasm. He was always challenging his friends to a game of tennis, chess, or a discussion of some topic in psychology, politics, or films. He organized seminars where we discussed research we had done or were doing and he created an academic environment for the clinical community in Indianapolis. Eventually most of us went back to academics.

Nearly everyone in psychology in Indiana was from somewhere else, mostly New York or Chicago. We had a common bond in our dislike for the right-wing politics and anti-intellectualism of the general community. While there I became involved in the local Civil Liberties Union, which had an activist, black lawyer as director who believed in setting up his cases against segregation with sit-in challenges. We went on sit-ins in restaurants, bars, and an amusement park. It could get quite interesting at times, like when we were ordered out of a tavern at gun-point. We left without argument. Passive resistance has its limits.

I began to realize that I enjoyed doing and talking about research more than testing and treating patients. I preferred intellectual activities that provided real answers, no matter how many new questions they raised. I also enjoyed the papers and late parties at conventions where one could "talk psychology," flirt, or just get drunk and disinhibited. These days I primarily go for the papers. Sensation seeking does decline with age.

At this point one of those chance events that determine our fates occurred. A psychiatric research institute opened at the Indiana University Medical Center next door to Carter Hospital, where I was working. By then I was ready for full-time research. John Nurnberger, a research-oriented psychiatrist, hired me as a member of an interdisciplinary team of biochemists, microbiologists, and experimental psychologists. We were expected to find the causes and cures of schizophrenia within a few years and no one discouraged this delusion among the politicians who funded the institute. For me it was the beginning of my interest in biological approaches to behavior. These were four productive years during which I worked largely on problems of personality assessment.

Toward the end of my stay at the institute, I began the experimental study of sensory deprivation that became my primary area of research for the next eleven years. The first exciting reports of sensory deprivation experiments on humans came from McGill University. The method was simple. Volunteer subjects were placed in dark, soundproof rooms, with tactual deprivation and movement restrictions. Their basic toilet and food needs were taken care of in the room. They were asked to report any unusual occurrences. Some reported hallucinations, and others had illusions or even delusions. Most showed a progressive slowing of brain-wave alpha activity. Most complained about cognitive inefficiency, saying that they could not concentrate on anything for any length of time. Some were bored, others got panicky, and only about two-thirds of the subjects could endure more than two days of sensory deprivation. Ten hours was the limit for the more severe water-tank immersion type of sensory deprivation.

It seemed to me that an experimental method had been devised to explore psychopathology as a transient state (I hoped) in otherwise normal volunteers. A group of investigators in Boston used an iron lung to confine the movements of their subjects. I found an old one in the storeroom of the medical center and began to use it in eight-hour studies, comparing the effects of sensory deprivation with mere confinement in the iron lung without sensory or social isolation. These effects were quite variable from subject to subject, but included some increase in anxiety in most subjects, complaints of conceptual disorganization, and visual hallucinations in some subjects. In subsequent experiments in sensory deprivation conducted at Brooklyn College, Adelphi University, and Einstein Medical Center, we switched to an ordinary bed in a soundproof room.

In the Fall of 1959 I returned to New York and started my first academic job as an assistant professor at Brooklyn College. This move coincided with a divorce, personal therapy, and a period of great personal turmoil and growth. Perhaps it is not coincidental that it was at this time that I developed an instrument to measure a trait that I decided to call "Sensation Seeking." In most of our studies we gave subjects standard personality tests before the experiments to see if we could predict their responses to sensory deprivation. Affective responses to sensory deprivation were variable, ranging from boredom to panic.

Sensory deprivation has been called a "walk-in inkblot." The analogy is with the Rorschach ink-blot test where personality is supposedly revealed by one's unique interpretations of the ambiguous blot forms. Sensory deprivation is an ambiguous situation where nothing is required of subjects and they may interpret the darkness and silence in any ways they like. It is not surprising that people who have a strong anxiety trait become anxious in the sensory deprivation situation, just as "field-dependent" people became anxious because of the lack of a structured environment.

However, since a major source of stress was the deprivation of sensory stimulation, it seemed reasonable that a personality trait based on differences in need for stimulation might be predictive of anxiety in sensory deprivation. The theoretical basis for this hypothetical trait came from an idea of Wilhelm Wundt, the founder of psychology, that neither too little nor too much stimulation and sensation was optimal. For each sensory modality there was an optimal level of stimulation at which people felt best. Others proposed that this optimal level might apply across sensory modalities to a generalized stimulation or arousal level. Some suggested that there might be individual differences in this generalized optimal level of stimulation and arousal. I predicted that persons with a high optimal level should be more stressed than persons with a low optimal level by the deprivation of external stimulation. Since there was no standardized measure of such a trait we set out to devise one.

With an undergraduate assistant I began to write items for the first form of the Sensation Seeking Scale (SSS). We were encouraged to find that diverse kinds of items, incorporating many sensory modalities and complex kinds of experiences, did intercorrelate enough to justify our assumption of a broad multimodality factor. The essence of this factor was the seeking of sensory experiences that satisfied a desire for novel, complex, and intense experiences, and restlessness and boredom when the social or physical environment was unchanging. The items also measured a willingness to accept physical or social risks in order to have these kinds of experiences. Later analyses of new experimental forms revealed four subfactors in the SSS:

- Thrill and adventure seeking: Seeking unique and intense sensations through such sports and activities as parachuting, scuba diving, etc.
- Experience seeking: Seeking novel sensations and experiences through the mind and senses; music, art, travel, drugs, and unconventional life styles.
- Disinhibition: Seeking sensation through exciting people, parties, drinking, and sex.
- Boredom Susceptibility: An aversion to sameness in people or environments and a restlessness when such sameness is unavoidable.

We first applied the SSS to predicting the outcomes of sensory deprivation experiments conducted at Adelphi University and later at Albert Einstein Medical Center. This was what I had designed the scale for. I was then thinking of sensation seeking as a rather narrow trait, of relevance to only a small range of situations. If the scale predicted reactions to sensory deprivation, the results would support my theory, which was based on individual differences in optimal levels of stimulation and arousal.

While the general SSS did not predict affective reactions to sensory deprivation, it did predict random body movement, or restlessness, during an eight-hour period of confinement, with or without sensory deprivation. This result suggested that movement restriction was a major source of stress for high sensation seekers in the situation. Subsequent studies demonstrated that increasing the degree of movement restriction markedly increased the subjective and physiological measured stress response to sensory deprivation. One study showed that when sensation seekers were given a choice between working for bland visual stimulation and brief time periods to get off the bed and move around, they usually chose the opportunity for movement. However, in another study where they were not given this choice they responded more to view bland slides. Finally, in a situation where subjects were confined with another person, and had the opportunity to talk, listen to music, or view slides, it was the low sensation seekers who were more emotionally distressed; the highs tended to enjoy the stimulating situation.

During my brief appointment at Adelphi University I became involved in the struggle for civil rights. I joined the local chapter of the Congress for Racial Equality (CORE) and was arrested in a "lay-in" in the lobby of an apartment house in Long Beach where blacks had been refused rentals. I spent an evening in the local jail. Since CORE was not able to make bail the next morning, I was handcuffed and taken in a van to jail. Fortunately, after a few hours I was bailed out. The total experience was an interesting one, but a little beyond my own "optimal level of stimulation." This is not to say that sensation seeking alone explains dangerous protest activities. The trait is highly correlated with liberal values in general, which is not surprising since liberals, in contrast to conservatives, are people who are not afraid of change. Given particular political orientations and sets of values, sensation seeking probably determines the level of risk one is willing to take for the sake of a strong belief. Personally, I wanted to do something beyond picketing and writing letters to my congressman, but I knew I did not have the courage to risk death, like the Freedom Riders who were trying to end segregation in travel facilities in the south. Many forms of sensation seeking involve risk, and sensation seeking partly determines the level of risk one will tolerate for the sake of the experience or "the cause."

I subsequently learned that the administrators of Adelphi University were not pleased with newspaper photos of me lying prone in the police station. The students were delighted but Adelphi was a conservative university and in 1963 protest was not yet fashionable. I was told that even if I were not fired I would not have been given tenure. Fortunately, another job opportunity had come up at a new research facility at Albert Einstein Hospital research labs in Philadelphia.

Harold Persky, a former biochemist colleague from the Indiana Institute of Psychiatric Research, invited me to join a group in endocrine research just formed at Albert Einstein. He wanted me to work with him on studies of the biochemistry of anxiety, depression, and hostility. I looked forward to the chance to add some psychophysiological and hormonal measures of reactivity to my sensory deprivation experiments. I joined the new Society for Psychophysiological Research and began learning the techniques of this field for use in sensory deprivation studies. At that time I viewed biological measures as indices of stress and emotional reactions rather than as biological traits which might play a causal role in personality.

At the end of the decade of the 1960s I again had to deal with a crisis involving both my work and my personal life. Albert Einstein Medical Center was a research facility founded on "soft money" without institutional back-up. By this time my entire salary was paid by my own research grant. In 1968, after ten years of support from the National Institute of Mental Health (NIMH) for sensory deprivation research, I was told that a proposed continuation would not be approved. NIMH decided that everything had been learned about the subject and new research could not contribute more. This was a great surprise to me since I had many new ideas for research. I suddenly realized that there *is* a difference between "soft" and "hard" money, and a tenured academic position began to look quite attractive. But looking for an appropriate position when one is 40 can be an unsettling experience, and at the time of this work crisis, my second marriage dissolved.

Fortunately, I managed to get an appointment at the University of Delaware, where they were just starting a new graduate program in clinical psychology. When I took the job I never dreamed I would be there for the next twenty years. From early childhood my life had involved frequent changes of location and such stability was almost inconceivable. Delaware provided the security I needed to develop a basic research program without the frequent periodic search for external funding and the pressure to tie one's work to clinically relevant topics.

A lack of large-scale funding was a problem, because sensory deprivation research is expensive. I therefore decided to focus my work on sensation seeking itself, without reference to sensory deprivation. I wanted to see what the SSS could predict in the natural behavior of college students, as well as their tastes, preferences, and styles of life. In the early 1970s there were three kinds of revolutions going on in colleges and elsewhere: the political protests against the war in Vietnam and racism in America; the sexual revolution changing American mores about pre- and postmarital behavior; and the widespread experimentation with drugs.

Sensation seeking in college students was related to participation in all three of these revolutions. Low sensation seekers were conservative, nonactivist, and passive resisters in the sexual and drug revolutions. High sensation seekers tended to be politically active, or if they were conservative they joined the Army to see "the action" in "Nam." They tended to have more varied sex with more partners and to smoke, drink, and use drugs more than low sensation seekers. They were overrepresented among volunteers for any kind of unusual experiments or activities like hypnosis, sensory deprivation, drug experiments, and encounter and sensitivity groups, but did not show an equal interest in experiments involving learning or social interaction. They tended to participate in such risky sports as parachuting, scuba diving, skiing, auto racing, and hang gliding, but did not like monotonous sports like swimming, running, or aerobic exercise. The high sensation seekers preferred novel and complex designs to familiar, simple, and symmetrical ones. They liked jazz or rock music and disliked "easy-listening" or movie-sound-track music. They enjoyed X-rated or horror movies but did not spend much time watching television.

There is hardly any area of psychology that has not been studied in relation to sensation seeking. Recently, studies have been done on cognitive and attentional processes and social interactions of couples in the laboratory setting. We found that sensation seekers have a strong focused-attention mechanism, and sensation seeking women tend to focus their eyes on their love object more than low sensation seekers. The phenomenal pictures of the sensation seeker and sensation avoider have been delineated by the research efforts of psychologists and psychiatrists around the world and have suggested a breadth of explanatory power for the trait going far beyond what I originally expected.

The first questions we ask about a new personality trait are "What is it?" and "What can it predict?" These are never fully answered since there are always new phenomena to be explored, and critical studies that could change our precise understanding of the trait. But sooner or later an investigator must ask more basic questions like "Where does it come from?" and "How is it formed?" Depending on one's approach, this can lead to studies of the family background of persons at high and low ends of the trait distributions, or to studies of their biological characteristics and genetic influences. I decided to take the latter research strategy.

David Fulker, Sybil Eysenck, and I did a large-scale "twin study" of sensation seeking in London. The study showed a stronger genetic component for sensation seeking than what is typically found for most personality traits. But genetic studies cannot tell you what biological mechanisms are inherited to form the basis for the trait.

Somewhat earlier we began to use psychophysiological methods in the study of sensation seeking. Sensation seekers appear to be behaviorally alert and interested in novel situations or novel things in their environment, but they do get bored by repetition. This suggested the possibility that we might find differences in the strength of the orienting reflex and its habituation. Specifically, could the basis for their general interest in the novel be a stronger (or a weaker) than normal physiological reaction (e.g., skin conductance or heart rate) to novel stimuli? And could their boredom be caused by a strong habituation mechanism?

The answers from our studies of the orienting reflex suggested that the answer to the first question was "yes." High sensation seekers showed a stronger reaction to novel stimuli than lows, but no differences were found between high and low sensation seekers on subsequent presentations of these stimuli. The answer to the second question was "no," since no difference was found between high and low sensation seekers in the rate of habituation beyond the second presentation.

A second line of psychophysiological research involved a more direct measure of brain reactivity—the cortical evoked potential. Unlike the first studies, these studies varied the intensity, rather than the novelty, of stimulation, using a method developed by Monte Buchsbaum. A pattern of increasing cortical response to increasing stimulus intensity is called "augmenting." A pattern showing no such increase or actual decrease in evoked potentials at the highest stimulus intensity is termed "reducing." We found that the high sensation seeker tends to be an augmenter of cortical response to high intensity stimuli, while the low sensation seeker tends to be a reducer. The significance of this finding may be that high sensation seekers have an inborn physiological tolerance for high levels of stimulation and can work and feel better than low sensation seekers in such conditions. Low sensation seekers have brains that protectively "tune out" strong stimulation.

Turning our attention to the biochemical level, Reid Daitzman and I discovered that sensation seeking was strongly related to levels of gonadal (sex) hormones in males, not just testosterone but estrogen as well. We also found that gonadal hormones were related to social assertiveness and heterosexual experience in young, unmarried males. A newspaper report of this research suggested that low sensation seekers had "shrunken testicles." Besides insulting low sensation seeking males, this report was quite inaccurate, since the lows had normal testosterone levels, while the highs had very high levels.

But the most exciting discoveries came from studies conducted by investigators at the NIMH. These results led to a new model for sensation seeking, deemphasizing differences in cortical reactivity and pointing to limbic brain monoamine systems activity as the basis for the trait. In two separate studies, investigators found significant *inverse* relationships between sensation seeking and the enzyme monoamine oxidase (MAO). Although MAO is assessed from blood platelets in living humans, in the brain it is a vital enzyme in the regulation of three important neurotransmitters—dopamine, norepinephrine, and serotonin, collectively called "monamines." These findings made me curious about these systems, their behavioral functions, and their possible role in sensation seeking trait differences. But first I had to learn some basics in the field of psychopharmacology, a science virtually unknown to me at the time.

During the last 15 years I have become an avid student in the fields of comparative behavioral psychopharmacology and biological psychiatry. Some preliminary findings have linked sensation seeking with the monoamine norepinephrine, assayed from cerebrospinal fluid in normal humans. On the basis of these findings and a great deal of theoretical "free-flight," I have attempted to build a new theory of sensation seeking that goes "beyond the optimal level of arousal" to specific reward and arousal brain systems mediated by catecholamines.

Apart from the security of tenure, one of the benefits of teaching is that it forces you to read and think beyond your narrow research focus. I have only once taught a course in my specific topic of interest (sensation seeking); my usual courses are in the broader areas of personality and psychopathology. A responsible teacher must also be a scholar. But reading for one's personal interest does not yield the depth of understanding that comes with the necessity to explain things to students. With colleagues you can hide your limited understanding of the phenomena in the esoteric language of your field. With students you must be prepared to explain all concepts in the most basic terms. Teaching personality theories required me to think about how sensation seeking fit into the broader structure of personality.

In the last several years I have attempted to determine the biological basis of sensation seeking and to formulate hypotheses about the "psychobiology of personality." This research may be startling to some and would have been to me when I began in psychology at mid-century, but both the field and I have changed. Research and life lead one down some strange, unanticipated paths. One must be willing to change and learn. This willingness to change is the positive aspect of sensation seeking. One of the so-called big-five personality traits has been labeled "Openness to Experience." A researcher must be open to unexpected findings, new methods, and new theoretical approaches in order to discover something of value. At the same time theoreticians must not give up too easily on a model because of a lack of positive findings in a specific study. As in stimulation and arousal seeking there is an optimal level of changeability. The theory may apply to our personal lives as well. Too often, however, you do not realize you are beyond an optimal level until it is too late.

The study of sensory deprivation combined with my continued interest in personality assessment led to the study of sensation seeking and the development of a scale for this study. But a willingness to shift my interest from sensory deprivation to what was originally a minor interest in a new personality trait resulted in something of importance. Admittedly, the discovery of sensation seeking was determined by personal factors as well as scientific ones. Perhaps for a time I was a sensation seeking voyeur in a state of sensory deprivation. Then for a time I became an active sensation seeker. But some sublimation is necessary for hard scientific work. A really dedicated sensation seeker cannot spend much time in the laboratory or at home writing papers and books.

The development of the sensation seeking scales and theory was also influenced by environmental factors somewhat beyond my control, like the rejection of my grant renewal for sensory deprivation research, which resulted in my return to academia and less-expensive research. This event forced a decision about a failing marriage and the beginning of a new and happier relationship, which has endured to this time. What would have happened if NIMH had renewed my grant for another five years? There are no controlled experiments in life. These accidents of life may be more important than we believe in the shaping of personality.

SUGGESTED READINGS

BUCHSBAUM, M. S., HAIER, R. J., & JOHNSON, J. (1983). Augmenting and reducing: Individual differences in evoked potentials. In A. Gale & J. A. Edwards (Eds.) *Physiological correlates of human behavior, Vol. 3* (pp. 120–138). London: Academic.

SCHOOLEF, C., ZAHN, T. P., MURPHY, D. L., & BUCHSBAUM, M. S. (1978). Psychological correlates of monoamine oxidase in normals. *Journal of Nervous and Mental Disease, 166,* 177–186.

ZUBEK, J. P. (1969). *Sensory deprivation: Fifteen years of research.* New York: Appleton-Century-Crofts.

ZUCKERMAN, M. (1979). *Sensation seeking: Beyond the optimal level of arousal.* Hillsdale, NJ: Erlbaum.

——— (1984a). Sensation seeking: A comparative approach to a human trait. *Behavioral and Brain Science, 7,* 413–471.

——— (1984b). The neurobiology of some dimensions of personality. In J. R. Smythies & R. J. Bradley (Eds.) *International review of neurobiology. Vol. 25* (pp. 292–436). New York: Academic.

——— (1990). The psychophysiology of sensation seeking. *Journal of Personality, 58,* 313–345.

——— (1991). *Psychobiology of personality.* Cambridge, MA: Cambridge Univ. Press.

——— (ED.). (1983). *Biological bases of sensation seeking, impulsivity and anxiety.* Hillsdale, NJ: Erlbaum.

——— BUCHSBAUM, M. S., & MURPHY, D. L. (1980). Sensation seeking and its biological correlates. *Psychological Bulletin, 88,* 187–214.

*L*ARY *SHAFFER* (D. Phil., Oxford University) is currently Professor of Psychology at State University of New York at Plattsburgh. He has done research in behavior ecology of seagulls and chipmunks and has studied the development of sheepdog behavior. He has made numerous scientific documentaries on animal behavior for the BBC and Time/Life and is a regular reviewer of natural-history books for the London Times Literary Supplement. He is just completing photojournalistic work based on his two months in the People's Republic of Congo. Dr. Shaffer is a biking enthusiast and recently made a solo cross-country bicycle trip.

5

Cracking the Crab Case

—————— ❖ ——————

My first brush with research occurred when I was an undergraduate psychology major in the mid-1960s. One of the fashions in research at that time was to attempt to unravel the evolutionary development of learning. A commonsense viewpoint suggested that so-called "lower" or "primitive" animals—such as fish, salamanders, and turtles—had more limited learning capacities than animals considered to be "higher" or "more evolved"—such as rats and college freshmen. This enterprise was called comparative psychology because of the presumption that the behavior of nonhuman animals was only of interest if it was compared to other animals' behaviors, specifically the behavior of humans.

Because a large body of knowledge on the learning of rats and freshmen already existed, I decided to focus on turtles and salamanders in order to have a research niche that could offer new challenges. My undergraduate honors project was a study of learning in the red-spotted newt, a type of salamander.

Learning has been defined as a relatively permanent change in behavior resulting from practice, and comparative psychologists often looked for it to happen within the confines of T-mazes. The T-maze, as its name suggests, consists of a straight runway which leads to a choice point. At the choice point, the animal can turn either left or right. Classically, one of these choices is rewarded and one is not. Since newts normally live in damp places, it occurred to me that I could perhaps teach a newt to turn in a particular direction in order to find a damp paper towel.

Before setting off with the T-maze itself, I attempted to establish some baseline information about the damp-seeking response of newts. I wanted to demonstrate that this behavior was, in some way, systematic, predictable, and amenable to scientific measurement. To collect this pilot data, I built a small straight runway which had a start box at one end and a goal box, with a wet paper towel in it, at the other. I water-deprived several groups of wild-caught newts for periods of time ranging from 15 minutes to 2 hours. My hypothesis was that the more deprived groups of newts would run faster to reach the damp towel. I expected to determine the ideal level of water deprivation of the newts in the runway and

I planned to use this information in the subsequent learning study using the T-maze.

The behavior of the newts in the runway was very predictable; it consisted of a systematic attempt to escape from the apparatus. Different deprivation times made no difference in running speed to the supposedly rewarding damp towel. Infrequently and seemingly by accident, the newts would amble down the runway to the towel upon release from the start box. It was much more typical, however, for the newts to sit still with what appeared to me to be confusion written on their little faces. Those who chose not to sit still would wander around a little and then try to climb the walls of the runway.

Undaunted by this I tried to demonstrate newtonian learning in the T-maze anyway and achieved results similar to those obtained in the runway. Research in the wild has since demonstrated that species of newts can perform prodigious feats of homing: finding their home stream by its smell from 15 miles away. From these data it is clear that the newts were easily capable of finding a paper towel from a distance of two feet, had they so desired. I now believe that they were willing to forgo the joys of a damp towel in exchange for a concerted effort to get out of the runway, out of the lab, and return to their home swamps. In retrospect, I would do the same thing if I were in their position. They were daring and adventuresome escape artists and, in spite of my best attempts at security, I would often find the little crispy and dry corpses of escapees under books and behind furniture. The caged lab-newts were trying to tell me something, but I was not ready to learn from them.

Near the end of the newt episode in my life I was assigned, as part of some course work, to read Niko Tinbergen's classic paper *The Shell Menace*. Tinbergen and his research group were studying animal learning, but they were using wild animals living in their natural habitats. Tinbergen's approach was called Ethology and it had grown as an offshoot of European biology. He was finding that animals are remarkably good at learning to solve problems when the problems have relevance to their everyday life. The additional appeal of his work was that the animals fed and watered themselves and they lived in remote places which were exciting and wonderful. I was sold.

As an undergraduate at SUNY–Plattsburgh, a small college in a state university system, I doubted that it was realistic to even consider applying for graduate study with the great Tinbergen at Oxford University. My long-suffering honors-project advisor, Henry Morlock, belittled my fears and pointed out that even if Tinbergen did not answer my letter, I had nothing to lose but the cost of an airmail stamp. I applied. Tinbergen responded with application forms for me to fill out and a handwritten letter apologizing for the forms. His apology was longer than the forms themselves. In February of my senior year the impossible happened, Tinbergen invited me to join his research group. He was polite about a copy of the newt honors project which I had sent and briskly suggested that I might like to work with seagulls on Walney Island in the Irish Sea.

Assuming that Oxford would be a very formal place, I bought a new tweed three-piece suit, which was the most British-looking garment I could find in Gloversville, New York. When I arrived for my first formal meeting with Tinbergen, I was resplendent in my new suit, while he was wearing well-worn and carefully patched army fatigues. He was a modest and humble man who, from the first, could not do enough to see that I had every opportunity to learn about animal behavior. Although his secretary had assured me that he wanted to be called "Niko," not "Dr. Tinbergen," I was very uncomfortable being that familiar and I avoided all direct address for the first few months. As Tinbergen casually hand-rolled and chain-smoked cigarettes, he told me about the graduate program, or non-program, at Oxford. My degree was a research degree. There would be no formal classes and only one big oral exam. I would do a substantial piece of research which would, upon completion, be examined by some zoologists who had played no role in the shaping of the research. I might finish within three years but I must finish within five years. At Oxford, graduates were not spoon-fed, but he would be happy to give me advice. Did I have any questions?

I walked away dazed by what was certainly either staggering good fortune or daunting and impossible responsibility; I could not decide which. Nevertheless, after meeting the other research students, who were mostly dressed in jeans and sweatshirts, I rolled up my suit, crammed it into the bottom of my trunk, and got to work.

During the autumn and winter in Oxford I learned that animal behaviorists are often faced with the same kinds of tasks as crime detectives. Faced with some glimpses of a puzzling story, they are confronted with clues, suspects, and seemingly unrelated bits of information; they have to guess, think hard, make more observations, and often do a great deal of plain leg work. Animal behaviorists persevere because they have a faith—often seemingly irrational—that eventually a fascinating story will emerge.

In March I moved from Oxford to the Animal Behaviour Research Group field base on Walney Island, in the Irish Sea off the northwest coast of England. Walney is the home of a mixed breeding colony of about 50,000 pairs of Herring Gulls and Lesser Black-backed Gulls. The first walk through the gull colony was a great adventure. The gulls flew up from their nest sites and whirled overhead screaming at the tops of their lungs and making occasional dive-bombing runs. Their aim was excellent, and I was often wiping warm gull crap off my face. The bombing tactic had the effect that the gulls desired; we kept out of the breeding colony except when it was absolutely necessary.

During the winter in Oxford, I had heard the beautifully integrated research stories developed by some of the graduate students who were almost finished, and I now grew alarmed because I had no inkling of how I was going to produce a coherent project from the seeming chaos of seagull behavior. Niko was very patient and sat with me for hours during the first weeks on Walney, just watching gull behavior. His philosophy was that if an observer with basic biological and evolutionary training watched long and carefully, questions about behavior would begin to arise. Attempts to answer these questions almost always raised more questions than they answered. In the process of asking and answering questions, a story about behavior would emerge.

Morning after morning Niko and I went to a secluded observation post where we could watch the gulls without disturbing them. Niko taught me that, with intensive study, it is possible to recognize wild animals as individuals. They are as unique as we are and once I had watched them for a while, I could recognize some individuals with no difficulty. Individuals differ slightly in shape and color as well as in characteristic behavior. Niko reminded me that, to most people, all dogs of a certain breed appear to be similar, but no dog owner would confuse his or her dog with another, even if they were of the same breed.

In the gull colony I came to understand that daily life requires that gulls constantly learn about new sources of food and new sources of threat. The gull is not a clockwork machine responding to a few stimuli, but an animal that must constantly consider a number of alternatives and make decisions about what to do next. I was going to be studying animal learning of a very complex kind and the days of the puzzled little newts in their runway seemed very far away.

I had decided to do a study of Herring Gull feeding behavior, reasoning that the gulls had to eat *something* and so I could be certain of getting *some* results. The gulls are omnivorous feeders. They scavenge for food at garbage dumps, plunge-dive for fish at sea, follow the farmer's plough at sowing time, and prey on the broods of other birds, even each others' eggs and young. As part of their courtship, the male adult gulls feed the females at the nest sites. They regurgitate or discard indigestible parts of their food, and these remains of the varied diet surround the nest sites throughout the gullery. It occurred to me that I could collect some data by marking a number of these nests with numbered stakes, checking them every few days, and recording the different kinds of food remains I found. When I patrolled my 120 study nests I found the remains of almost everything: fish bones, mussel shells, starfish, prawns, thumbnail-sized pink shells of the Baltic Tellin, and shells of the large sea snail called the Dog Welk. From the dumps there were chicken bones, butter wrappers, rubber bands, large ham bones, as well as pieces of glass and many other odds and ends.

The interesting thing about the distribution of these remains was that the gulls clearly had individual food preferences. Some gulls would have large quantities of fish bones near their nests week after week, while others had almost none, preferring the dumps or other feeding grounds. It was clear that many of the gulls had learned individual feeding preferences and they were experts at finding certain types of food. Several of these feeding specialists baffled me because I could not imagine how they could find such large quantities of certain foods that seemed to me to be quite scarce in their environment. I decided to closely investigate one of these feeding specialities to try to discover how it worked.

There were twelve nests in this colony of 50,000 nests that were surrounded by great piles of shells or carapaces of the Edible Crab, *Cancer pagurus*. While this species is familiar to those who like crab salad, they did not seem to be plentiful around the shores of Walney. I wondered how these gulls found large quantities of crabs. I knew that under big rocks there were some of these crabs which were exposed at extreme low tide, but I could not imagine how the gulls could get the crabs out from under the rocks.

I tried putting an observation hide, or blind, in a position to observe a crab-hunting gull's nest. This blind was a small enclosed tent with slit windows through which animals could be watched. Hidden in the small blind, I tried to follow the gulls' outward flights, but had very little success. Although I could recognize individual gulls when they were close at hand, I would quickly lose the crab-hunting gull as it flew out away from the colony through a cloud of a hundred or so of its neighbors. This clearly was not the way to discover where the gulls found crabs to eat. In the end, a solution was stumbled upon by accident.

During my spare time I often took long walks over the sandy low tide beaches with Niko and his wife, Lise. One day, when looking for sand eels and other interesting beach life, Lise happened to dig up what she thought must be a round, flat stone buried under a low flat dome of sand. The stone, which she intended to skip out over the water, turned out to be an Edible Crab. Further searching turned up large numbers of Edible Crabs buried under such domes. We noticed much variation in the appearance of the domes. Some were mere cracks in the sand, which could be seen only by very close observation. These domes were very difficult to see when they happened to be surrounded by ripple marks in the sand. Other domes were so pronounced as to cast black oval shadows that could sometimes be seen from as far away as 50 feet. I wondered if these oval sand domes, about $1/4$-inch high and often slightly cracked along one edge, could be the sign that the gulls learned to use to locate buried crabs.

Extensive beach walks soon revealed that gulls often pecked at irregularities in the sand that somewhat resembled crab domes. Among the most common of these mistakes were pecks directed at small domes caused by air bubbles trapped under wet sand. It seemed that these air-bubble domes were mistaken by the gulls for crab domes. This was a nice example of what Niko called a "natural experiment"; nature had deposited fake model domes for us, and the animals misread these signs and reacted according to their mistaken interpretation. Such phenomena are often useful in behavioral studies because they may alert one to some of the stimuli to which an animal responds. From this particular natural experiment it appeared that it would be possible to test the gulls to see if they responded to the characteristics of the domes, rather than to some other cues, such as movement of the crabs under the domes.

This stimulated me to conduct a number of tests to determine the extent of the visual discrimination that had been learned by the crab-hunters. When the tide began to fall, I went to the beach and built fake model domes of sand in a variety of shapes and sizes. Returning just before the incoming tide reached the tests, I recorded the frequency with which the gulls had pecked at each of the models. I presented each dome characteristic I wished to test in a series of identical groups. Each group contained five different models, and each of these models was presented 100 times. For instance, to test the characteristic of size (the vast majority of crabs found on the beach being between 64 mm and 120 mm), five domes, ranging from very small (25-mm wide) to very large (250-mm wide), were built along the top of a long sand dune–type ridge on the low-tide beach where the gulls often found buried crabs. On the next ridge another set was built, and so on until twenty sets had been built at each tide. Variables such as size, shape, height, presence or absence of a crack, and shape of crack were tested. The results showed that the gulls responded to a few very specific characteristics of the crab dome, rather than to just any disturbance in the sand. In general, the more a fake model looked like a real crab dome, the more it was pecked by the gulls. The crab-hunting gulls had learned to hunt for very specific signs of their prey.

I also began to wonder how the domes were formed. Since I was trained as a scuba diver, I decided to spend a number of days swimming in the icy Irish Sea over the intertidal zone while the tide was falling in order to try to find crabs digging into the sand. Even with a wet suit the water was painfully cold where it rushed into the suit around the wrists, ankles, and neck, and only slightly warmer by the time it reached more interesting parts of my body. For all my discomfort and effort, I never spotted a digging crab. It is a general principle of field research that while there may be no gain without pain, there can be pain with no gain.

To get some idea of what was going on, I captured a few dome crabs one day and took them out into the water and watched them. When digging in was done under water at a falling tide, the crab's back was covered with sand washed over it by tidal action. By the time the waterline had receded so as to leave the crab high and dry, the crab was completely buried. During the time that the sand was very wet, no dome was visible. The only sign showing the presence of the crab was a small funnel-shaped hole in the sand directly above the crab's mouth parts. But as the sand dried, the crab pushed itself up with its legs and claws, and this formed the dome with the typically sharp crack along the front. The crab breathed through this crack in the sand during the long wait for the returning tide.

I was interested in watching the gulls while they were hunting for crabs. My first idea was to take one of our canvas observation blinds to the beach and set it up during low tide. This was a complete failure. The gulls were on the beach that day but none of them would come within 500 feet of the blind. I needed a way to have the blind there all the time, so the gulls would get used to it. To accomplish this I constructed a raft with oil-drum flotation and heavy timbers that accommodated a 4' x 4' x 4' canvas observation blind on its deck. The raft was anchored over a section of beach which was uncovered by water for several hours at each low tide and where I had found many crab remains. On my raft's first night in the water a stiff breeze sprang up and in the morning the blind was, literally, gone with the wind. I sheepishly entered it in the Walney Equipment Log as "lost at sea" and signed out another blind. This time I did not leave the blind erected but left it folded up in a wooden box that I bolted to the deck of the raft. The next morning, after a night of gale-force winds, the whole raft was gone. I searched the shore and found it about two miles down the coast of Walney. It had dragged its rock-filled oil drum anchor and was sitting on the beach waiting for me. Clearly sterner measures were indicated. During one of my walks, I had seen a real ship's anchor, about 10 feet long, abandoned far out on the low-tide beach. I darted down to it during the next low tide, jacked up its massive flukes, tied them to the back bumper of our Land Rover, and with some difficulty managed to drag it back to where I wanted the raft. With that, the raft stayed put.

A few days later the keeper of the lighthouse on the tip of Walney Island told me that the harbor master had radioed and he wanted to talk to me immediately. I put on my best clothes, which smelled vaguely of the gull colony, and headed my motorcycle to the mainland. The sparkling mahogany and brass and crisp white charts of the harbor office made me feel as scruffy as if I had been washed up by the tide. The harbor master was a giant of a man who towered over me when he asked if the obstruction in the harbor approach was mine. It was clear that he was making reference to my raft. I said that it was. He then roared at me so loudly that his eyes bulged out as if on stalks, making him look like the crabs I was studying. Did I know what would happen if a ship mistook that raft for the buoy at the tip of the island? Did I have any idea what a damn-fool irresponsible thing it was to anchor anything in a harbor approach without permission of the harbor master? Did I know that any new object in a harbor approach was required by maritime law to be the object of a written warning to all shipping published by the harbor master? What in the hell did I think I was doing out there anyway?

By the time he ran out of breath, I was pinned against the wall and his face was about two inches from mine. I weakly started to tell my cute little story about gulls and crabs and he slowly backed off. Amazingly, the idea of the specialist feeding gulls caught his fancy and he asked a few questions. As our talk gradually took on the air of a friendly chat, he seemed to forget that I was being charged with attempted shipwrecking and, in the end, offered to issue the appropriate warning to mariners. He advised them of the position of my raft and even asked them to give it a wide berth so as not to disturb me.

Returning to Walney I began a routine of raft observations. In subsequent days, as the tide began to fall, I would wade or swim to the raft and prepare to start observations. This was a simple arrangement on days when the sea was calm. The blind could be easily removed from its box on the deck and hoisted onto the framework of its supporting poles, just like putting up a small tent. On windy days, however, I was faced with a deck awash with breaking waves and the task of erecting an unruly blind, which was just like putting up a large sail. Once the blind was up I would huddle in it, clinging to the pitching deck, which all too soon taught me the meaning of sea sickness. After an endless series of sharp bumps as waves picked the raft up and dropped it on the beach, the raft would be left behind by the falling tide and I could begin my observations. The gulls quickly became accustomed to the raft and soon they ignored it altogether.

During the course of the next few weeks I was able to watch the gulls pursue many crabs. From my ringside seat, I watched with great fascination while the Herring Gulls employed one of two methods of searching for Edible Crabs. Some searched on foot while others searched from the air. The foot-searching gulls walked back and forth along the receding waterline, defending their feeding area by chasing away other gulls who tried to land in this narrow zone. They generally found crabs by spotting crab domes near the waterline. The gulls that searched the beach from the air used a very characteristic gliding flight that combined looking down and scanning the beach with sideways-turning movements of the head. These gulls generally found buried crabs quite a way up the beach from the waterline.

Crabs found by footsearchers were eaten on the beach, while those found by air-searching gulls were prepared in a special way. The gull would take hold of the crab by a claw and use the claw as a handle to give the entire crab a sharp shake. This would break off the claw. The same process was followed with the other claw and then the legs. The gull then grasped the mutilated body in its bill and flew back to its nest site in the colony. I presume that this stripping of the crab's appendages prevented it from damaging the gull during flight. It was these gulls who had first attracted my attention by the masses of crab carapaces discarded near their nests.

Only 12 gulls out of 100,000 had become sufficiently proficient at finding crab domes to earn a living. These gulls had learned about crab domes and had learned the complex skills involved in preparation and transportation of the crabs. I color-ringed the offspring of the crab hunters to see if perhaps parents had a role in the teaching but, although I saw these young in subsequent years, there was no evidence that they had become crab eaters. It is more likely that gulls learn this kind of feeding trick by watching other, unrelated gulls at a feeding site. Parents do not stay with their young much beyond the beginning of the autumn following the breeding season, so they have only a short time in which to influence their offspring. It is also possible that gulls do not learn about crab domes by watching other gulls, but that they stumble upon them and figure it out by themselves.

Exploration of the gulls' behavior raised further questions concerning the behavior of the crabs. Biologists hold the Darwinian faith that animals will do the things that benefit themselves. Those who look out for themselves are the ones most likely to survive and breed. Their offspring will also put their own interests first. In this way, over generations, the successful animals should come to be well adapted to look out for themselves in the environment in which they live. While it was kind of the crabs to offer themselves as dinner for the gulls, it did not make any sense from the viewpoint of the crab's survival.

My first move in trying to piece together this puzzle was to go to the library to dig out anything I could about crab behavior. To go to the library in Oxford was an adventure in itself. There are many libraries, but "the library" appropriate to my needs was the imposing Radcliffe Science Library. At my first appearance at the information desk an imperious librarian asked me if I had "sworn in." I had no idea what that was, so I guessed that I had not. The librarian produced a dog-eared card and instructed me to read it out loud and warned me that she had to hear every word. As amused students walked past, I stood on display at the main desk and read a promise not to deface library materials or to commit a number of other specific misdemeanors. The last forbidden activity on the list involved promising "to kindle no flame" within the library. I presumed, at the time, that this referred to smoking, but after several bone-chilling sessions sitting in the cold and drafty stone building, I realized that it might be considered a real temptation to build a little campfire on the floor had one not forsworn such activities.

Searching the indexes for articles about crabs, I discovered that the library was both a disappointment and a gold mine. There had been almost no *recent* work on the behavior of crabs. However, I discovered that several naturalists around the turn of the century had done astonishingly meticulous studies on the life history of the Edible Crab. Most note-worthy among these studies was a series of early-20th-century papers by H. C. Williamson, who had relentlessly pursued these crabs and record-ed everything he found in minute detail. Later, when I replicated some of Williamson's observations, my respect for him grew even more as I became aware of the vast amount of time that he must have spent scam-pering around looking under rocks near the low-tide mark, at night, in the winter, with icy North Sea gales blowing in his face. His dedication left a remarkable legacy of information about the crabs, tucked away in the *Annual Report of the Fisheries Board for Scotland* and seemingly just waiting for me to come along.

Armed with the references to Williamson's promising papers, I went to the catalogs of library holdings and discovered that there was no list-ing for the *Annual Report of the Fisheries Board for Scotland*. With some trepidation, I approached the steely-eyed librarian again and asked if she could help me order some articles on interlibrary loan because they were not in the Radcliffe. Her eyebrow shot up in a pointed arch and she gave me that look of disgust and disdain that Americans reserve for dogs that they find defecating on their lawns. The very suggestion that the magnif-icent Radcliffe would not have something as commonplace as turn-of-the-century Scottish fishery reports seemed to raise her hackles several notches. She defiantly swept to the catalogs and triumphantly produced the Fisheries Reports filed under *Scotland, Fisheries Board for, Annual Report*.

The Edible Crab is largely nocturnal, feeding and moving around at night and becoming inactive during daylight. The sexually mature ani-mals spend the winter in offshore water more than 20 fathoms deep. In spring they move inshore, and are only rarely found above the low-tide mark.

The crabs are distributed by age on the sea floor. Crabs from the postlarval stage to 64 mm (to three years of age) remain all year in the shallow water where they were hatched, and are found under rocks between the high- and low-tide marks. Crabs from 64 to 102 mm wide (three to five years of age) inhabit water just below the low-tide mark and the larger, adult crabs live at an even-greater depth. Most female Edible Crabs are mature when they are about 140 mm wide (eight years of age). Most males of 105 mm (five years of age) or over are mature. With thanks to Williamson, I turned back to the problem at hand.

Every school kid knows that science operates by having scientists form hypotheses, or statements of belief about why or how a natural phenomenon takes place. According to the textbooks, the next step is to test these hypotheses under rigorously controlled conditions. I was faced with a dilemma at this stage in my research because I had no hypothesis about what the crabs were doing on the beach. I not only had no hypoth-esis, I did not know where to get one. I was starting to discover that a great deal of the work of science does not involve doing experiments and testing hypotheses. Often years of preliminary observations or little trial experiments, called pilot studies, have to be done before the scientist knows how to phrase a hypothesis in a way that is testable.

Niko agreed that perhaps the best thing to do was just to measure and record everything that I could about the crabs that were found under domes. Our hope was that some sort of answer would emerge if I collected a sufficiently large mass of data. At the time, it did not occur to me that I might end up with heaps of information about the dome crabs and no idea at all about what they were doing on the beaches.

The first and easiest thing to do seemed to be to measure crab carapaces collected from the gull colony. I discovered that I had a valuable source of data lying right there on the ground. From these measurements it appeared that the width of crabs found under domes on the beach varied from 41 to 146 mm, distributed normally, with a peak or mode at about 90 mm. Although there was no way to assess maturity from the carapace itself, I suspected that most or all of these crabs were sexually immature juvenile crabs, since they fit so beautifully into the 64- to 140-mm-width limits of crab adolescence described by Williamson.

Niko suggested that perhaps the crabs brought back to the colony by gulls were not representative of the population of dome crabs; maybe the gulls were bringing back only the small ones. I did not believe that and I do not think he did either, but he was trying to teach me to be cautious. To answer his objection, I collected gull-killed carapaces from the high-tide line after each tide. These were the carapaces of crabs killed and eaten on the beach that day. They fell into the same size class as the carapaces from the colony. Niko then suggested that perhaps the gulls were not finding all the crab domes and that there might be larger or smaller crabs on the beach which the gulls missed.

The only way I could counter this challenge was to go to the beach and look myself. Although it would be very time-consuming, it occurred to me that I might shed some light on the crab question if I did this every day and recorded everything I could.

Field workers with tight budgets have to learn to find inexpensive ways to do things and the project at hand presented another engineering challenge. I wanted to permanently mark a large section of the beach so that it could be searched every day at low tide. I decided that I could use plastic one-gallon bottles for markers, since these were washed up on the tide line in considerable numbers. The bottles would need to be anchored on short ropes so they would float up as the tide came in and would not be covered by the sand that drifted as the tide went in and out. For anchors I decided to use concrete blocks salvaged from an old World War II gun emplacement along the shore, which was being undermined by the sea and was falling down onto the beach in sections.

Early one sunny morning at low tide, I went to the old fortifications and backed the Research Group's Land Rover up to a fallen wall. It took very little effort to loosen quite a number of blocks, and I loaded them in the back and drove off down the low-tide beach. I marked out a large rectangular section of beach, 100 m wide, extending from the high-water mark to the low-water mark. I placed the markers 50 m apart around the edge of the study area. I had no surveying equipment other than a long tape measure, but I was able to check the accuracy of my measurements by measuring the diagonals of each 100 m by 50 m rectangle. Both diagonals were the same; so the area was a true rectangle.

After a while, the tide had turned and I had placed quite a number of these bottle markers and was generally pleased with my efforts. I decided to do one or two more before retreating, thinking that I could easily finish the next day. I started the Land Rover, put it in gear and let in the clutch. As it started to roll forward I felt one back corner drop slightly and felt the wheels start to spin. I was glad that the Zoology Department had had the wisdom to supply us with four-wheel drive vehicles for field use. I shifted the Land Rover into four-wheel drive and let in the clutch. Again the wheels spun with no forward motion. Upon inspection, it appeared that a back wheel had settled into a wet spot in the sand and was spinning. Because the Land Rover was down in one back corner, it was up in one front corner and that wheel, too, was spinning. I was stuck. The rising tide was about 45 minutes away from the time when the Land Rover would begin to be submerged. In a panic I sprinted back to the field base to get tools and help.

I woke up fellow-researcher Mike MacRoberts, found a couple of shovels, and we tore off back to the beach on my motorcycle. By the time we got back, we had about 20 minutes to do something. We decided to dig a ramp behind the stuck rear wheel and build a road up and out. We surfaced the little road with concrete block rubble, which we made by breaking up some of the blocks which were still in the Land Rover. We tried to dig under the stuck wheel a bit and to push rubble under it as well. With minutes left, I got in the Land Rover, put it in its lowest gear range and shifted into reverse. I was aware that I would not have another chance to free it before the water came washing under it. With my heart in my throat, I eased in the clutch and the Rover shuddered and climbed out. Although still in low-range reverse, I slammed my foot to the floor and the Land Rover went screaming backward to high ground at about 15 mph. The next day I carried the concrete blocks required to finish the study area down the beach by hand.

I searched the beach study area during each daylight low tide through one spring and early summer. Previous observations had shown that this was the season when the crab domes were to be found on the beach. Each crab found was measured and sexed. This was easy because the abdomen of the female was much wider than that of the male. Next, each crab's location within the study area was determined by measuring the location from two of the plastic-bottle markers. These data were used to make maps of the area, showing the location of all crabs for each low tide. I marked each crab by painting a number on its back with nail polish and filing a notch in the edge of its carapace. The edge of the carapace had regular pinch marks, like a classic apple-pie crust, and by filing these systematically I could give each crab an individual identification. The crabs were then reburied in the location where they were found.

While I was operating without a hypothesis, I did have some expectations. I expected that as the days went by I would find the same crabs over and over, and I planned to be able to plot maps of the successive stranding of individual crabs. In all, I marked more than 500 crabs in the study area, but I never saw any of them again. The gulls continued to work the beach on both sides of my area, and I collected the carapaces of their kills from the tide line and the breeding colony. They never found one of my marked crabs either. This was an indication that I was probably dealing with a very large, highly mobile population and I had marked such a small percentage of the animals that the probability of a recapture was low.

One of the first surprises from the beach area was that on most days there were almost no dome crabs at all and then suddenly there would be days when crabs were all over the place. On these busy days I would be running around frantically trying to get all the crabs marked, sexed, measured, and located during the short low-tide period.

My daily counts over prolonged periods revealed that on most days only a few crabs were found under domes; but in each 28-day lunar cycle there were a few particular days when the beach was suddenly riddled with crab domes. At first it was not obvious why those days were so special.

I think the role of insight in science has been somewhat underplayed in the textbooks. In reality, scientists become absorbed with research problems and end up spending most of their free time mentally churning them over. It is not surprising, then, that solutions to problems may pop up in quite unexpected ways and at unexpected times. Rather suddenly one day, when I was sitting in the field base cleaning my camera, a flash of insight revealed that during the days in which there had been a frantic rush to get all the crabs processed, the tide had been low in the middle of the morning. Across the lunar cycle, the time of day at which the tide was low would be about one-half hour later each day. It seemed more than a coincidence that there would suddenly be many dome crabs during the few low tides that occurred in the mid-morning. On checking the data collected in earlier years from the crab-nest gulls and from less-systematic beach-searching, more such peaks of crab availability were discovered. Each of these peaks, like those found in the beach study area, occurred on days when the tide was low at about 10 A.M. After a long period of feeling baffled, it was at least a little comforting to find that some of my data followed a reliable pattern. All I had to do was to figure out what the pattern meant. I puzzled over this for days while walking on the beach and one day, in another flash of insight, I had a plausible explanation.

The days when the tide was low around 10 A.M. were also days when it had been high at about 4 A.M. I knew from the scientific literature that these crabs were active at night and inactive during the day. What had happened, then, was that these crabs wandered around feeding during the dark hours on the beach that was covered by the high tide. When the sun rose at about 4 A.M. the crabs dug into the sand to avoid being washed around by the currents during their inactive daylight period. Since the tide was high at the time of this digging-in, there was a maximum chance that the crabs were digging in on land that would later be exposed as the tide went out. As the morning progressed, these crabs were left behind on the beach as the tide receded and they formed domes in the way I had observed. On days when the tide was high much earlier or later than 4 A.M., much less of the area between the high- and low-tide line would be submerged when the crabs were digging in, so the chances were decreased that crabs would, unknowingly, dig in on sections of beach that would fall dry later as the tide changed.

Since crabs were found under domes only from late March to mid-June, and in considerable numbers only in April and May, their appearance under domes corresponded with the migration of the mature crabs to inshore water. If the juvenile, dome-making crabs were living just below the low-tide waterline the rest of the year, it is likely that aggressive competitive pressure from the inward-migrating adults, either for food or, more likely, space, drove them yet farther inshore, where they became stranded at low tide. The stranding is not intentional and the dome formation is a response to the unpleasant surprise of being stranded. Doubtless, hiding under the sand will protect many such crabs from predation on beaches that are not adjacent to gull colonies. However, on Walney, some gulls have learned the secret of the crabs.

Niko's first impulse was that the crab domes had something to do with the peculiar tidal currents on Walney. He had worked on the coast of Britain for 20 years and was a very skilled observer of nature, but he had never seen crab domes before we found them on Walney. He was particularly adamant that this did not happen on the beach at Ravenglass, slightly to the north, where his research group had maintained a field base for years and where many scientists, including Niko himself, had spent a great deal of time studying various animals on the beach. As soon as we could get away, we traveled to Ravenglass and immediately found crab domes on the beach there. Subsequently we found them on many British beaches. Although he was grumpy about it at first, Niko was quick to admit that he must have overlooked the domes for years. He cheered up as he realized that it nicely illustrated the point of much of his research on food-searching in animals: most of us animals see things when we know what we are looking for, but we are likely to overlook even quite obvious things that we do not expect to find.

SUGGESTED READINGS

ALCOCK, J. (1984). *Animal behavior: An evolutionary approach.* Sunderland, MA: Sinauer.

BITTERMAN, M. (1965). The evolution of intelligence. *Scientific American, 212,* 92–100.

MORRIS, D. (1979). *Animal days.* New York: Bantam.

TINBERGEN, N. (1958). *Curious naturalists.* London: Country Life.

―――― (1963). The shell menace. *Natural History, 72,* 28–35.

――――FALKUS, H., & ENNION, E. (1970). *Signals for survival.* London: Oxford Univ. Press.

TWITTY, V. (1966). *Of scientists and salamanders.* San Francisco: Freeman.

WILLIAMSON, H. C. (1900). Contributions to the life history of the Edible Crab *(Cancer pagurus). Eighteenth Annual Report of the Fisheries Board for Scotland for the year 1899, 77*–143.

ROY S. MALPASS *(Ph.D., Syracuse University) is Professor of Behavioral Science at the State University of New York, College at Plattsburgh. He has published extensively in the area of face recognition and eyewitness identification. He has been the Editor of the* Journal of Cross-Cultural Psychology *(1982–1986), and is past President of the Society for Cross-Cultural Research, and President of the Division of Psychology and Law of the International Association for Cross-Cultural Psychology. Professor Malpass was born and raised in New York's Mohawk Valley, and continues to spend as much time as possible at his boathouse on a scenic lake in the Adirondacks. When out of the laboratory he may often be found pursuing his hobby of photography or his collection of antique cameras and photographs. During summer months he is more likely to be found rowing or paddling on Adirondack lakes.*

6

They All Look Alike to Me

--- ❖ ---

The data are always right, but they are not always the right data.

Lots of people think they are good at remembering faces. Names may be a problem, but faces are memorable. Of course, you may find yourself at a social gathering staring at someone you are just sure you've met before, but you have no recollection of when or where. But most difficult is when you stare blankly into the face of someone who has just said "Huddsfupple (your name)—I wondered when we'd meet again!"—and you have absolutely no memory for this person. But if you think these situations could be upsetting, let me tell you about an acquaintance of mine who was consulting for a well-known international agency. When she arrived in the exotic foreign location she was met by a member of the agency staff who escorted her to a hotel. She checked in, and he left her to get settled, have a nap after traveling, etc. When she went to the coffee shop she spotted him in the lobby, and waved hello. He didn't respond, and she was surprised. She took a stroll near the hotel, and again saw and greeted him. Again he did not respond. As she walked on, puzzled at his behavior, she looked up only to see him again! But this time he was dressed very differently. It was then it dawned on her that as a European in an Asian city for the first time, she was a victim of one of the oldest clichés in the book: "They all look alike to me!"

She was an experienced traveler, and was able to have a good laugh at herself for not having figured it out sooner. This is only one of the many forms of interpersonal perception and behavior in which we respond to people in terms of their group identification rather than their individuality. It is interesting, not only in its own right, but also because it represents a larger group of phenomena that are perhaps more central to intergroup identity and conflict: stereotyping and other forms of ethnocentrism. It is intriguing because it is not easily explained. A small group of researchers has been working at it for more than 20 years with some interesting findings, but no definitive explanation to show for it. This chapter is a brief description of portions of my work on this problem and how it has developed over the last two decades.

HOW DID IT ALL START?

Inquiry is driven both by theory and by the need for practical understanding. Research can take very different shapes depending on what drives it.

During the spring of 1968 a colleague and I were part of a community-action group in the Midwest. We were evaluating the examinations used to test applicants' qualifications for positions in such agencies as the fire and police departments. The town had a substantial number of black citizens, but the fire and police departments did not. We were trying to assist in the qualification of blacks on the fire and police examinations by writing training materials, and by attempting to identify any blatantly discriminatory aspects of the examinations.

We had done this for the fire department examination, and turned our attention to the police exam. The police department was cooperative, and set us up in a conference room. When we opened the examination to the second question we had a surprise. There, spread across two pages, were the photographs of eight men. Next to each photograph was a variety of facts about it. Eight minutes were given to the applicant to study this information. When we turned to the next page, there were photos of four of the eight men, and questions about the information previously given about them. All the faces displayed were white.

On the face of it (sorry) there was something discriminatory about this test when given to blacks. We thought it would be very likely that black applicants would have more difficulty recognizing white faces than black faces. We had each heard our share of racist remarks about blacks, and prominent among these was the comment that they all look alike. But that was pretty easy to understand. In the late 1960s, before school integration was widely implemented, before discrimination in housing and real-estate sales was diminished, and before black faces began to appear more widely in advertising and other media, most whites interacted with very few blacks at all, and rarely on anything like an equal basis. So there would be little personal experience as a basis for learning about them as individuals rather than as more or less equivalent examples of a category. It seemed likely that blacks' perception of whites would work the same way, and that they would have jokes about how all those whites look alike. Anyway, it seemed very likely that this particular test item would be more difficult for black than for white applicants, and therefore was an instance of racial discrimination.

As we left the police station I volunteered to go to the library to find the relevant literature documenting this problem. We agreed we would consider what to do once the nature of the evidence was known. At the library I was absolutely unable to find any literature bearing directly on this problem. I decided it must be my own incompetence in the library; so

I sent my graduate assistant to find the relevant studies. He found none. Then together we convinced a couple of undergraduates to try. They reported only one marginally relevant study, but it was one more than we had gotten. We set out to design research that would give us some information on the problem. The basic question was, of course, whether there really was differential recognition for own- vs. other-race faces.

Before going on I ought to comment on the concept of "race" and how it ought to be understood in this area of research. There seems to be no good and consistent way to refer to all the various "races." To refer to a white person as "Caucasian" appears to give credence to a theory of race that has Europeans deriving from a population living at one time in the area of the Caucasus mountains. Identifying modern individuals with historical geographical populations appears to assume a kind of stability of population and within-group marriage/mating that may characterize some areas of the world well, but others not at all. Whether or not English, Poles, and Italians interbreed in Europe, people with these origins do so with great frequency in the USA, as do people of more diverse geographical origins. Similarly with "blacks." Whites in the USA tend to call anyone with discernibly "African" features "black," but in other parts of the world many more categories are used. So the old racial names just don't seem to work, especially in complex multiethnic societies. The color names also will not work, at least not consistently. While "black" and "white" are in popular usage, "yellow" will simply not do for Asians, and "black" just does not differentiate sufficiently between subgroups. "Hispanic" describes language and not even much of culture, not differentiating between Central American aboriginals and European Chileans. National "extraction" also provides difficulties. What do you call an American whose father was German/Italian, and whose mother was English/Chinese, especially if his appearance is somewhat Asian? For purposes of research on facial recognition, a typology of facial appearance might be useful. Maybe the real issue is what "traditional" group a person's appearance fits into. But then a large number of people may be unclassifiable. This problem has not been solved in a satisfying way. We have to acknowledge it, and get on with the inquiry about facial recognition— even if we have to communicate by using some not so terribly appropriate terminology. But in doing so, we have to be sure that when we translate our research findings into inferences about the real world we do not forget the convenient fictions we accepted in order to get on with it!

NAILING IT DOWN: THE FIRST STUDY

There were important things to do. First was to obtain a suitable sample of faces to use in the research. Second was to recruit subjects, and third was to design an appropriate memory task. Fourth, although I didn't know it at the time, was a problem of the index of recognition that we would finally use. Research of this nature usually can't be done by individuals working alone. Undergraduate students often play important roles in the planning and implementation of research projects. On this project we had support for undergraduate participation in the research from the National Science Foundation, which paid the students' project expenses and provided them stipends.

We obtained photos from a variety of sources in Illinois and at Howard University, in Washington, D.C., where Jerry Kravitz, a friend from graduate-school days, was on the faculty. Kravitz had more experience with studying memory than I did, and was a good person to consult about the structure and design of the memory task for the research. My initial inclination was to stay very close to the form of the police examination that started us on this line of research. That would make it a "paired-associates" task, where faces and information about the person (face) would be associated. The test could be to produce the facts associated with each face, recognize which facts were associated with a particular face, or vice-versa.

But there would be a problem with interpretation. When the data were in, it would not be clear whether the findings had to do with recognition of facial images, with the association of verbal information with the stored representation of the images, or both. Kravitz counseled that, for sake of clarity, a simple recognition task should be used. This seemed like good advice, and so the first experiment used a simple recognition task. We first showed subjects 20 faces (10 white, 10 black) mixed semi-randomly (no more than 3 black or 3 white faces could appear in sequence). Then we showed them these 20 faces mixed in with 60 more (30 white, 30 black, again mixed semirandomly). Each time a face was displayed we asked the subjects to answer "yes" or "no" to "Was it one of those shown in the first set?" (of 20).

We conducted this experiment both at Illinois and at Howard. When we were through we wrote up a basic report on the study and circulated it among a small group of researchers who we thought might be interested, and who might offer us their critical comments. We preferred to get the first round of comments from friends rather than from a journal editor's anonymous reviewers! The responses to our paper brought a very interesting surprise—one that has been influential for me in many ways. Harry Hake, an experimental psychologist of considerable reputation, returned the paper with a number of helpful comments. And at the end of the paper he penciled a note asking whether I knew about "signal-detection theory." He also offered the opinion that if I published the study as it was, the human-engineering types would eat me alive.

I knew nothing about signal-detection theory, and frankly the phrase "human-engineering types" scared the hell out of me. These guys know a lot of technical stuff, and I didn't see that in my future. At the same time the prospects for continuing ignorance didn't seem so great either, so I got on the phone to Harry. He offered to come to my office and discuss it with me over a bag lunch.

Before going on, I want to emphasize the social aspects of professional life. I have learned a lot of interesting and important things from friends and colleagues over lunch and at social occasions of various kinds. Discussing ideas in a social setting is central to professional success. Do it early, and do it often.

Harry Hake did indeed come to my office, and gave me the first lesson in what has become a major interest for me—the response-decision processes that interpose between whatever it is we know personally and the actions we take on the basis of this knowledge. We often say more, less, or different from what we know, and we do so to serve our own interests. Think what the world would be like if we always said just what we have seen, thought, or remembered! In a face-recognition experiment, if we think it is important to identify as many as possible of the faces we are asked to remember (called "hits"), we will probably be willing to say "yes" to a face that looks even remotely familiar. As a result, we'll probably make some mistakes—saying yes to faces we actually didn't see before (called "false alarms"). So both hits and false alarms increase because we are more willing to say yes. If we really wanted to *avoid* making false alarms—as we might to avoid a mistaken identification of an innocent person in a police lineup—we would want to be much more careful about saying yes, and probably say it less often. So both hits and false alarms would decrease. But our ability to tell faces we saw before from faces we didn't see before probably would not be different. Only our willingness to say yes would be different. So if we want to know about recognition accuracy apart from people's willingness to say yes in the experiment, we need a way to adjust the accuracy score for the false-alarm rate. Signal-detection theory does that (and much more—but that's another story).

We reanalyzed our data using signal-detection-theory procedures, and what seemed like mildly confusing results were cleared up. The results and their interpretation seemed pretty obvious. First of all, there was a difference in recognizability between the white and black faces used in the experiment, for both the groups at Howard University and at Illinois. White faces were more often recognized on the average for both groups of subjects. In addition, there was a "statistical interaction" between the "race" of the faces and the "race" of the subjects, indicating that faces were better recognized by subjects of their same race.

APPEALING TO THEORY: INVESTIGATING THE OBVIOUS, AND LEARNING ABOUT WHAT ISN'T

Now what did we really have? We had a perfectly good experimental result that partially confirmed a conjecture (we can hardly call it an observation) from "real life." We had at least dragged this idea into the domain of scientific study, but two problems remained. First, we did not have a good explanation for the finding. Second, while many theories might be used to help understand this phenomenon, it was not going to be their testing ground.

The second of these—that the finding of a cross-race recognition differential would not likely be the testing ground of theories—is an important illustration of how "science" works, and deserves further comment. The primary focus of psychological research is testing propositions derived from theory, and modifying existing theory in accordance with the research findings. Development of new theory is a related activity. Theory-testing takes place in a context of well-defined techniques and methods. Theories understandably focus on problems that lend themselves to investigation and measurement in ways that are relevant to the theory. As a result, the questions that receive the major focus of research and theory do not necessarily represent the questions "out there" awaiting explanation. At any time, many interesting phenomena and processes exist that are the focus of no theory. Therefore, they are either not investigated at all, or they are investigated as a function of their importance in contemporary social events. If existing theory addresses these phenomena they may be "brought into theory." If not, their understanding may have to wait for the development of new theory. In the meanwhile, researchers busy with their own theory-driven research can hardly be blamed for not getting excited when someone says, "Yeah, but your theory can't explain my favorite phenomenon." While investigating a phenomenon that is interesting in its own right but not generated by existing theories one can feel slightly homeless.

Anyway, we began our investigations of the basis (cause) for differential recognition across race in what might be called the quarter-finals approach so well known in sports. We assembled the major contending explanations and started elimination rounds. We began with the most obvious potential explanations and set out to collect data that would allow us to choose among them.

The first study was based on the idea of "communication accuracy," which had been well worked out in the (then) newly flourishing field of language and cognition. Communication accuracy is the idea that those objects that can be more reliably described and identified from their verbal descriptions should be more reliably recognized visually. According to the theory, this is because verbal descriptions become part of the memory code for objects, and later help to trigger their memory. Observers see an object in a recognition experiment, generate a linguistic label or description of the object, and the label activates associations with other objects or concepts. Later, when the observer sees the label, the previously generated associations help to elicit the object's image. The more reliable or consistent the verbal description, the better the visual recognition. We knew from a previous study that there were differences in the verbal descriptors used by blacks and whites to refer to facial features. So we reasoned that if verbal descriptions were important in facial recognition, these differences might explain the differences in facial recognition.

Henry Lavigueur, David Weldon, and I designed experiments in which subjects received different amounts of training in describing faces. More verbal-description training ought to make their descriptions more reliable, and subjects ought to get better at recognizing faces on the basis of a verbal description. So we designed a test of communication accuracy to detect whether verbal training was having this effect. Subjects also ought to get better at recognizing faces—particularly other-race faces. So they were also tested for recognition of own- and other-race faces.

The results were interesting and informative. Verbal-description training did substantially improve the communication accuracy of face descriptions, but it had no effect on visual recognition, for either own- or other-race faces. The absence of a verbal–visual relationship surprised us. We thought that perhaps face recognition might just be very difficult to improve through a relatively short training program. But in a second experiment a relatively short series of trials in which subjects were punished (by electric shock) for recognition errors brought own- and other-race recognition to the same (high) levels. Improvement was possible, it seemed, but verbal training didn't get it done.

It appeared that cross-race recognition has something to do with the outcomes of subjects' experience with the facial images, but that verbal processes weren't an important part of it. Therefore differences in verbal references to own- and other-race faces could not be used to explain differential recognition. These results told us something about where *not* to look for an explanation of cross-race face recognition: just what the "elimination rounds" approach does in the scientific process.

Other research programs have produced similar findings. This creates an important practical problem. If the police want to construct an image of a wanted criminal, the obvious way to do it is through the descriptions of witnesses and their verbal comments on attempted constructions. But attempts to create such images are notoriously unreliable. My conjecture is that it's because they all depend on verbal access to the subject's facial memory, *but facial memory does not use verbal categories to any great degree.* We appear to recognize faces in very short spaces of time, and we are aware of a face's identity before we are aware of its descriptive attributes.

Other studies followed, looking for other "obvious" explanations of the recognition differences in terms of well-known and important concepts. For example, we examined the relationship of racial attitudes to face recognition. If whites and blacks possess negative attitudes toward each other, racial attitudes might explain differential recognition. But we were unable to find any relationship between intergroup attitude and face recognition, in a number of studies. Other researchers have also failed to find this relationship. Our inability to find a satisfactory explanation in existing theory has been one of the things that has kept my interest in this work at a high level for many years. In many ways, it's a mystery story! Another reason is its practical implications.

TAKING IT TO COURT

We began this line of research after observing what we believed to be a racially biased test item on a police-qualification examination. From there we dug deeper into psychological theory and research until we had clearly described the differential recognition phenomenon. Later on, Bob Bothwell, Jack Brigham, and I examined a series of studies in our laboratories and elsewhere and found that differential recognition (often called the "cross-race" effect) was a stable phenomenon, applying to blacks and whites alike. We did not yet fully understand the basis of the cross-race effect, but there it was, facing us (sorry, again), as real as anything. So when I was first asked to go to court as an expert witness in a trial of a black man identified by a white man I had a sense of returning to the community from which I had derived this interesting problem that had been so good to me professionally.

Good to me professionally? I ought to explain that. How can a phenomenon like differential face recognition be good to an academic psychologist? It's simple, really. This phenomenon is inherently interesting, and it gives me a chance to work on something challenging, something that draws from a wide range of theoretical approaches and areas of psychology. But even better, it has implications for the real-world from which it was originally derived. That's a nice, diverse, but integrated package. Beyond that, however, I have been identified with the cross-race effect, since the paper I published with Kravitz in 1969 was the first (and hence "classic") study on this problem. Since the phenomenon is memorable, so is my connection with it. One should not underestimate the degree to which that opens doors, helps to begin conversations, leads to invitations to attend conferences, participate in symposia, present papers, review manuscripts and grant proposals, and many other things that enrich the life of an academic psychologist. The way it all began seems like a happy accident. But my work on this problem since that time has been very rewarding, both personally and professionally. That's how it's been good to me.

But back to court! There are some difficulties involved in testifying in court about cross-race identifications. First, it is not the role of an expert witness to make judgments about whether the identification in a particular case is or is not valid. Rather, it is the expert's role to assist the jury in their evaluation of the evidence—including the accuracy of the particular identification involved. So the expert can testify only to findings in general. Therefore, before one testifies one ought to be satisfied that there is a basis for testimony (that the own-race/other-race differential actually exists), and that the basis generalizes over populations studied, measurement techniques, and conditions of observation.

If one is satisfied on these counts, it seemed to me, one could make a real contribution. If the haunting problem of mistaken eyewitness identification is being increased by errors of cross-race identifications, it makes an already bad situation worse. Further, if it is true, as most would suspect, that white identifications of black suspects would be far more numerous than black identifications of white suspects, a note of social injustice is also added to the problem. Surely it would be a good thing to contribute our knowledge to the courts to prevent as many errors as we reasonably and practically can.

For cross-race recognition the issues are sometimes less than straightforward. We have found that a reasonable interpretation of cross-race recognition difficulty is that people are less able to distinguish other-race faces from each other. That is to say, other-race faces appear subjectively more similar to each other than they would to an own-race observer. This has two important implications.

First, when white witnesses sift through a set of black mug-shots in the process where witnesses "nominate" possible suspects, they may be more likely to identify an innocent person who looks similar to their recollection of the offender. Since these faces will appear subjectively more similar to each other, such mistakes are easily understood. At this point in the process, then, other-race nominations may be more likely to incriminate an innocent person. Also, if the identification used by the police was a "show-up," where the witness is offered a single individual for identification, there are circumstances that could easily produce an identification error. If the suspect was chosen on the basis of a good verbal description, one would understand if the suspect was similar in appearance to the offender, and also if the witness confused one for another.

Second, in some circumstances an other-race lineup might be "fairer" than an own-race lineup. The fairness of a lineup is related to the similarity of the lineup members to each other. In a chapter published in 1983, Trish Devine and I showed that, with the limitation that they must not be look-alikes, greater similarity generally means a fairer lineup. So if the lineup is otherwise appropriately constructed, the increased subjective similarity due to the lineup members being of an other race than the witness would appear to make the lineup fairer than would be true for an own-race lineup. This would be a better protection for the innocent suspect, but at the same time it might work against the identification of a guilty suspect.

Attempts to actually take our work on the cross-race effect to court met with limited success, but from my point of view it had some interesting side-effects. One day in the late 1970s I had a phone call from a public defender in a northeastern state who had read of our work. He asked if I would testify in a case that would shortly go to trial. After we discussed the case, what questions he would ask me and what my responses would be, he did invite me to offer my testimony as an expert witness in the trial of a young black man accused of assault and robbery. My testimony was to center on the question of whether white witnesses would be less able to make an accurate identification of a black offender/suspect—whether an innocent black suspect would be more likely than an innocent white suspect to be wrongfully identified as the offender. My experience as an experimental psychologist active in studying this matter qualified me, at least potentially, as an expert who could assist the jury in determining the facts of the case. But first, the judge had to decide whether the jury would be allowed to hear my testimony.

To make a long story short, the judge heard my testimony in the absence of the jury (the normal procedure) and then decided that the jury would not hear it (not an unusual result). The trial judge has great discretionary latitude in such matters, but there are certain standard issues that structure the decision. One issue concerns the probative value of the testimony—whether the information an expert would contribute would actually assist the jurors in their attempt to decide what the facts of the case actually are (for example, whether or not the witness' identification was made in error). Another is whether the information the expert would contribute comes from an established and recognized field of knowledge. And still another is whether hearing testimony from an expert would tend to influence the jurors to give excessive weight to what the expert had to say. There are plenty of factors for the judge to balance, and also lots of room for the judge's personal evaluation of the issues to enter the decision.

I happened to see the judge later that day in the hallway, and I was very curious as to his reasons for disallowing my testimony. He came over to me and said he thought our research was very interesting. When I asked him why, then, he had not allowed my testimony, he began to give his legal reasoning (having to do with its probative value). I stopped him and said yes, I understood that, but I was curious about why he came to view my work as lacking in probative value. He observed that all my studies had used photographs of faces, projected as color slides on a screen, and asked what that had to do with what happens to some poor guy outside a bar at two in the morning (referring to the case in which I had testified). I had to acknowledge that this was a good point.

Whether laboratory results generalize very far beyond the laboratory was an unanswered question. Later on, as a direct result of this interaction with the judge, Trish Devine and I addressed this problem in a series of studies in eyewitness identification. We did a series of "staged crime" studies to explore differences in eyewitness identification decisions in laboratory and "apparently real" settings. We found some interesting and unexpected things. For one, it appears that if you can manipulate the beliefs witnesses have about the consequences of making an identification you can modify their willingness to make an identification in a lineup. For example, if witnesses are led to believe that the people running the lineup think the offender is actually present, they will be a lot more willing to choose someone from the lineup and say he is the offender. Of course in our system of justice the question of who is the offender is a matter for the jury to decide. It is a bit premature to make it the basis for witnesses' willingness to make an identification!

An unexpected finding concerned the witnesses' belief in the severity of punishment. We thought that most people would be particularly careful about making identifications if the consequences of mistaken identification were particularly severe. Nobody wants to cause great injury to others, at least not by mistake! But in a study where our "experimental vandal" had destroyed scientific equipment belonging to a visiting lecturer in front of an audience, members of that audience were unwilling to make identifications if the consequences for the offender would be trivial, while many were quite willing if the consequences were severe. They appeared to be quite upset by the "crime," and willing to assist the police so long as he wouldn't just get his hand slapped! Reference to these studies is in the "suggested readings," if you're interested. At the same time, research documenting a cross-race recognition differential in natural social environments has yet to be done.

Still, there were other possible explanations that seemed interesting, and we pursued a number of these in our laboratory. One promising possibility, suggested by June Chance and Alvin Goldstein, was that people may naturally look at own-race faces in a way that connects with existing information in each person's cognitive system. That information may have to do with judgments about the person's personality (e.g., their honesty, how friendly they are). In contrast, other-race faces may be seen in a more superficial, less-connected way. There was already evidence that if subjects were directed to consider aspects of a face requiring cognitive elaboration and social inferences (personality judgments, for example), recognition would be better than if subjects were directed only to superficial information (like whether the person is white or black; whether the nose is big or small).

The idea was worth checking. Trish Devine and I did a study in which we manipulated whether subjects were oriented to inferential (e.g., honest or dishonest) or superficial (e.g., black or white) attributes of own- and other-race faces. We expected an orientation to complex attributes to result in a decrease in the cross-race recognition difference. It didn't happen. Even though orienting to superficial facial information does hurt recognition, it appears people spontaneously look at all faces in an inferential way regardless of race. So, we still had to look elsewhere for an explanation. And in the meantime, with many studies being reported which searched for possible relationships between other-race face recognition and either social attitudes or personal cross-race experience, these perennial favorites still did not come through as the explanation we were looking for.

TOWARD A THEORY OF FACE RECOGNITION AND SOCIAL EXPERIENCE

Restricted social experience with other-race persons has always been the favorite explanation for the cross-race effect. And that makes good intuitive sense: how can you learn to tell "them" apart if you don't know many of "them"? For this reason it is particularly surprising that since the very first study, subjects' reports of how many other-race persons they know (and how well they know them) have been unrelated to recognition for their faces. It is possible that there are problems with the sample of subjects involved (e.g., extremely little cross-race experience, and little variation) or it could be that we simply are not asking the right questions.

Brian Mullen of Syracuse University suggests that information about small minorities (e.g., Asians, in most northeastern cities) is actually processed cognitively in different ways than information about large minorities or majorities (e.g., women or men). Mullen and his colleagues have tried to explain the cross-race effect on this basis. My own view is that we have not asked the right questions about experience. For example, people generally don't know much about the differences among U.S. nickels unless the differences are important. Similarly with people. If it is useful to differentiate among other-race individuals we will find ways to do it. For example, as I think back to my first days in school I have a couple of vivid memories of the school playground and "recess." Recess, as I remember, was not supervised to any great degree. There were mean kids there, older and bigger than I was. I can remember a couple of them very well, even now, nearly 50 years later.

If the mean kids wore black hats, like the villains in old cowboy movies, we wouldn't need to know anything more than the color of their hat to know who's what. But when there are no other markers that indicate who has good things for you, who will tease and humiliate you, who will protect you, who will hurt you, who will be friendly and cooperative, it is important to be able to identify people as individuals so you can remember whether they are one of the good guys or not. I think that's why we're pretty good at recognizing members of our own groups. Likewise, when you can identify entire categories of people that are socially irrelevant, or which can be categorically avoided with little personal or social cost, then there is little need to learn how to distinguish among them as individuals. In the absence of black hats, other social-category markers will do. This is roughly what I think is the important aspect of intergroup social experience, at least as far as intergroup face recognition is concerned. To study this idea we ought to examine the ways in which people have personal significance for each other.

This is the problem on which I will focus much of my own energy in the years ahead. I am hoping that my recent paper dealing with this issue will provide a platform for further research in cross-cultural contexts where the variations of intergroup experience may allow us to get a better look at this interesting but yet unexplained phenomenon.

If you'll pardon one final personal digression, this line of thinking about social experience relates to another of my early memories. My father collected coins, nickels in particular. He was always waiting for the one to turn up that would make us millionaires. He examined every nickel that crossed his palm. He would provide anyone who would listen with lots of details about the different types of nickels. He never found that nickel.

They all look alike to me.

Suggested Readings

Bothwell, R. K., Brigham, J. C. & Malpass, R. S. (1989). Cross-racial identification. *Personality and Social Psychology Bulletin, 15,* 19–25.

Devine, P. G., & Malpass, R. S. (1985). Orienting strategies in differential face recognition. *Personality and Social Psychology Bulletin, 11,* 33–40.

Loftus, E. F., & Ketcham, K. (1991). *Witness for the defense: The accused, the eyewitness, and the expert who puts memory on trial.* New York: St. Martin's.

Malpass, R. S. (1990). An excursion into utilitarian analysis. *Behavior Science Research, 24,* 1–15.

——— & Devine, P. G. (1981). Eyewitness identification: Lineup instructions and the absence of the offender. *Journal of Applied Psychology, 66,* 482–489.

——— & ——— (1980). Realism and eyewitness identification research. *Law and Human Behavior, 4,* 347–358.

——— & ——— (1983). Measuring the fairness of eyewitness identification lineups. In S. Lloyd-Bostock, & B. Clifford (Eds.), *Evaluating witness evidence* (pp. 81–102). London: Wiley.

———— & ———— (1984). Research on suggestion in eyewitness identification. In G. L. Wells, & E. F. Loftus (Eds.), *Eyewitness testimony: Psychological perspectives* (pp. 64–91). New York: Cambridge Univ. Press.

———— & KRAVITZ, J. (1969). Recognition for faces of own and other "race." *Journal of Personality and Social Psychology, 13,* 330–334.

————, LAVIGUEUR, H., & WELDON, D. E. (1973). Verbal and visual training in face recognition. *Perception and Psychophysics, 14,* 285–292.

MULLEN, B. (1991). Group composition, salience and cognitive representations: The phenomenology of being in a group. *Journal of Experimental Social Psychology, 27,* 297–323.

WAGENAAR, W. A. (1988). *Identifying Ivan: A case study in legal psychology.* Cambridge, MA: Harvard Univ. Press.

DUANE **M. R**UMBAUGH *(Ph.D., University of Colorado) is currently Regents' Professor of Psychology and Director of the Language Research Center at Georgia State University and Affiliate Scientist at the Yerkes Primate Center, Emory University. He is editor of* Language Learning by a Chimpanzee: The LANA Project, *a book that summarizes his team's work with Lana—the first chimpanzee to learn language-relevant skills at a computer-monitored keyboard. His wife and colleague, E. Sue Savage-Rumbaugh, jointly founded the Language Research Center at Georgia State University. He has a research history of 33 years with primates, is widely published in the areas of comparative learning and ape-language research, and serves on the editorial boards of three journals. His interests include conservation and enhanced care of primates, and boating.*

7

Learning About Primates' Learning, Language, and Cognition

❖

Major developments in our lives are, in retrospect, profoundly directed by what appear to be relatively matter-of-course events of the day. So it was when I learned in 1955 that I was to be retained by the Department of Psychology at San Diego State College. During the preceding year I had taught courses for a professor who had been on sabbatical leave. Now I needed my own courses. What would they be?

Wolcott Treat, then department chairman, called me in and together we searched through the college catalogue to find courses that were not already defined as "turf" of other faculty. There were, of course, the several opportunities to teach sections of general psychology and statistics, but what would be my specialty?

With a degree in general-experimental psychology and animal-learning research from the University of Colorado, I had always thought that an ideal career would be to study animal behavior. That I had, in error, discounted the prospects of finding such a position became clear when Wolcott said, "Now here's a course—Comparative Psychology. We haven't offered it in some time. Would you like to be our comparative psychologist?" My answer was simply, "I certainly would!" By a process of exclusion whereby other alternatives were pre-empted by other colleagues, a gem had fallen into my hands. I would have a chance for a career learning of animals' behavior and psychology.

The first problem to solve was that there had never been an animal laboratory on campus. Temporarily, an empty treatment room in the hospital of the San Diego Zoo provided space for research to be conducted with—would you believe—mazes and rats. Looking back, I'm appalled that I wasted time working with rats in the setting of a magnificent zoo! But, at the time, I was a captive of research ideas and tactics that I had learned in graduate school, and research with zoo animals was not generally accepted as "scientific."

Shortly thereafter my work was interrupted by the Suez Canal crisis of 1957. The navy commissioned me as a research psychologist in the Medical Service Corps and sent me to the Naval Medical Research Institute in Bethesda, Maryland, for training in the summer of 1958. It was there that I first worked with primates—squirrel monkeys and marmosets—and gained my first insight into what I would do upon my return to San Diego. A view advanced by William A. Mason portrayed an ordering of the species of Primates as approximating the evolutionary course that led to the emergence of our own species—Homo sapiens. From prosimians to New and Old World monkeys and continuing on to the great apes and humankind, there were trends toward enlargement of body, prolonged gestation and maturation, elaboration of the brain's cortex, and the possible emergence of new processes of self-recognition and primitive thought.

To THE SAN DIEGO ZOO

The wonderful primate colony of the San Diego Zoo would provide an opportunity for research into the relationship between evolution of the primate brain and the emergence of competence for learning complex tasks and concepts. In response to an invitation from the zoo, I asked for a small facility within which to have the apes tested in a modified Wisconsin General Testing Apparatus. This apparatus was developed by Harry Harlow at the University of Wisconsin for his now-classic 1949 studies of learning set—the process whereby primates might come to be one-trial, "insightful" learners, rather than just laboring trial-and-error learners, as a function of a specifically defined opportunity to try to learn each of a long series of discrimination problems. A typical discrimination problem might be, for example, an aspirin tin presented with a bottle cap. Let us say that chance has determined that choice of the aspirin tin will be reinforced with food, to be found in an underlying foodwell, whereas choice of the bottle cap results in nothing but the next trial a few seconds later. The right–left position placements of these two items on the tray change unpredictably so that the learner must attend to the qualities of the objects to be discriminated (i.e., learned). After a small and fixed number of presentations (i.e., six times, or trials), this stimulus pair is discarded and the next problem ensues. It might consist of a match box and a part from a child's toy. Again, chance determines which object is correct (i.e., reinforced with food if selected), and this problem also is given for only six trials—whereupon the next problem begins. This

FIGURE 7.1
One of several modified Wisconsin General Testing Apparatus used by the author in research, about 1960, at the San Diego Zoo. The primate being tested for the effects of irrelevant visual foreground cues (note $^1/_2$-inch wire mesh behind the fronts of the plastic bibs) is a gibbon (*Hylobates lar*), a form of lesser ape.

method of training might continue for several hundreds of problems, with each problem consisting of a randomly paired set of objects. Across the course of these problems with the learner just trying to learn, the shape of the learning curve changes from one of gradual improvement to the point where performance/choice is essentially correct after the first trial on any new problem. This radical alteration in efficiency of learning is due to the experience of the learner in this discrimination learning situation, and its formation is called *learning set*.

The Wisconsin General Testing Apparatus (see Figure 7–1) was known to be an efficient device for conducting object-discrimination learning studies with primates that resulted in the formation of learning sets. Learning set, the learning-how-to-learn phenomenon, was known to be sensitive to both maturation and brain damage. Hence, it was promising as a method for studying the complex-learning abilities of great apes and monkeys whose brains varied widely in terms of complexity and, in particular, cortical development. Comparative studies of such abilities might help us understand the biobehavioral roots of one of our most cherished competencies—*intelligence*.

Initial efforts in the research program taught me more than it taught the apes. Their cleverness at avoiding the opportunity for "higher education" was underscored by one young orangutan who took the opportunity to become a truant when a door was left unlocked. She ran through the woods and then climbed, of all things, a television broadcasting tower that seemed to soar interminably into the sky! As she climbed rung by rung up that tower, I saw my newly established research effort vanishing forever. That was it! I was done! The orang would be electrocuted and I would be out on my ear. But then, a friend, who was a keeper, came to my assistance. He entered his nearby work area and returned with a bottle of milk. A call to the orang got its attention and, at the sight of the milk, she scampered down from the tower and ran to the keeper's arms. In a very real sense, both the orang's life and my life, at least my research life, had been saved "by the bottle!"

SPECIES DIFFERENCES

Over the years, the apes learned-how-to-learn and defined for us nice relationships between their levels of brain maturation and abilities to learn discrimination tasks. Their rates of learning problems increased as they worked on hundreds and hundreds of them (e.g., they developed learning sets and became more facile at learning new problems). Interestingly, one form of ape, not a great but lesser ape—the gibbon, proved to be very, very poor at learning in our test situation. They simply failed to improve with experience. Then one day, an idea came to me as I saw one of them rub its hand on the front of one of the transparent bins that contained the objects to be discriminated, as though to feel its surface. Plexiglas bins had been devised and used to ensure that the animals would not steal or destroy test objects from the Wisconsin General Testing Apparatus. The animals had been given training intended to teach them to attend to and to learn discriminations between objects presented. The improvements in all great-ape primate subjects tested were evidence that they had continued to look through the front plane of the bin to see the objects within. But what about the gibbons? Might they be attending primarily to the frontal planes of the bins (i.e., its abrasions and reflections) rather than to the objects within and, consequently, just selecting one of the bins randomly?

By systematically enhancing visual noise (i.e., irrelevant visual cues, provided by $1/2$-inch wire-mesh inserts) either in front of or behind the objects that constituted the problems to be learned, we discovered the problem. Gibbons were not looking through the frontal planes of the bins. But why?

Subsequent research with still other primate species revealed an orderly relationship between how arboreal (tree-dwelling) versus how terrestrial (ground-dwelling) primate species were in nature and how likely they were to attend to visual cues that were closest, most proximal, to their eyes—in our instance, the fronts of the bins. Doing so in nature might serve to protect their eyes from twigs and branches, but in my test situation it precluded their learning, if they were highly arboreal, as is the gibbon.

That lesson underscored my long-standing concern about the equity of the test situation for members of different species and age levels. In point of fact, there was no way of knowing whether the test situation was as fair and equitable for the gibbon and gorilla as, say, for the squirrel monkey or orangutan. Species differ in size, appetites, strength, what they attend to, and so on. The search for more defensible and equitable testing procedures had to be intensified.

COMPLEX BRAINS ASSIST TRANSFER

A window of opportunity presented itself during a sabbatical in 1962 which I spent at the San Diego Zoo. Analysis of data from a discrimination-reversal experiment revealed an interesting finding. The experiment had consisted of presenting gorillas, chimpanzees, orangutans, gibbons, and macaque monkeys a long series of two-choice, discrimination problems comprised of paired junk objects (e.g., bits of toys, plastic, etc.). One object was randomly defined as "correct," in that choice of it resulted in a reward—a prized piece of food—whereas choice of the other object did not. But then after the first few trials, the "correct" object became incorrect, and the initially "incorrect" stimulus became correct (e.g., choice of it now resulted in food).

Analysis of data across species revealed very interesting differences. Some of the great apes took the reversal cues seemingly in stride and were so efficient in doing so that they did appreciably better on the reversal trials (e.g., once the food-payoff values of the objects were reversed) than they had done on the initial trials. Another way of summarizing their performance was that some, but not all, great apes continued to improve throughout each problem (except on the trial or two that followed the reversal of cues). Now, that struck me as very interesting because the squirrel monkeys and marmosets generally had done very poorly on the reversal trials. The strong suggestion was that if the reversal trials were viewed as tests of transfer-of-learning from the initial acquisition trials, great apes' transfer of learning was positive whereas squirrel monkeys and marmosets transfer was negative.

The prospect emerged that a hallmark of evolution of the primate brain, and in particular the elaboration of the cortex, is the ability to transfer learning in one situation to another with a positive advantage rather than to a negative disadvantage. Subsequent research with my Transfer Index demonstrated clearly that the higher the level or amount of learning, the better (i.e., more positive) the transfer by the great apes (with the most-complex brains of the nonhuman primates) but, by contrast, as the amount learned was increased for the smaller primates (with brains of lesser complexity than the great apes), the more disadvantageous (i.e., negative) the transfer.

An important functional role afforded by elaboration of the cortex with primate evolution became clear—it served to facilitate transfer of even small amounts of learning to an advantage. And increased levels or learning served to enhance the consequences of transfer. Thus, as students, you probably have found that the more you learn about principles in one class, the better you do in the next class. But, if you were the squirrel monkey or marmoset, you would find quite the contrary, because you then would be learning each topic or "problem" in a very specific way. Rather than learning principles, you would find that the more you learned in one class, the *worse* you would do in the next. (A horrible dilemma would then be presented. For you to graduate, you would have to make certain that you didn't learn very much in any one class along the way—to learn a great deal would serve only to devastate your cumulative grade-point average.)

COMPLEX BRAINS ALLOW FOR NEW LEARNING PROCESSES

But what were the learning processes put in place by elaboration of the cortex that "made the difference"? Did they simply enhance transfer of learning or were new processes of learning introduced with expansion of the cortex? Several psychologists of earlier years—Yerkes, Kohler, Nissen, and Schneirla, for example—had speculated that new kinds of emergent learning processes occurred as the primate brain evolved. (An emergent process is one that is the product of interaction between other processes and/or elements; thus, airplanes take off and fly when the thrust from engines increases the flow of air and thereby produces a vacuum over their wings, water is produced when hydrogen is "burned" by combination with oxygen, and green is produced by the mixture of blue and yellow pigments or paints.)

Abilities to learn of relationships and to generate hypotheses/strategies were thought to come into play as the cortex became more complex. "Thought," rather than just stimulus-response associations, might emerge as a consequence. (As students, you know that if you understand material you can do more with it than if you have only learned it by rote memory.) How to detect such a shift in learning processes became the challenge.

The next several months were spent in devising as experimental procedure to ferret out such differences, and it worked wonderfully well. Predictions were upheld, and it was concluded that elaboration of the primate cortex serves to enhance transfer because learning processes shift from those that are predominately the association of specific stimuli with specific responses to those that provide for relational and mediational learning—learning that I view as the first traces of primitive thought.

HUMANS AND ANIMALS: COMMON GROUND

Humans are an egotistical lot. Many people maintain that although there might be similarities in the anatomies of animals and humans, animals cannot think or experience feelings or learn language as do we humans. Such thinking has been all too common ever since Descartes, who advanced the view that only humans can think. He argued that animals are beast-machines that cannot think. Consequently, they cannot feel anything (i.e., joy or pain); neither could they "sin." Pain and punishment are the consequences of sin, Descartes argued, and because humans sinned, from time to time they had to suffer pain as punishment. But because animals were held incapable of sinning, since they were *non*-thinking beast-machines, God would not punish them with pain. Thus, while animals might appear to suffer, they really were not, for if they really suffered, God would be unjustifiably imposing suffering upon them for sins—sins for which they were incapable. Because God is just, he would not do that. And so, animals could not suffer. And so, the argument has gone on and on.

PRIMATE ROOTS FOR LANGUAGE

In particular, many humans hold that language is the feature that distinguishes them from animals. Yes, parrots might "talk," but not as humans. The Latin root for language is *lingua*—tongue. Speech is language, and language is speech. None but our kind can speak and use language with competence—so the argument has gone. With Chomsky's assertion that language is the product of a mutation unique to *Homo sapi-*

ens, one that resulted in a posited Language Acquisition Device that provided for the universal/basics of language learning and grammar, the possibility that animals might have language was presumed to be ruled out forever.

Despite that, however, efforts were renewed to explore apes' abilities for language. No, the efforts didn't necessarily call upon the ape to talk with its voice—though the one (unsuccessfully) attempted by the Hayses did. But they did call upon them to talk with their hands or with bits of plastic that were to serve as symbols—methods pursued by the Gardners of Nevada and Premack of California.

A golden opportunity presented itself in the spring of 1969. I got a call asking if I would be interested in joining the Yerkes Regional Primate Research Center. Now an opportunity would be at hand that would provide for the collection of additional data to evaluate the primitive thinking abilities of the great apes. A related and more demanding effort would be to determine even more definitively the ape's ability for language.

The language research method that I advanced through discussions with Harold Warner, a biomedical engineer of the Yerkes Center, was to develop a computer-operated keyboard on which each of a large number of keys would be embossed with distinctive geometric symbols. Each symbol would serve as the functional equivalent of a *word*. Speech, though clearly a uniquely evolved and highly efficient means of expressing language, was not to be held as the essence of language. Rather, the use of symbols whose meanings would be defined by social experiences would become the medium for expressing language.

In concert with scientists from the University of Georgia and Georgia State University, where I served as Chairman of the Department of Psychology from 1971 to 1989, the LANA project (the *Language ANAlogue* Project; also the name of our first chimpanzee subject, Lana) was launched in 1971. Operation of the computer-based system started in late 1972. Our chimpanzee's progress was remarkable. Not only did she learn the function of individual symbols on her keyboard, she learned to use them in combinations or what we called "stock sentences" in order to bring about consequences for which she was motivated. By use of her "sentences," Lana could ask for a variety of specific foods (PLEASE MACHINE GIVE MILK; PLEASE MACHINE GIVE PIECE OF BANANA, etc.) and drinks (PLEASE MACHINE GIVE COKE) or a movie or slide show (PLEASE MACHINE MAKE MOVIE or SLIDE), a view of the outdoors (PLEASE MACHINE MAKE WINDOW OPEN), or a friend to enter her room for a bout of grooming, tickling, or chasing (PLEASE TIM/SHELLY/BEV COME INTO ROOM; PLEASE TIM/SHELLY/BEV TICKLE/GROOM/CHASE LANA). Not a bad life, especially for a chimp (see Figure 7–2).

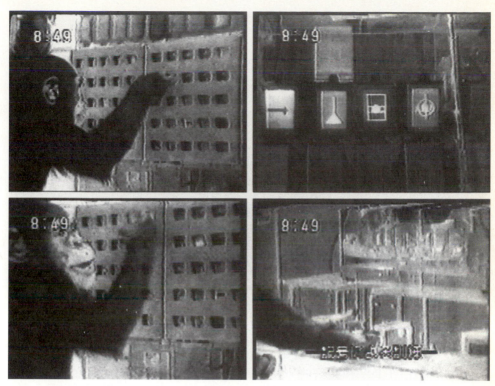

FIGURE 7.2

Lana at her computer-monitored keyboard, about 1973. She asks for a food available, such as "PLEASE MACHINE GIVE PIECE OF BANANA," then catches it as it is delivered by an automatic feeder.

Lana surprised us with all kinds of skills. Not only did she use her stock sentences to obtain "the good life," she used them, both in their original form and in variations thereof, to solve problems—such as bringing to the attention of people present the fact that one of her vending machines was not working or that she wanted what they had. She also gave evidence that having names for objects probably enhanced her accuracy in making same-difference discriminations when one object of a pair was presented visually and the other presented only for palpation or touch. Early on, she readily learned the names of six test objects (a shoe, ball, box, bowl, cup, and can) and the six colors in which each could be presented (red, green, black, yellow, orange, and purple). Upon specific request she would tell us either the name or the color of the object. Her color perception proved to be very similar to that of a human. Her colors enabled her to ask for things for which she did not have names. Hence, a cucumber was termed "banana which-is green"; an apple was requested as "ball which-is red"; and a purple purse carried by a woman visitor was called "box which-is purple"; and so on.

In subsequent years, the LANA Project spawned other projects, including one at the Georgia Retardation Center in 1975 with children and young adults with severe and profound mental retardation who had otherwise failed to learn words and communication systems. About half of them benefited significantly from being taught in accordance with principles derived from the LANA Project. In particular, one young boy was able to carry out a well-structured conversation through use of the keyboard so as specifically to request a container of chocolate pudding, that it be opened, that he be given a spoon with which to eat, and to comment that it was delicious! Without the benefit of our technology and principles derived from research with Lana, he probably never would have been able to develop such skills of symbolic communication. There was no doubt, in the views of parents and teachers, that Lana had made a contribution that enhanced the communication skills and quality of life for those individuals.

In 1975 another primate finished a Ph.D. at the University of Oklahoma. Her name was Sue Savage. I did not meet Sue in person, but as author of a manuscript that I was called upon to review in 1973. On the basis of that manuscript, I knew that Sue would make her own distinctive contributions to our knowledge of chimpanzees! After our meeting at the Fourth International Primatological Congress of 1974 in Japan, Sue joined the language project of Georgia State University and the Yerkes Regional Primate Research Center in 1975 as a research associate.

Sue's primary interest of 1976 was to determine whether chimpanzees might learn to communicate with one another through use of lexigrams, the symbols originated in the LANA Project. Sherman and Austin (chimpanzees) joined the project when they were about two-years-old. Sue set about to teach them the meanings of symbols and, then, how to use them to coordinate in the solving of various tasks.

Several kinds of tasks were used, but two of them merit special consideration. A variety of puzzle boxes were designed and built so that each could be locked in unique ways. Special tools were required to open them so that Sherman and Austin could extract prized foods and drinks locked within them. One required a lever, and others required a key, a special wrench, or a stick, and so on. Once they had learned how to use specific tools to open the array of boxes and had learned the lexigrams for each tool, important test trials were conducted. On those trials, only one chimpanzee could watch to see which box was "baited" with the prized incentive. That chimpanzee then had to use the lexigram keyboard to ask the other chimpanzee, positioned in an adjoining room, for the specific tool needed. The second chimpanzee "read" the first chimpanzee's request on a projector and then, if all went well, went to its "tool box" and picked out the tool requested. Next, it vended the tool through a small window so that it could be used by the first chimp. Once the food or drink had been extracted from the puzzle box, it was shared so that both chimpanzees were rewarded for their coordinated efforts.

Sherman and Austin also learned to use their symbols so as to ask one another for a variety of foods and drinks available to them on a tray. They took turns so that each could ask for a desired food/drink while the other chimp served. (The advantage in being the requester was that requesters could get what they wanted. The advantage in being the server was that servers could, most assuredly, get the larger portion!) The chimps enjoyed working together on such tasks and chorused loudly whenever preparations for such tasks began (see Figure 7–3).

Sherman and Austin were, thus, the first nonhumans to coordinate their social behaviors through use and comprehension of symbols that stood for things—things that were not necessarily present in time and space. That the symbols had basic semantic meaningfulness was demonstrated in a study where, in the final test, they were presented with 17 lexigrams, each of which stood for a specific food or tool. These were lexigrams that had been used and learned in the studies of the kind referenced above. In this task they were to classify each lexigram as either a *tool* or a *food* through use of appropriate lexigrams. That they were able to do that with only one error between them was interpreted to mean that as they saw each lexigram, in turn, they were able to conjure a representation (a mental construction) of what it stood for—that is, what it meant. Next they had to decide whether the "thing it represented" was something that they ate or something that they used to open puzzle boxes. As stated, there was only one error: Sherman called a sponge a food. But when one acknowledges that Sherman literally ate a lot of sponges, which were used to soak up soft drinks contained in deep tubes, one can understand why, for him but not Austin, a sponge was a food. It was something he ate—after using it as a tool.

Sherman and Austin spontaneously commented on things they saw (such as a scary thing out the window) and on activities in which they were engaged (such as tickling and play-biting.) They also came, quite on their own, to announce or to make a statement about what it was that they were going to do. For example, they could go into a room where they found a tray of foods and drinks, randomly selected for presentation to them across visits. They would look at the tray, return to the keyboard in an adjoining room, announce through use of the appropriate key the specific food/drink that they had selected, then return to the tray (out of the experimenter's view) and select the item announced. Upon returning to the room in which the keyboard and experimenter were located, they received praise and shared the food/drink with one another. In brief, they could make plans, announce them, and then carry them out—almost without error! (Who says that animals can't think?)

FIGURE 7.3
Sherman and Austin in the food-sharing situation.

In the early 1980s, bonobo chimpanzees (erroneously, but commonly called pygmy chimpanzees) were made available to us. The bonobo is much more like us than is the so-called common chimpanzee. It stands and walks erect more comfortably, has a more vaulted brain case, and can modify its vocalizations more than the common chimpanzee can, and so on.

Great efforts were invested to teach lexigrams to a wild-reared bonobo, Matata, but she did not learn well. Matata had been raised in the field until about six years of age, during which time she learned how to adapt to all of its challenges; but that learning apparently interfered with her learning lexigrams and the challenges of our laboratory. (That she was from "the old country" made it difficult, it appeared, for her to learn the language and ways of the Western World.) Her adopted son, Kanzi, by contrast, received no formal training during Matata's training sessions or at any other time. He just played and watched. Notwithstanding, he learned! When he was 2 $1/2$ years old, Matata was assigned to the Yerkes Field Station for breeding. That was the first opportunity to work with Kanzi apart from Matata.

Surprisingly, it became clear that Kanzi needed no instruction. He had learned all that Matata was intended to learn—and more! He had learned his lexigrams and how to use them to name things, to ask for things, and to announce what it was that he was doing or what he intended to do. With that finding, we decided not to give him any of the planned training but, rather, to just see what he might continue to learn in his world of living throughout each day with people and other chimpanzees, all of whom used lexigrams and, in the case of the humans, speech to coordinate activities.

Kanzi is, at the time of this writing, 10 years old (see Figure 7–4). He now understands human speech in detail far greater than ever expected for a chimpanzee. He has demonstrated an ability to understand novel requests that are spoken to him in controlled conditions that preclude

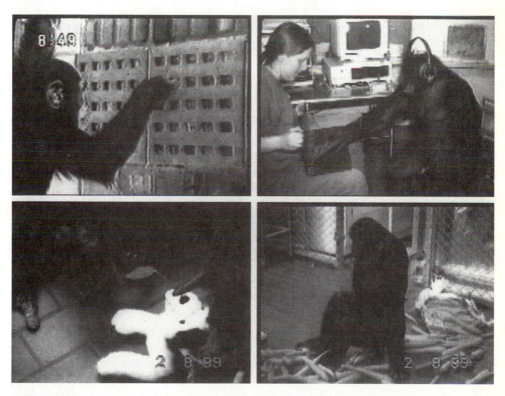

FIGURE 7.4

Kanzi (*Pan paniscus*) can understand speech—either single words (upper right) or novel sentences of request that are spoken to him under controlled test conditions. At lower left, Kanzi carries out the novel request of "MAKE THE DOGGIE BITE THE SNAKE'; lower right, he is pushing carrots to Rose after being asked, "KANZI, CAN YOU GIVE ROSE A CARROT?"

cuing. By carrying out the requests, we know what he can and cannot understand. He understands a variety of types of requests: GET THE LETTUCE THAT'S IN THE MICROWAVE; PUT WATER ON THE CARROT; TICKLE LINDA WITH THE BUNNY; MAKE THE DOGGIE BITE THE SNAKE; POUR THE MILK IN THE JELLY; POUR THE JELLY IN THE MILK; and so on—at the level of the child (Alia, whose mental age was 2 $^1/_2$ years) who received similar requests. Both Kanzi and the child (Alia) fully carried out about 60 percent (to be correct by chance in sentence comprehension approximates 0 percent) of the approximately 700 novel requests spoken to them. On the remaining sentences, they were generally partially correct (for example, when Alia was asked "Make the doggie bite the snake," she bit the dog! They were far more similar than they were different in their efforts and in the kind of errors made.

Kanzi can also now make sharp chips of stone by striking one rock with another. He works until he gets a good one, one large and sharp enough to cut a rope so as to open a box that holds a ball or some other prized object.

There is little doubt about it. At every point along the path of better than 30 years, primates have continued to teach us things that we "had known" were well beyond their abilities. Chimpanzees have important language abilities. They can also count, that is, they can count an arbitrarily determined quantity of boxes upon request in a video task. In sum, there is continuity in the advanced cognitive processes of humans and chimpanzees—a finding that attests to an evolutionary link which we shared in the not-so-distant past.

Our lives in research have produced still other important and exciting ventures. Communications with NASA in 1986 stimulated our thinking about how we might help enrich the lives of rhesus monkeys while they serve in biomedical experiments in a NASA shuttle so that more can be learned about how the adaptation to weightlessness can be enhanced. (Weightlessness for long periods of time causes the bones to lose calcium, muscles and the cardiovascular system to weaken, etc.—all of which can adversely affect performance of astronauts during flight and their well-being after flight.) An earlier observation that language-competent chimpanzees could readily learn to use a joystick and perform a wide variety of complex computer-based tasks portrayed on a monitor directed our attention to the possibility of having rhesus monkeys do the same. Grave reservations about the probability of success were based on 40 years of literature which said that rhesus could learn to differentiate visual cues/objects only if they actually touched them. To teach them to use a joystick, some 8 to 10 inches from the center of a monitor's screen, to indicate their choice of stimuli on a monitor in learning tasks would, by implication, be very difficult, if not impossible. Notwithstanding all this, we tried. We bet that the literature of long standing would not apply to video-formatted tasks if we took the correct approach to teaching the monkeys what to do.

As it turned out, it was very easy to teach them to learn to use the joystick with precision—to chase, capture, and pursue moving targets; to shoot bullets of light and hit targets; and even to learn the relative values of all numerals 0 through 9. In the present instance, findings obtained through use of the Wisconsin General Testing Apparatus over the course of 40 years did not apply to our Language Research Center's Computerized Testing System (LRC-CTS). Although rhesus monkeys had to have their fingers close to, and preferably directly on, the stimuli which constituted problems "to be learned" in the Wisconsin General Testing Apparatus, such was not the case in the LRC-CTS. (Lessons of the past learned through use of one set of research tactics might not generalize to others.)

Research with the LRC-CTS (see Figure 7–5), with David Washburn, has proven to be very efficient and has allowed us to explore a wide

FIGURE 7.5
A rhesus monkey (*Macaca mulatta*) working on a number task presented by the Language Research Center's Computerized Testing System (LRC-CTS).

variety of questions that otherwise would have been impracticable to pursue. For example, we have learned that the monkeys differentially "lead" the target in the laser task in response to changes in the speed of the target and the distance of the moving target from the turret. Also, they "abort" or recall bad shots that are clearly going to miss the target. By aborting bad shots they move up in time the opportunity to try again. In brief, they predict where they must aim in order to shoot to hit the target—whereupon they get a prized piece of food. (The monkeys work at the task as they wish and are not deprived of either food or water.) If they compete with one another in shooting at the same target on a monitor, each monkey fires more shots per minute, recalls shots more frequently, and the target is hit more quickly than if the monkeys are working alone—that is, not in competition.

Our two most-experienced monkeys, Abel and Baker, have worked in cages in the same room since they came to us in 1986. Interestingly, if they are placed one-to-a-room so they can neither see nor hear one another, their rate of working at the LRC-CTS drops off very substantially—as does the promptness and accuracy with which they work!

In our "select" task, the monkeys can choose among five tasks on which to work. They do significantly better on tasks when they can specifically select them than if they are arbitrarily assigned to work on them by the experimenter. (Don't we all? True. But no one knew before that it made a difference to animals.)

Abel and Baker also have learned the rank-ordered values of all numerals 0–9. In the LRC-CTS, if they chose, for example, 7 when paired with 5, they got 7 rather than 5 pellets of food. If, given 3 and 6 to choose between, they chose the 3, they got 3 rather than 6 pellets. Thus, they didn't have to choose the larger numeral in order to get pellets—but the numeral selected did determine how many pellets would "come down the shoot" from the vending device controlled by the computer's software. Seven novel combinations of numerals had been reserved for a critical test to determine whether they learned which numeral was the better one to choose in each specific pair, or whether they had learned in a more comprehensive, relational manner the relative values of all numerals 0–9. One monkey made no errors; the other made only 2 errors. Thus, we conclude that they had learned something that might be described as a matrix of relative values that differentiate the numerals. Thus, they might have learned that, yes, 7 is greater than 5 more than it is greater than 6; so, upon the first presentation of 6 and 5 they chose the 6! And so on. There seems little doubt that animals have many important competencies that only now are being revealed because (1) we are asking better questions, (2) we are getting better at designing procedures for teaching and/or accessing those competencies, and (3) modern technology, and computers specifically, assist us in conducting research.

FIGURE 7.6

A schoolboy who, because of mental retardation, uses a computer-monitored keyboard to assist him in communication with classmates in public school. Such keyboards were pioneered in the LANA project of 1971, where, in all probability, the first successful development of a computer-monitored/controlled system was devised for research into the basic processes of language.

Because of our research program with apes and its benefits for children (see Figure 7–6) and biomedical research, Georgia State University built the Language Research Center and dedicated 55 acres of surrounding forest in 1981 to advance our efforts. The Center is operated in cooperation with the Yerkes Primate Center, the institution that brought Sue and me to Atlanta.

Mary Ann Romski, Robin Morris, Rose Sevcik, David Washburn, William Hopkins, Shelly Williams, Dan Cerutti, and Lauren Adamson— all faculty; a large number of staff and students; and a substantial number of other scientists from here and abroad are working with us to achieve a clearer definition of language and cognitive skills from a comparative perspective that includes studies of our nearest living relatives—the great apes and other primates. We hope our work will also help to foster a better understanding and appreciation of primates and other animals in relation to ourselves. Only by doing this can we hope to succeed in saving vital and irreplaceable parts of our natural world and heritage—one part being our own species.

Acknowledgments

I thank the National Science Foundation for research support during the 1960s and the early 1970s, the National Institute of Children's Health and Human Development and the Institute for Comparative Medicine of the National Institutes of Health for continuing support from 1971, the National Aeronautics and Space Association for support from 1986, and the College of Arts and Sciences of Georgia State University for support from 1971. I also want to thank the following primates, by species in alphabetical order, for highly significant contributions to the research referenced in this chapter: *Gorilla*—Albert, Alvila, Vila: *Homo sapiens*—James E. Crouch, Clyde W. Faulkner, Robert W. Harwood, Oscar J. Kaplan, Frederick A. King, Robert and Carolyn Lee, Carol Rice McCormack, Austin H. Riesen, Leonard A. Rosenblum, E. Sue Savage-Rumbaugh, Richard Simmonds, Judy Sizemore, Robert Voas; *Hylobates*—Cong, Gabrielle; *Macaca*—Abel and Baker; *Pan*—Austin, Kanzi, Lana, Mulika, Panbanisha, Panzee, Sherman, Tamuli; *Saimiri*—Joe, Pete, Ghengis. I also thank San Diego State College (as it was then known), the San Diego Zoo, Georgia State University, and the Yerkes Primate Center of Emory University for continuing support.

SUGGESTED READINGS

FOBES, J. L., & KING, J. E. (1982). Measuring primate learning abilities. In J. L. Fobes & J. E. King (Eds.), *Primate behavior* (pp. 289–321). New York: Academic.

RUMBAUGH, D. M. (1990). Comparative psychology and the great apes: Their competence in learning, language, and numbers. *The Psychological Record, 40,* 15–39.

——— HOPKINS, W. D., WASHBURN, D. A., & SAVAGE-RUMBAUGH, E. S. (1989). Lana chimpanzee learns to count by "Numath": A summary of a videotaped experimental report. *The Psychological Record, 39,* 459–470.

——— & PATE, J. L. (1984). The evolution of cognition in primates: A comparative perspective. In H. L. Roitblat, T. G. Bever, & H. S. Terrace (Eds.), *Animal cognition* (pp. 403–420). Hillsdale, NJ: Erlbaum.

——— RICHARDSON, W. K., WASHBURN, D. A., SAVAGE-RUMBAUGH, E. S., & HOPKINS, W. D. (1989). Rhesus monkeys (*Macaca mulatta*), video tasks and implications for stimulus-response spatial contiguity. *Journal of Comparative Psychology, 103,* 32–38.

SAVAGE-RUMBAUGH, E. S. (1986). *Ape language: From conditioned responses to symbols.* New York: Columbia Univ.

———— MURPHY, J., SEVCIK, R. A., WILLIAMS, S., BRAKKE, K., & RUMBAUGH, D. M. (1993). Language comprehension in ape and child. *Monograph Series of the Society for Research on Child Development*, in press.

WASHBURN, D. A., HOPKINS, W.D., & RUMBAUGH, D. M. (1989). Video-task assessment of learning and memory in macaques (*Macaca mulatta*): The effects of stimulus movement on performance. *Journal of Experimental Psychology: Animal Behavior Processes, 15*, 393–400.

NORMAN FREDERIKSEN *(Ph.D., Syracuse University) is currently Distinguished Research Scientist Emeritus at the Educational Testing Service, Princeton, New Jersey. He is the co-editor of* Test Theory for a New Generation of Tests, Diagnostic Monitoring of Skill and Knowledge Acquisition, Administrative Performance and Personality, *and* Prediction of Organizational Behavior, *and many journal articles, including the influential* The Real Test Bias: Influences of Testing on Teaching and Learning *(American Psychologist, 1984). In his spare time he makes furniture in his woodworking shop.*

8

Changing Conceptions of Intelligence

❖

In my early teen years I was quite a bookworm. I spent hours in our small-town public library and I borrowed two or three books almost every week. I remember borrowing a book with the word *psychology* in the title because I was curious as to what psychology is (or was). I read chapters about hearing, seeing, smelling, learning, perception, and intelligence, but I don't remember much about any of the topics except that intelligence was supposed to be inherited.

PREPARATION FOR A CAREER IN PSYCHOLOGY

I didn't think much about going to college, although my high-school teachers saw to it that I took all of the "college prep" courses. However, a friend of mine told me that he was going to attend Nebraska Wesleyan University, and he urged me to go along. I agreed, and at the appointed time he drove up to my home in his Model-T Ford with his suitcase strapped to a front fender. I strapped mine on the other fender, said goodbye to my parents, and we were off to Lincoln in the depth of the great depression (the economic one).

When we arrived in Lincoln I learned that I was supposed to apply in advance for admission to college. I was told to wait while the admissions committee checked on my credentials; the next day I learned that I had been admitted. I managed to find two part-time jobs—stacking books in the library and sweeping out classrooms—so with help from home and a summer job in an ice-cream factory I had adequate financial support.

Remembering the psychology textbook I had read, I signed up for the course in introductory psychology. Eventually I took all of the psychology courses that were offered. Looking back, I realize that what I learned had little resemblance to what is taught to undergraduates today. For example, there was much interest in

111

instincts, which were thought to be inner "drives" or sources of motivation for various kinds of behavior, and there was much debate among
psychologists as to how many and what instincts there were. (However, there was no argument about the existence of sex and hunger
instincts!)

I learned in the introductory course that much of the research on
intelligence involved attempts to trace the descendants of feeble-minded
people. Two families (the pseudonyms were "the Jukes" and "the
Kallikaks") were studied in detail. In such studies the emphasis was on
such things as "defective mentality" and "bad blood," but, as I recall, little attention was given to environmental factors.

I did learn something about "intelligence" tests—the Binet test, the
Stanford version of the Binet, the Army Alpha test, etc. During World
War I there was an urgent need to find ways to classify recruits
with respect to their assignment to different kinds of duty or training,
and the Army Alpha proved to be quite useful. After the war, many
off-shoots of the test were developed, usually in multiple-choice form. I
took one such test as part of a course in educational psychology.
I remember one of the items: "A Korean has ___ legs: (2), (4), (6), (8)." I
knew the answer because I had seen a Korean and heard him give
a lecture; I suppose most students had not. At any rate, I decided that
there must be more to intelligence than remembering such bits of information.

I was graduated from Nebraska Wesleyan with an A.B. degree and
little understanding of intelligence. Nevertheless, I applied for (and was
granted) a research assistantship at the University of Nebraska at $400 a
year. I didn't know it at the time, but my mentor at Nebraska was a man
who was to become one of the major figures in psychology because of his
contributions to knowledge about intelligence. His name was Joy Paul
Guilford, although he became known to his students and friends as JP.
Years later I consulted with him on what tests I might use in various
research projects I was working on.

JP's interests were broad; his research at Nebraska involved sensory
processes, psychophysical judgment, attention, affectivity, interests,
and personality traits, all from a psychometric point of view. Another
major interest was factor analysis, a mathematical procedure for sim-
plifying a mass of data by reducing a large number of variables
to a smaller number by putting together similar variables to form
subgroups. For example, suppose 15 tests were administered to 100 students and five of the tests measured arithmetical skills, another five
measured verbal skills, and a third group measured writing ability; fac-
toring the intercorrelations of all the tests would no doubt reveal the
number and nature of the factors and reduce the number of variables
from 15 to 3.

When JP moved to California his interests turned toward factors
in intelligence. His major contribution was his Structure of Intellect

model of intelligence. In this model the many components of intelligence were arranged to form a three-dimensional structure, one that until recently was probably greater in its coverage of intellectual abilities than any other factor model.

Acting on the advice of another professor at Nebraska, I applied for admission to Syracuse University, where Floyd Allport was a leading figure in social psychology. I earned my board and room there by serving as a dormitory proctor and later as a part-time instructor, both on campus and at an extension center. I took several graduate courses in biology and genetics as well as psychology, but I don't recall a course that had much to do with intelligence.

My first full-time job was at Princeton University, where I was an instructor with a Ph.D., a wife, and a salary that started at $2,000. My primary duties were to teach social psychology and to get started on my own research program. It didn't turn out to be a very happy situation because I wasn't really interested in social psychology, and there was too much competition among some of the senior faculty. So, when World War II came along and I was offered a job working on a war research project, I accepted. Harold Gulliksen was the Project Director, and I was the first member of his staff. This was my first real opportunity to learn about measuring abilities, whether or not they can be called intelligence tests.

SELECTION AND TRAINING OF MILITARY PERSONNEL

The Navy wanted us to do research on (1) improving their ability to make appropriate assignments of recruits to service schools, and (2) improving instruction in the service schools. Those most involved were gunner's mate, torpedoman, electrician's mate, fire controlman, basic engineering, and machinist's mate schools.

It seemed that the best beginning was to determine the validity of the tests then used by the Navy for assigning recruits to training schools, i.e., how well the tests predicted performance in the assignments made. This would now be called predictive validity. The Navy's "Basic Battery" of tests for enlisted men included the General Classification Test (a sort of general intelligence test), a reading test, an arithmetic test, and three mechanical tests: the Mechanical Aptitude Test, the Mechanical Knowledge Test (Mechanical), and the Mechanical Knowledge Test (Electrical). All were multiple-choice tests. The criteria against which the tests were to be "validated" were the service-school grades, which were based on written tests, oral tests, and instructors' judgments.

The gunner's mate is to guns what the garage mechanic is to automobiles; he must be able to diagnose malfunctions and correct them and make adjustments to improve performance. The gunner's mate must not only be able to take guns apart and put them back together; he must also understand the functions of the parts and their relations to each other. One would expect that the mechanical tests would be better predictors of performance than the verbal tests. But such was not the case.

To my surprise, the best predictors of grades in gunner's mate schools were found to be the verbal tests—the General Classification Test and Reading. How could this be accounted for? Apparently the students learned more from lectures and reading technical manuals than from assembling and disassembling guns. Perhaps the instructional methods were faulty; maybe there was more talking and reading than playing with guns.

The Gunner's Mate School

I was sent to the gunner's mate school at Bainbridge, Maryland, to find out what the instruction was like. Even though I was ignorant about guns, it didn't take long to find out about the teaching. The lecture-demonstration method of teaching was used, with chairs in the classroom for the students and a podium for the instructor. The students listened and watched (and sometimes napped) as the instructor demonstrated the steps involved in disassembling and reassembling guns. Homework involved reading the technical manuals. Students spent only about a quarter of their time working with guns.

The training of gunner's mates took five weeks, with one week on each type of gun: small arms, Browning machine guns, 20-mm guns, 40-mm guns, and the 5"/38-caliber antiaircraft gun. At the end of each week an examination was given; it consisted of a paper–pencil test of names and functions of gun parts, oral questions, and judgments of mechanical ability as observed by the instructors. The correlations between the school grades (based on the weekly examinations) and the tests of the Basic Battery were low; predictions were poor for both the verbal tests and the mechanical tests. I was not surprised to find the low correlations on the General Classification Test, Reading, and Arithmetic, because (I thought) these skills would have little to do with learning to assemble gun parts. The low correlations for the mechanical tests must have resulted from comparatively little opportunity for hands-on learning.

The results of this validity study were duly reported to the Bureau of Naval Personnel (BuPers), along with the recommendation that *performance* tests be used for the assessment of learning. Presumably because of this report, orders came down from BuPers to develop performance tests—tests that require students to demonstrate with their hands their ability to find and correct faults in guns.

With the help of the instructors, it was not difficult to develop performance tests. We chose, for example, such tasks as adjusting the oil buffer of a 50-caliber Browning machine gun for maximum rate of fire; removing and replacing the hammer, striker pin, and breech face piece, and reassembling the breechblock of the 20-mm gun; removing and replacing a faulty interlock carrier spring from a 40-mm gun; and replacing an extractor plunger from the breechblock of a 5"/38-caliber gun.

The instructors predicted that the students would not be proficient in performing these tasks, and of course they were right. However, the instructors were quick in responding. The first changes were to move the chairs and the podium out of the classroom and to bring in tables and gun mounts to hold the guns, and the students were encouraged to perform under the eyes of the instructors (see Figure 8–1). Students began to spend much more of their time practicing the skills needed to adjust and repair guns and to find faults (introduced by the instructors). Students were very interested; they even came in after hours to compete with one another: "If you can do it in 45 seconds, I can do it in 40." Thus students acquired a better understanding of the inner functions of guns and skills in disassembly, assembly, diagnosing faults, and repairing them. And there were changes in the correlations of Basic Battery tests with gunner's mate school grades. Correlations with the General Classifications Test, reading, and arithmetic tests dropped, while the correlations with the mechanical tests rose; the correlation was highest for the MK(M)—knowledge of mechanics. More important, students in each class improved in performance from week to week as they progressed through the school. Furthermore, performance improved from class to class as the newcomers learned from the students ahead of them.

After the results were reported, the use of performance tests was mandated by BuPers, not only for all of the gunner's mate schools, but also for other service schools, including torpedoman, electrician's mate, and basic engineering, with similar results. Some of the tasks became too easy, and more difficult tasks had to be devised to encourage broader coverage and more-skilled performance. Thus our research made possible better selection and training—not only in gunner's mate schools but also in other schools that required mechanical or electrical skill and knowledge. Presumably performance aboard ships also improved.

It is usually assumed that the curriculum leads teaching and testing; in this instance assessment led to both teaching and curriculum.

The Amphibious Training Base

Another assignment from BuPers sent me to assist in the development of tests to assess the skills taught at the Amphibious Training Base, which was located on the "silver strand"—a beautiful beach near Coronado, California. When I arrived, a large number of tests had already been

FIGURE 8.1
A room in gunner's mate school.

developed and were in use, including blinker receiving, buoy recognition, flag-hoist, maneuvering signal (semaphore), beach marker, boat
checking, and engine checking—even knot tying. All the tests were simulations of real-life situations that one might have to deal with in preparing for a landing on a beach—a sound approach to test development.

    When I tried out some tests in other formats I found that one test—
the beach marker test—posed a potentially serious problem. After a section of an enemy beach had been taken and occupied, additional personnel and materiel had to be landed in order to provide food, more guns
and ammunition, medications, and other supplies. Beach markers were
large pieces of canvas with symbols that were set up to indicate where
the landing craft were to land. For example, a marker with a large red
cross meant "land medical supplies here." Two important markers indicated the location of each end of the beach that had been taken; a horizontal strip of canvas indicated the left end of the beach and a vertical
strip indicated the right end of the beach (or was it the other way
around?).

Some of the tests were very easy, and the beach-marker test appeared to be one of the easiest. However, a substantial proportion of the trainees (about 10 percent) made errors on the markers of the left and right flanks—errors that could be costly, if not deadly. The part of the beach beyond the flank markers could be dangerous because of a rocky shore or the presence of the enemy.

When I observed a class being taught beach markers, it became clear why the flank markers were often incorrectly marked on the test. The trainees sat on outdoor bleachers where they could see a string of minia-ture beach markers hung on a wire strung between two posts. The instructor used a long rod to touch the various markers, and the trainees called out their names. The positions of the markers on the wire were never changed; the right-flank marker was always on the right and the left-flank marker always on the left. Thus trainees could respond on the basis of observed position—left or right—without attending to the vertical–horizontal cues. The remedy was obviously to present the mark-ers singly, so that responses had to be based on the vertical–horizontal cues.

This experience and others involving gunner's mates helped me to understand the value of realistic simulations in teaching and learning. Ideally, teaching and testing should be done with problems that reflect all of the important properties of relevant real-life situations. Without realistic simulations of problems, generalization of what has been learned is less likely to occur.

THE USE OF SIMULATIONS IN ASSESSMENT

Assessing the Competence of Air Force Officers

Somewhat later I got involved in another military project, this time at the Air University in Montgomery, Alabama. The Air Force Personnel and Training Research Center was concerned about how to evaluate the effectiveness of instruction at its Command and Staff School (CSS), and the Educational Testing Service was asked to develop prototype assess-ment instruments. The students at the CSS were majors and lieutenant colonels—officers who had been selected for training in preparation for greater responsibilities in the Air Force.

The first phase of our project was to make a study of the CSS curricu-lum and objectives. The courses offered included organization, manage-ment, personnel, operations, and intelligence. (In this instance, "intelli-gence" was a term associated more with the CIA than with the Army Alpha.) A colleague and I spent a good deal of time interviewing instruc-tors and school officials to find out what Air Force officers do and what skills might be improved as a consequence of CSS instruction. To be more specific, we tried to collect instances in which the officers had (or had not) been successful in dealing with important Air Force problems.

We collected several hundred stories about successes and failures—obviously too many to deal with separately in developing assessment methods. To reduce the load, we sorted the stories into a dozen or so important behavior categories, and after discussions with the CSS staff it was reduced to four categories that would serve as foci in scoring the assessment instruments. They were (1) makes efficient use of routines by using standard operational procedures; (2) flexibility, or willingness to introduce change; (3) foresight, or anticipation of future conditions or events; and (4) effective evaluation of data.

After several days of discussion with school officials and instructors about *what* was to be assessed, my colleague and I returned to our bachelor quarters to ponder separately *how* these abilities could be assessed. After an hour or so with paper and pencil, we got together to compare notes. My colleague had started writing multiple-choice items. I had been considering a quite different approach—to create realistic simulations of situations in which problems are posed for Air Force officers to deal with.

I had noticed that on every officer's desk there were two baskets, one marked IN and the other marked OUT. The IN basket, I assumed, contained the letters and memos that had accumulated during the past day or so—communications that might have important implications. The OUT basket, I presumed, contained the officer's responses to the in-basket items. We decided that in-baskets might provide a suitable format for assessing the executive skills of Air Force officers.

The idea was to prepare the contents of an in-basket: the letters, memos, directives, records of in-coming phone calls, etc., that had been delivered to an Air Force officer. These communications were addressed to an officer who had just been killed in an automobile accident, and the student was to be told that he had been transferred to another wing to replace the officer. His first task was to respond to the items in the officer's in-basket.

After a good many trials and errors, our staff produced four in-baskets. Here is an example of an "item" that was placed in the commanding officer's in-basket. This is a relatively simple problem consisting of only one document.

To: Commandant
From: Adjutant
For: Action
File: C446   Date: July 3, 1956
Subject: Correction of the Log of Classified Documents
Remarks:

1. The administrative Inspector, HQ, 99th AF, discovered a discrepancy between our Log of Classified Documents and the File of Classified Documents.

2. The missing document is Secret Letter MV 162-092-21, Dated 16 March 1956, from HQ AMC.

3. The report of the Administrative Inspector contains no mention of the specific missing document, but merely mentions a discrepancy between the Log and the File of Classified Documents, which must be corrected.

4. The document described in Paragraph 2 was burned by the undersigned after appropriate action on the letter had been taken. There were unfortunately no witnesses; the undersigned was new at the job and did not realize the importance of the action.

5. Permission is requested to correct the Log of Classified Documents by drawing up a new Log which omits the listing of the document described in Paragraph 2, and to destroy the present Log of Classified Documents.

(signed)   John T. Smith

Major, USAF Adjutant

Question for the reader: How would you respond to this item if you were the Commanding Officer?

Other items dealt with a wide variety of problems, e.g., a memo from the wing commander about a morale problem, a letter regarding misconduct of an Airman Third Class, a letter about how punishment had been escaped by an airman through a hardship discharge, and a memo from the civilian personnel officer regarding a visit by a delegation of civilian employees who had a grievance. We obtained such items as these and many others through an arrangement with the McGuire Air Force Base in New Jersey; we were allowed to search their files for what might become appropriate items; they were then rewritten to match the simulated wing and to protect the privacy of any individuals involved. Thus the test was, I thought, a good simulation of an important part of the real world of Air Force officers.

In preparation for taking the tests, each student was given a good deal of information about the hypothetical wing to which he had supposedly been transferred. The information included a statement of the mission of the wing, maps, rules and regulations, a roster of its officers, etc., etc. And when the students arrived to take the test they were given oral instructions something like the following: "Today you are to assume the role of [blank] Wing. The previous director of personnel, Lt. Col. Hart, was killed in an auto accident, and you are to take his place. The envelope on your desk contains the materials that have collected in Hart's in-basket, together with additional background material placed there by the adjutant for your assistance. Your job is to read Hart's mail and take appropriate actions as though you were actually on the job. Write the appropriate notes, memos, letters, or directives. Take as much action as you can with the available information."

Our next task was to investigate the validity of the in-basket tests. As I noted previously, the typical procedure is called "predictive" validity; it consists merely of computing the correlation between a predictive test and a "criterion." For example, the SAT is often "validated" by correlating it with freshman grades; the higher the correlation, the greater its predictive value.

There is another way of viewing validity, called construct validity. A construct was defined as "some postulated attribute of people, assumed to be reflected in test performance," and construct validation is "not essentially different from the general scientific procedures for developing and confirming theories" (Cronbach & Meehl, 1955). We had no opportunity to carry out the scientific procedures, but at least it was obvious that dealing with the contents of one's in-basket (even a simulated one) resembles the work of an Air Force officer much more than being a student at CSS reading textbook assignments, listening to lectures, and doing the assignments required by the CSS instructors.

Assessing the Competence of Elementary-School Principals

It is difficult to assess the work of a school principal because there is little opportunity to observe his or her work, and because the number and nature of the problems encountered vary very (!) widely. We proposed to use in-baskets as tests for such evaluations, so that identical problems could be presented to all of the principals to be assessed. A grant from the U.S. Office of Education enabled us to proceed with the project, and as one result, 232 elementary-school principals from schools all over the U.S. were recruited to serve for a week as principal of a simulated Whitman School.

The principals were assembled in small groups at different times and places, from Maple Valley (Washington) to Swampscott (Massachusetts). The first part of a week was spent in their getting acquainted with the Whitman School by means of films, tape recordings of school-board meetings, records of school surveys, a statement of policies and by-laws, a school census, etc. In addition, a variety of tests, questionnaires, and inventories were administered (including the National Teacher Examination), and the subjects were asked to prepare and deliver a speech for the PTA (to a tape recorder).

Several Whitman School in-baskets were presented to the subjects during the latter part of the week. Some examples of their contents: a letter from a college professor who wanted permission to use the students in an experiment, a memorandum about parent conferences with teachers, requisitions for supplies, requests from a mother for a meeting regarding her daughter's school problems, student transfers, and complaints about slow progress of children. By the end of the week each principal had read and responded in some way to most if not all of the communications. Between in-baskets, other information was obtained, including ratings of the speech, and various demographic variables, such as age, experience, and education. Altogether, the total number of variables was 165, not including the in-basket scores.

After the week was over, many principals stated voluntarily that the in-basket problems were very similar to the work encountered at home, and several reported that they felt no different doing simulated in-baskets than they did at their own desks at home.

In preparation for developing a scoring procedure, competent judges made notes of how the problems were handled (e.g., "compulsive," "postpones decisions," "overly critical," etc.). These were sorted into categories, 40 of which were chosen for further analysis. To reduce still more the number of descriptors, a factor analysis reduced the number to eight.

Factor A: Exchanging information

Factor B: Discussing before acting

Factor C: Complying with suggestions

Factor D: Analyzing the situation

Factor E: Maintaining organizational relationships

Factor F: Organizational work

Factor G: Responding to outsiders

Factor H: Directing others

The correlations of some of these in-basket factors with the other variables provided a reasonably good basis for claiming construct validity for at least some of the in-basket scores. For example, the National Teacher Examination tests—especially those named Administration and Supervision, Elementary Education, and Social Studies—correlated substantially with Factor A (Exchanging Information), Factor B (Discussing with Others), and Factor C (Complying with Suggestions). Several items from a Scorers' Check List also correlated with similar factors.

What is the significance of all this? There were several possible applications of the findings: (1) to provide a better basis for the selection of people for their first job as a principal; (2) to provide materials for use in training school administrators; and (3) to provide materials for the study and teaching of school administration.

Industrial Applications of In-Baskets

The president of Educational Testing Service (the original one) went to the Psychological Corporation to discuss the possibility of its marketing in-basket tests, but the people there were not interested. Douglas Bray (a psychologist employed by AT&T) picked up the idea and prepared an in-basket test for use by AT&T in training middle-management employees. Many other companies, including Dayton Rubber, Boeing, Proctor & Gamble, the Port of New York Authority, and many others used in-baskets for assessment, selection, and/or training. ETS is now working on an in-basket test that can be scored by a computer.

A couple of years ago I encountered Doug Bray at a meeting, and I asked him if in-baskets were still being used. His answer was, yes, almost every large company has its own in-baskets and uses them for training and/or selection. And, according to a recent article in the *American Psychologist*, virtually all assessment centers use in-baskets.

TESTS OF SCIENTIFIC THINKING

At the first session of a high-school or college course someone is likely to raise his or her hand and ask "What will the tests be like? Multiple-choice or essay?" Depending on the answer, students will tend toward different methods of preparing for the examinations. If the answer is multiple-choice, the students will tend to look for and remember names, dates, places, formulas, theories, and other pieces of factual information. Such tests are usually easier for the students, and also easier for the teacher to prepare and to grade.

Essay questions are usually more difficult for students to prepare for (and more difficult for the teacher to write and to grade). Smart students who believe that the answer is "essay" are more likely to pay attention to the textbook headings and chapter titles and try to understand their content. This type of preparing for an exam may lead to a higher level of mastery of the material—and incidentally it also facilitates the learning of names, dates, places, etc., because it provides a better context for such learning.

Since multiple-choice tests had been criticized on the grounds that they fail to measure the more complex cognitive skills and encourage the learning of "basic skills," I made a try at developing tests that might help in teaching skills requiring Higher-Order Thinking Skills (HOTS). One test I developed was a paper–pencil test called "Formulating Hypotheses." Its purpose was to provide opportunities for students to think of hypotheses that might account for events, situations, or occurrences that were described. The items did not require advanced knowledge, but they did require the ability to see relationships and to recognize information that is meaningful in the relevant context. The items in the test were concerned with such mundane events as changes in employment rates in an industry such as mining, and changes in work stoppages resulting from labor-management disputes.

One of the items in the test was based on the work of a scholar who had collected data on death rates, and had prepared a graph (see Figure 8–2) showing death rates from different causes. Below the graph was his statement of the findings: The rate of death from infectious diseases has decreased markedly for each 10-year period since 1900, while the rate from diseases of old age has increased. The task of the examinee was to consider possible reasons for the difference and to write hypotheses ("possible explanations") for the finding. Here are some examples of students' answers: "Compulsory inoculation laws produced a decline in infectious diseases, but not for old people" (half right); "Old people die more often than young people" (poor); and "As treatment of infectious diseases has become more successful, more people survive to old age, and, since everyone must die, death from diseases of old age increases" (good).

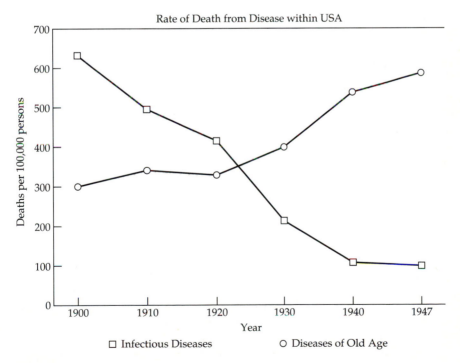

FIGURE 8.2
Sample Formulating Hypotheses Item.

I computed the correlations of Formulating Hypotheses scores with several tests that are more conventional—tests of vocabulary, reading comprehension, interpretation of data, and general information. The correlations were very low. The interpretation of my colleagues was that the Formulating Hypotheses test was worthless. My interpretation was that the *conventional* tests measured knowledge and some basic skills, but they were worthless for measuring HOTS.

I wrote an article describing the test and the results of the tryout, complete with means, standard deviations, correlations, etc., and sent it to a well-known journal for publication. It was rejected—the only time this has happened to me. Little interest was displayed by the editors or by my colleagues at ETS, possibly because the multiple-choice format was viewed as preferable because of its economy and efficiency. There has been little interest in free-response testing until recent years, when the development of cognitive psychology has revealed the importance of tests that go beyond a format that permits students to choose from a set of options, and doesn't require them to think of answers for themselves.

Years later the Graduate Record Examination (GRE) board expressed interest in finding methods to assess HOTS. In response, a colleague and I suggested that it seemed appropriate to make a test that might eventually be useful for the selection of students applying for admission to a graduate school for work in psychology. It seemed even more appropriate when we found that GRE was willing for us to use GRE testing time (time that normally would be used for trying out new test items), and to do the testing in sessions where the Advanced Psychology Test was also given (thus making available to us all the GRE scores). We developed a new Formulating Hypotheses Test and three other tests relevant to problems facing young scientists. Collectively, we called them the "Tests of Scientific Thinking" or TST. All four tests were administered to about 3,500 candidates for admission to graduate school in psychology, along with the GRE. We generated two kinds of scores from the new tests. One set of scores were what we called Number scores, and the other were Quality scores. The latter were based on judgments of the *quality* of answers, and the number scores were based on the number of ideas, the number of *good* ideas, and the number of *unusual good* ideas.

A correlational analysis revealed that the Quality Scores were moderately correlated with the GRE tests (the Verbal and Quantitative aptitude scores and the Advanced Psychology Test), while the number scores (especially the Number of Unusual Responses) were unrelated to these conventional tests. This strongly suggests that the GRE as it exists today would be good for predicting the more basic skills, but not for selecting students who are imaginative and creative.

The following April, when most of the students should have been nearing the end of their first year of graduate study, a questionnaire was sent to those students who had given us permission to do so. The purpose of the follow-up was to investigate the relationships of the TST and the GRE scores to graduate-school performance, as reported by the questionnaire.

Some of the questionnaire responses that were significantly related to the TST number scores were: Did collaborative research; Worked with research equipment; Published an article; Presented a paper at a professional meeting.

In contrast, the correlations of these questionnaire variables with GRE scores were very low. Such performances appear to be better indicators of HOTS than the GRE.

Test Formats: Multiple-Choice and Free-Response Tests

We have been studying free-response tests that elicit behaviors that apparently require higher-order skills, but we have little understanding as to the nature of these skills. We thought that a comparison of a free-response test with a multiple-choice version of a similar test might provide some leads as to the nature of HOTS.

So we developed a multiple-choice version of a Formulating Hypotheses test that appears to require many original ideas for dealing with problems. The two forms were identical except that instead of spaces for writing hypotheses we provided nine multiple-choice options. These options were chosen in a way that made them representative of answers actually written by subjects who had previously taken the same test in a free-response form.

The students were also given a battery of tests that were intended to assess the usual aptitudes and several aspects of creativity. The factor analysis of these tests yielded seven factors: vocabulary, quantitative reasoning, induction, logical reasoning, cognitive flexibility, expressive fluency, and ideational fluency. The last three are, of course, the ones most likely to predict creativity.

The purpose of all this was to determine the correlations of the two forms of Formulating Hypotheses tests on the seven factors and the GRE. The most important finding was that the correlations of the free-response Number scores with the Flexibility and Fluency factors were *much* higher than those for the multiple-choice version. In contrast with the multiple-choice form, the free-response form requires one to think for himself, to be original—to develop the skills that the future demands.

CONCEPTIONS OF INTELLIGENCE

It appears that the typical psychologist's concept of intelligence is extremely narrow, as compared with the range of skills and comprehension that are required in different environments. Intelligence testing is generally restricted to problems that can be presented on paper and scored by a machine. Testing for a broader range of skills will require the use of realistic simulations and observations of real-life performance and its products.

TOWARD A BROADER CONCEPTION OF HUMAN INTELLIGENCE

The best way to summarize what I've been trying to say is to cite the abstract of my article that was published in the *American Psychologist* in 1986. The title of the article is "Toward a Broader Conception of Human Intelligence."

ABSTRACT: It is argued that the typical psychometric model of human intelligence is limited because the data-base fails to take account of many manifestations of intelligent behavior that are displayed in the world outside the testing room. The data for factor-analytic studies of intelligence are generally restricted to scores on academic tests that employ only the multiple-choice format and are administered under standard conditions. A review of research studies involving tests that simulate real-world problem situations suggests that the cognitive processes involved in taking a test are influenced not only by test format but also by the situation or setting in which the test is administered and by such personal characteristics as the examinee's level of expertise. The structure of intelligence of the future may not be a static model, but one that varies as subjects change and as circumstances are altered. [Copyright 1986 by the American Psychological Association. Reprinted by permission of the publisher.]

THE LIFE AFTER . . .

I retired from the Educational Testing Service in 1979 with the title of Distinguished Research Scientist Emeritus and with office space as long as I care to use it. I also have a budget, but I never did ask how large it is. I get the services of a very competent secretary when I need one, and I know many competent psychologists and psychometricians who give me advice when I need it—which is quite often.

My present activities include editing (with two competent co-editors) a book to be named "Test Theory for a New Generation of Tests"; working on a research project on the influence of minimum competency testing on the performance of students; and writing a chapter for a book that is edited by a couple of psychologists at Plattsburgh, NY, which will be entitled *The Undaunted Psychologist*. When I get one of these finished, something else will probably turn up. If it doesn't, I'll have more time to spend in my woodworking shop.

P.S. I just received a "draft for review" of a committee report on assessing the performance of military personnel. It is 450 pages long, and they want my comments as soon as possible. What should I do?

SUGGESTED READINGS

CRONBACH, L. J., & MEEHL, P. E. (1955). Construct validity in psychological tests. *Psychological Bulletin, 52,* 281–302.

FREDERIKSEN, N. (1984). The real test bias: Influences of testing on teaching and learning. *American Psychologist, 39,* 193–202.

_____(1986). Toward a broader conception of human intelligence. *American Psychologist, 41,* 445–452.

_____JENSEN, O., & BEATON, A. E. (with a contribution by B. Bloxom). (1972). *Prediction of organizational behavior.* Elmsford, NY: Pergamon.

_____SAUNDERS, D. R., & WAND, B. (1957). The in-basket test. *Psychological Monographs, 71,* 1–28.

ROGOFF, B., & LAVE, J. (EDS.). (1984). *Everyday cognition: Its development in social context.* Cambridge, MA: Harvard Univ. Press.

STERNBERG, R. J., & WAGNER, R. K. (EDS.). (1986). *Practical intelligence: Nature and origins of competence in the everyday world.* Cambridge, MA: Cambridge.

THORNTON, G. C., & BYHAM, C. C. (1984). *Assessment centers and managerial performance.* New York: Academic.

DAVID C. MCCLELLAND *(Ph.D., Yale University) is currently Distinguished Research Professor of Psychology at Boston University, after having retired from Harvard University where he was Professor of Psychology for 30 years, largely in the cross-disciplinary Department of Social Relations. He is the author of* Personality, The Achieving Society, Motivating Economic Achievement, Power: The Inner Experience, *many other books and articles, and most recently of an advanced textbook entitled* Human Motivation. *He has studied the effects of certain key human motives in the fields of economics, management, governing, education, social adjustment, physiology, health, and most recently, old age. He also enjoys swimming and his protea farm on the island of Maui, Hawaii—and his seven children, ages 5 to 48.*

9

Motives and Health

———————— ❖ ————————

The 1960s was a time of change and I found myself and my work very
much involved in the various social movements that swept through the
country at the time. Presidents Kennedy and Johnson were focusing the
nation's attention on the need for a war on poverty and oppression. Society was
seen as a source of all evils, and it could and should be changed. Opportunities
had to be opened for blacks, women, Hispanics, Indians, and other minorities.
They had to be trained for these new opportunities. Education had to be
reformed to teach the underprivileged more effectively.

How did these events affect my work? To begin with, I too was caught up by
the possibility of contributing to human improvement through education and
my research on achievement motivation seemed to hold obvious utility in helping to cure some of the ills of society.

Over the years, I had developed a standardized procedure for assessing
human motivation. The idea was simple enough and occurred to me, as I recall,
in 1946, as I was driving home with G. Richard Wendt, then chairman of the
Wesleyan Psychology Department, after a meeting of the Psychological Round
Table in Northampton, Massachusetts. That was a group of convivial but serious
young "experimenting" psychologists. Membership in the Psychological Round
Table stopped when you were 40, by which time you were supposed to be "over
the hill" as far as experimentation was concerned. There had been plenty of studies of the effects of hunger or hours of food deprivation on the behavior of rats.
Why not study the effects of hunger on humans? At least everyone agreed that
hunger was a motive or drive. But humans were obviously different from rats in
that they might learn what we were interested in, have some ideas about how
hunger should influence their behavior, and shape that behavior in accordance
with those beliefs. I had a distrust of what people believed and I was strongly
influenced by Freud's conception of unconscious motives. So John Atkinson and
I arranged to conduct an experiment on hunger in such a way that the subjects,
who were submariners at the naval base in New London, Connecticut, would not
realize that we were interested in studying the effects of hunger. This was done
simply by assigning them after supper to quarters where no food was available

and allowing them to sleep through breakfast, which they were glad enough to be allowed to do. They didn't eat again until noon the following day, so that we were able to get 16 hours of food deprivation before they were given various psychological tests. We also obtained the same measures one hour and four hours after eating, and in none of the experiments did the subjects realize that we were interested in investigating hunger.

But what behavioral effects should we look for? Initially we cast a wide net. Research had shown that poor children were apt to estimate a dime to be somewhat larger than rich children did if the dime was presented under sufficiently ambiguous conditions. This had stimulated much interest in the effects of needs on perception, and we thought it likely that hunger might lead people to overestimate the size of edibles like a cake. We also asked the subjects to rate how hungry they were, and found that there was not a direct increase in rated hunger associated with increasing hours of food deprivation. Instead, people rated themselves on the average no hungrier after 16 hours of food deprivation than they had after four hours of food deprivation, confirming my belief that they would tend to rate themselves as hungry as they ought to be considering the fact that in both instances the rating was taken just before meal time.

But our primary interest was in the effect of hours of food deprivation on thought content as obtained from imaginative stories written to pictures, using the method pioneered by Henry Murray in the Thematic Apperception Test (TAT). The stories were to be written around the following questions: (1) What is happening?; (2) What has led up to the situation?; (3) What is being thought?; and (4) What will happen? The general tone of the instructions urged subjects to be as creative as possible and not to think in terms of right and wrong answers.

What we found surprised us. There was not a regular increase in references to eating or edible objects as hunger increased, despite the conventional wisdom that hungry and thirsty people spend their time dreaming about eating and drinking. Our decision not to let the subjects know that hunger was under investigation turned out to be wise, since others have shown that if they had known, they would have filled their stories with eating episodes. On the other hand, stories referring to food deprivation and to implements related to getting food or eating, such as knives, forks, and spoons, did increase in direct fashion with hours of food deprivation. This confirmed another expectation, namely that the fantasy measure, the TAT, was a more sensitive indicator of degree of physiological hunger than self-rating of hunger was.

The next step was simply to apply this system which reflected the arousal of a motive to stories written under neutral conditions so that individuals could be picked out who were, so to speak, in a state of motive arousal even when there was no external reason for them to be so. This step was not taken with the hunger motive, but it played an important role in subsequent work.

Having detected the effects on fantasy of an aroused biological drive or motive, we next turned our attention to arousing a social motive to see what its effects on fantasy would be. At that time there was one way in which subjects were aroused in experimental situations that had been shown to affect their subsequent performance. It was called "ego-involvement." Subjects who were told that what they were doing would reflect how intelligent they were or how fit they were for leadership positions would typically perform better than they would without these instructions. So we decided to see what effects such "ego-involving" instructions would have on fantasy. The procedure was parallel to what we had done with the hunger motive. We compared stories written under standard or unaroused testing conditions to determine what kinds of story themes appeared more often after ego-involving arousal.

What we found was that stories written under ego-involving arousal referred more often to someone trying to do better in relation to some achievement goal, such as doing a better job or getting ahead in the world. We developed a scoring system around these differences in story content, which we labelled the need for Achievement or *n* Achievement because they referred to doing something better or achieving. Although we did not know it at the time, these achieving story characteristics, when they appeared under neutral testing conditions, turned out to measure individual differences in an important personality characteristic that would explain many things a person would do. Take, for example, the following story, which was written about a picture of a boy in a checked shirt sitting at a desk, with an open book in front of him:

1. The boy is taking an hour written exam. He and the others are high-school students. The test is about two-thirds over and he is doing his best to think it through.
2. He was supposed to study for the test and did so. But because it is factual, there were items he saw but did not learn.
3. He knows he has studied the answers, but he can't remember them all and is trying to summon up the images and related ideas to remind him of them.
4. He may remember one or two, but he will miss most of the items he can't remember. He will try hard until five minutes are left, then give up, go back over his paper, and be disgusted for reading but not learning the answers.

Obviously, here the boy is concerned about doing his best on the examination ("he is doing his best to think it through" and he is "disgusted for reading but not learning the answers"). Furthermore, there are a number of aspects of an achievement sequence specifically mentioned, such as the fact that it is his fault that he is not doing well ("he saw but did not learn"), and that he is trying out various ways of solving his problem ("trying to summon up the images and related ideas to remind him of them"). The fact that he is not successful in his achievement efforts is not taken to mean that the student who composed this story has a weaker achievement motive than someone who wrote a story in which his problem-solving activities were successful. In both cases there is a marked concern about doing better.

Psychologists often seem to expend most of their energy doing research on how college sophomores perform various tasks in the laboratory. The early research on achievement motivation was no exception to this rule. Out of it came the generalizations that people high in achievement motivation tend to seek out and do better at moderately challenging tasks, take personal responsibility for their performance, seek performance feedback on how well they are doing, and try new and more efficient ways of doing things. Then it occurred to us if individuals high in achievement motivation had the characteristics just reviewed, they ought to behave in ways that, under certain circumstances, would lead to greater success in the real world. I proposed that high achievement motivation should make people particularly likely to be interested in and able to do well at business, for business requires that people take moderate risks, assume personal responsibility for their own performance, pay close attention to feedback in terms of costs and profits, and find new or innovative ways to make a new product or provide a new service. I found that, generally speaking, young people higher in achievement motivation were in fact more attracted to business occupations in several countries. Further, business executives in three countries (the United States, Italy, and Poland) were found to have higher average achievement-motivation scores than other professionals of the same educational background.

As my work advanced, it became clear that if the need to Achieve could be increased it could be one of the keys to fighting poverty by stimulating economic growth; we had found that people who are concerned with doing things better (i.e., with a high need to Achieve) become active entrepreneurs and build growing business firms which by creating jobs help stimulate economic development. So we developed programs to train entrepreneurs in underdeveloped countries and underprivileged minorities at home in achievement motivation. These programs did stimulate business growth and employment.

Although some of these entrepreneurs we trained might be regarded as leaders, in the restricted sense that their activities established the base for the rise of a newly energized economic order, they were seldom leaders of people. The reason for this is simple: need for Achievement is a one-person game that need never involve other people. Children who are high in need for Achievement like to build things or to make things with their hands, presumably because they can tell easily and directly whether they have done a good job. A boy who is trying to build as tall a tower as possible out of blocks can measure very precisely how well he has done. He is in no way dependent on someone else to tell him how good his performance is. So in the pure case, people with high need for Achievement are concerned with improving their own performance regardless of the opinion of others. As an ideal type, they are most easily conceived of as a salesperson or an owner-manager of a small business, in a position to watch carefully whether or not their performance is improving.

While studying such individuals and their role in economic development, I ran head on into problems of leadership, power, and social influence. Need for Achievement clearly did not prepare one to cope with these problems. As a one-person firm grows larger, it obviously requires some division of function and some organizational structure. Organizational structure involves relationships among people, and sooner or later someone in the organization, if it is to survive, must pay attention to getting people to work together, or to dividing up the tasks to be performed, or to supervising the work of others. Yet a high need to Achieve does not equip an individual to deal effectively with managing human relationships. For instance, a salesperson with high need for Achievement does not necessarily make a good sales manager. As a manager, his or her task is not to sell, but to inspire others to sell, which involves a different set of personal goals and different strategies for reaching them.

I shall not forget the moment when I learned that the president of one of the most successful achievement-oriented firms we had been studying scored exactly zero in the need for Achievement! Up to that point I had fallen into the easy assumption that an individual with a high need to Achieve does better work, gets promoted faster, and ultimately ends up as president of a company. How was it possible for a man to head an obviously achieving company and yet score so low in need for Achievement? At the time I was tempted to dismiss the finding as a measurement error, but there is now little doubt that it was a dramatic example of the fact that stimulating achievement motivation in others requires a different motive and a different set of skills from wanting achievement satisfaction for oneself.

For some time now, research on achievement motivation has shifted in focus from individuals with high need for Achievement to the climate that encourages them and rewards them for doing well. No matter how high their need to Achieve may be, they cannot succeed if they have no opportunities, if the organization keeps them from taking initiative, or does not reward them when they do. As a simple illustration of this point, we found in our research in India that it did no good to raise achievement motivation through training if the trained individuals were not in charge of their businesses. Even though they might be "all fired up" and prepared to be more active and entrepreneurial, they could not do much if they were working for someone else, someone who had the final say as to whether any of the things they wanted to do would in fact be attempted. In short, people with high need for Achievement seldom can act alone, even though they might like to. They are caught up in an organizational context in which they are managed, controlled, or directed by others. To understand better what happens to them, we must shift our attention to those who are managing them, to those who are concerned about organizational relationships—to the leaders of people.

Since managers are primarily concerned with influencing others, it was not unexpected that we found that successful managers were characterized by a high need for Power, i.e., having impact, control, or influence over another person, group, or the world at large. If A gets B to do something, A is at one and the same time a leader (i.e., he or she is leading B), and a power-wielder (i.e., he or she is exercising some kind of influence or power over B). Thus, leadership and power appear as two closely related concepts. While research on the achievement motive led to a better understanding of business entrepreneurship, studying the power motive helped us understand important aspects of managerial, societal, and even political leadership.

One aspect of our research on power, however, was quite disturbing. I noticed that people with a certain type of power-motive syndrome act in many ways like those with Type A behavior as described by Friedman and Rosenman in their influential and popular book *Type A Behavior and Your Heart*. We called this the leadership motive syndrome because it is found more often in successful managers. People characterized by it are high in the need for Power (they strongly want to have their way)—low in the need for Affiliation (in having their way, they are not much concerned about the feelings of others)—and high in inhibition (they tend to hold their assertive impulses in check). Thus, they seem to be like the Type A's who are hard-driving, impatient, always sitting on the edge of their chairs, so to speak, and constantly ready to erupt into anger if frustrated, although normally such outbursts are kept under tight control. Friedman and Rosenman had collected evidence suggesting that such individuals are in a state of chronic sympathetic-nervous-system arousal in which the production of emergency-related hormones like adrenaline is increased with potentially damaging effects on the cardiovascular system in the long run. If individuals with the leadership-motive syndrome are characterized by Type A behavior, then they too might be characterized by chronic sympathetic activation.

One of my students, Robert Steele, showed that this might be true. He exposed groups of student volunteer subjects to four different types of treatments. One group listened to a tape recording of inspirational speeches such as Winston Churchill's speech on Dunkirk or Henry V's speeches in Shakespeare's *Henry V*. They contain much power imagery. Another control group of subjects listened to some tape-recorded travel descriptions. Steele attempted to arouse achievement motivation in a third group by giving ego-involving instructions relating to tasks they were performing and arranged an achievement-control condition by giving the same instructions in a relaxed, noninvolving manner. After the treatments, all subjects wrote stories to pictures that were scored for need for Achievement and need for Power. He also collected urine at the beginning and end of the experiment and analyzed it for the amount of epinephrine and norepinephrine present (signs of sympathetic activation). Power-related speeches produced the biggest increase in excretion of epinephrine, suggesting the greatest sympathetic activation in that condition. In the power-arousal condition there is a highly significant correlation between gains in epinephrine excretion and the need for Power score obtained at the end of the experiment. A similar significant correlation was obtained between gains in norepinephrine excretion and need for Power score. In other words, signs of sympathetic arousal were closely associated with the appearance of power thoughts when power motivation was aroused. The same was not true when it was not aroused or when achievement motivation was aroused.

If individuals high in need for Power have sympathetic nervous systems which are more responsive to power challenges, the next step was to see whether in time they would develop cardiovascular disease, which Friedman and Rosenman had suggested might be the outcome of chronic sympathetic activation. In several different samples, we found that, as contrasted with individuals lower in need for Power, those high in need for Power had significantly higher blood pressure, provided their inhibition score was also high. Our most impressive finding was that individuals with the leadership-motive syndrome in their early thirties had developed significantly higher diastolic blood pressure than other men some 20 years later. In fact, 61 percent of those with the leadership-motive syndrome had developed clinically significant signs of hypertension by their early fifties as compared with 23 percent of those in other motive categories, a highly significant difference. What it suggests is that some individuals have been continually having power thoughts that they block from expression in action over the years and that this thought pattern leads to chronic sympathetic arousal, which affects the cardiovascular system in ways that lead in the long run to high blood pressure.

It also seemed possible that stress hormones released by chronic sympathetic activation, like cortisol and epinephrine, might also damage immune function, making the body more subject to disease from viral and bacterial invasion. Several studies have been carried out to date to investigate this possibility, and all support in one aspect or another the following chain of events: individuals with the leadership-motive syndrome show signs of increased sympathetic activation, which is associated with lowered immune function, and with reports of having been more severely ill in the past year. This chain of events is more likely to occur if the individual also reports being under power stress—as from losing a job, failing an examination, fighting with parents, or being involved in competitive athletic events. In one study, college students varying in need for Achievement and need for Power were asked to fill out a life-events schedule patterned after the Holmes and Rahe schedule, in which they were to check potentially stressful events (like getting married, death of a parent, failing a course) that had occurred to them in the past year. They also listed any illnesses they had had in the past year and rated them for severity on a scale of 1–100. Three psychological variables influenced the severity of the illnesses the students reported—namely whether their need for Power was greater than their need for Affiliation score, whether their inhibition score was high, and whether they reported more than the average number of power stresses. Subjects who were high on all three variables or any two of them reported significantly more severe illness than other subjects. Most of the illnesses reported in this age group consisted of upper respiratory infections to which all students are exposed, so that what appears to be involved here is lesser immune defense against such infections. Furthermore, we demonstrated that it was power motivation and power stress specifically that related to the increased incidence of disease.

The reason for the increased susceptibility particularly to upper-respiratory infections is suggested by several studies that measured the concentrations of immunoglobulin A in saliva (S-IgA), the body's first line of immunological defense against viral cold infections. Individuals with the leadership-motive syndrome have significantly lower average S-IgA concentrations and significantly higher illness scores than other subjects. Furthermore, there is evidence that the impaired immune function associated with the leadership-motive syndrome is not limited to S-IgA, but also shows up in lower natural-killer-cell potency, a finding of potentially great interest because natural killer cells play a role in destroying some types of cancer cells.

One might object that the stresses reported in these studies are not "real" but are influenced by biases in memory and in the tendency to complain more or less about what is happening. Thus the relationship between reported stresses and reported illness severity could easily be due to such biases in subjective reporting of both types of events. John Jemmott, another one of my students, carried out a study in which the effects of known academic stress were investigated both on concentrations of S-IgA and illness reports obtained at different times during an academic year. In this case the students were in the first year of dental school, and the stress consisted of examinations conducted at different points during the year in which they had to demonstrate their proficiency in order to pass. Subjective reports confirmed the fact that these examinations were very stressful. In general, concentrations of S-IgA declined significantly for all subjects during periods of high stress during the year and increased again at the end of the year when the stress was over. Objective stress weakened immune defense. The mean concentration of S-IgA for those with the leadership-motive syndrome starts at about the same level as the mean for those with the opposite or relaxed affiliative-motive syndrome, (higher need for Affiliation than need for Power, low inhibition) but then it declines regularly throughout the year and fails to return to normal when the stress is over in July following the first year. As one would expect from this impairment of secretory immune function, the reported incidence of upper-respiratory infections increases to well above average for those with the leadership-motive syndrome in February–June, sometime after the concentration of S-IgA has shown its first major decline in November. In contrast, those with the relaxed affiliative motive syndrome are least affected by the stress: the decline in the average concentration of their S-IgA is slight and insignificant and soon recovers. Throughout the year their secretory immune function remains normal or above and their reported incidence of upper respiratory infections is also about average or what one would expect from students in this situation at the various times of the year reported.

Evidence is beginning to accumulate that the leadership-motive syndrome, an operant thought pattern, is not particularly good for your health. It promotes effective managerial behavior, but particularly if it is stressed it leads to physiological changes that in the long run make it more likely that you will become ill. In contrast the relaxed affiliative-motive syndrome is associated with better health.

IMPLICATIONS FOR MEDICINE

Let us suppose for the sake of argument that some or all of the relationships outlined are confirmed in further studies. What are the implications for the practice of medicine? They are potentially of far-reaching importance. Consider the problems inherent in evaluating the results of diagnostic procedures. Modern medicine insists that a patient should not be treated until it is known what is wrong, but finding out what is wrong often involves a number of stressful procedures. Even the simple procedure of taking blood, necessary for many diagnostic tests, increases epinephrine in serum much more for men than for women and probably much more in some individuals than others, if our inference is correct that individuals high in need for Power have more excitable sympathetic nervous systems. If we are further correct that increased sympathetic activation has consequences for the cardiovascular system and for the immune system, then we are talking about misreading diagnostic signs taken from these systems or in the worst case about an increase in the severity of disease brought about by the treatment process. Repeated diagnostic procedures may impair immune function and weaken the body's defense against disease, particularly in people with the leadership-motive syndrome. At the very least, doctors should take into account the psychological characteristics of the people they are treating in weighing the possible dangers against the benefits from diagnostic procedures. Clinicians who really know their patients undoubtedly have always intuitively taken such factors into account, but in this day of modern scientific medicine in which decisions are made based on "objective" blood, urine, or immune tests, it is important to remember that psychological variables affect the readings taken on such indicators.

Our research shows that positive feelings, as they are reflected in the relaxed affiliative-motive syndrome, tend to promote health. The point can be illustrated by a finding from a study in which students were exposed to films of various types in attempts to arouse different motivational states. We had some preliminary evidence that a negative anger-arousing film about the triumph of the Nazis in World War II lowered concentrations of S-IgA in those with the leadership-motive syndrome, presumably by releasing stress hormones that impaired lymphocyte function. We also tried to arouse feelings of love and compassion in students to see if that would stimulate lymphocyte function by showing them an emotionally moving film produced by the BBC on Mother Teresa of Calcutta who has spent her life loving and serving others. As it turned out, the Mother Teresa film had a powerful positive effect on S-IgA concentrations, and the negative film had no overall effect on S-IgA levels. This suggested to us a mechanism through which psychic healers, or traditional doctors for that matter, may improve the health of their patients. They may act in ways that create trust in their patients and help them feel loved and cared for, rather than inhibited, fearful, and angry, like subjects with the leadership-motive syndrome. The implications for the practice of medicine are obvious: whatever you do to or for the patient, try to do it in a way that makes the patient feel more positive, more loved, and more relaxed, for such a state of mind is associated with better immune function, which means that the body's own defenses against the disease process will be stronger.

Looking at health from this psychological perspective suggests why holistic health practices, particularly meditation, may often have beneficial effects. In its simplest form it involves sitting quietly in a comfortable position once or twice a day with a relaxed attitude while one focuses attention on an object, a phrase, or one's breathing in order to become disengaged from the endless chatter of one's inner thought processes. Its physiological effects are considerable. It decreases oxygen consumption and respiratory rate, muscle tension, heart rate, and also blood pressure if it is elevated. Together these all indicate a decrease in sympathetic activation, which the research we have just reviewed suggests may be responsible for cardiovascular disease and decreased immune defense against infectious disease. So, meditation may well decrease the psychological state that we found to be associated with sympathetic activation. That is, it probably decreases power motivation by training in a more relaxed attitude and by decreasing involvement in one's frantic inner attempts to cope with the world, and it directly decreases inhibition through training in relaxation.

Furthermore we found those who showed an increase in affiliative thoughts of a trusting nature after viewing the Mother Teresa film were the very ones whose S-IgA had increased in response to the film. And in other studies Affiliative Trust has turned out to be an important factor in promoting stronger immune responses and better health. The real payoff from such knowledge comes when treatment is specifically redesigned to take such factors into account. I have recently become involved in helping design and evaluate the effects of behavioral medicine treatments, which attempt to decrease the effects of power motivation, and inhibition through relaxation and to increase thoughts of Affiliative Trust, which allow the cardiovascular and immune defense systems to function in a healthier way. Some of the clinical effects of these new treatment programs have been quite spectacular in terms of helping patients recover from or deal with disease processes that have been unresponsive to traditional types of medical treatment.

Knowledge of psychological factors in disease also has larger implications for health; obviously certain types of environments at home or at work are more likely to elicit the leadership-motive syndrome or the relaxed affiliative-motive syndrome. The possibility that feature films might create emotional states that affect the immune system holds great promise, for if we can learn how to create emotional states that foster recuperation, we may in time be able to create hospital environments that include the right kind of films and music to help stimulate or restore natural immune functions. As it is, I strongly suspect that the depersonalization, haste, and confusion found in many hospitals is hardly calculated to produce a loving atmosphere of affiliative trust, as Mother Teresa does in dealing with the sick. Certainly the last time I was in the hospital I never saw the same nurse twice and was angered by several forceful attempts to give me the wrong medication because they had gotten the records mixed up and no one knew me or cared for me as a person. What happened to my immune defenses under this kind of stress one can only imagine!

The working environment is also an important source of stress and stress-induced illness. It has always surprised me that executives who worry so much about bottom-line profitability are not more concerned about the costs of absenteeism due to illness. At the executive level, the absenteeism may be permanent if a heart attack disables or kills a person, and the cost to the company may be very great indeed. Yet our data show that it is precisely the individuals with the leadership-motive syndrome who are apt to be most successful in management and who are also most likely to be susceptible to cardiovascular disease and other types of illness if they are put under power stress. At the very least, this suggests that corporations should be more aware of the dangers of power stress to the health of their executives and should either find organizational means of reducing the stress or help their executives to learn methods of reducing the sympathetic activation attendant on it. The very first step is finding out what motive patterns key executives have and what types of stress they are under so that corrective measures can be taken. Fortunately neither type of knowledge is difficult to come by using modern psychological techniques.

At other levels in the organizations, it often turns out that absenteeism due to illness is much higher in some sections than in others. Surveys will then often show that the organizational climate is much poorer in the sections where there is more illness than in the other sections. That is, the workers are more often angry, upset, or bored with their work. These emotional states may lead people to avoid coming to work if they can find an illness excuse, or, as our data indicate, their emotions may actually weaken immune defenses so that in fact they are more susceptible to upper-respiratory infections, the most common cause of absenteeism. Again better knowledge is the first step toward remedying the situation. The company can either reorganize working conditions or provide workshops for employees that help them understand better the causes of their anger either in their own makeup or in the working or home environment so that they can make plans to cope with it better. Such workshops have actually been carried out and found to be very helpful particularly for employees who are experiencing the stress of reaching a midlife plateau in their careers or of approaching retirement.

So a little psychological knowledge goes a long way here as everywhere else. Trends in thinking about power, affiliation, and inhibition turn out to have important physiological effects that make the person more or less susceptible to disease. Furthermore, even following the implications of these findings a little way has suggested how the practice of medicine might be improved and how environments can be better arranged to promote health.

SUGGESTED READINGS

FRIEDMAN, M., & ROSENMAN, R. H. (1974). *Type A behavior and your heart.* New York: Knopf.

HOLMES, T. H., & RAHE, R. H. (1967). The social readjustment rating scale. *Journal of Psychosomatic Research, 11,* 213–218.

McClelland, D. C. (1961). *The achieving society*. Princeton, NJ: Van Nostrand.
_____(1975). *Power: The inner experience*. New York: Irvington.
_____(1984). *Motives, personality, and society*. New York: Praeger.
_____(1985). *Human motivation*. Glenview, IL: Scott, Foresman.
_____(1989). Motivation factors in health and disease. *American Psychologist, 44,* 675–683.
_____Atkinson, J. W., Clark, R. A., & Lowell, E. L. (1953). *The achievement motive*. New York: Appleton-Century-Crofts.
Winter, D. G. (1973). *The power motive*. New York: Free Press.

*E*RIC *KLINGER* *(Ph.D., University of Chicago) is currently Professor of Psychology at the University of Minnesota, Morris and Minneapolis. He has published investigations and theoretical integrations in the areas of fantasy (including daydreaming), motivation, and emotion and their effects on cognitive processing and alcohol abuse and treatment. His recent research has also addressed hate, as a distinct reaction system. He is author of* Structure and Functions of Fantasy, Meaning and Void: Inner Experience and the Incentives in People's Lives, *and* Daydreaming, *as well as numerous chapters and articles. To maintain sanity, he swims, hikes, bakes bread, immerses himself in things Austrian, and dabbles in gardening, languages, and politics at skill levels below amateur.*

10

What Will They Think of Next? Understanding Daydreaming

❖

Wwe all daydream a large portion of each day. Much of it is mindwandering or brief flashes of spontaneous thought. Some of it is highly fanciful, images of ourselves as space travelers, evangelists, lovers, or billionaires. Forty years ago psychologists knew little about this activity that consumes perhaps half of our thoughts, yet many taught their students and the public that daydreaming is wasteful, regressive, and even dangerous to one's mental health. As a result of many people's research, we now have good reason to believe that daydreaming is an integral part of the way the human mind works, that it contributes to our productivity and is, under most circumstances, harmless. This is the story of one researcher's pursuit of the truth about daydreaming.

I became involved in research on daydreaming by a very circuitous route, a fact that reveals an important feature of the scientific enterprise. The stream of science is much like the stream of an individual's consciousness. Each is governed by overarching goals, yet each wanders from one focus to the next—from investigation to investigation or thought to thought—according to what excites us at the moment. Where we end up may have only a loose connection to where we started out.

My daydreaming research also reflects another attribute of science, one that marks science as a very human enterprise that is often governed by strong prejudices, even ideologies, that can control the course of investigation as stringently as a theocracy. Since the 1920s, American psychology has been heavily influenced by behaviorism—a movement that made enormously positive contributions to psychology and to our understanding of science. One of its axioms, however, was that private, inner experience was inherently beyond scientific investigation. For four decades, behaviorism became a creed, loyalty to which was a prerequisite to hiring, retention, and promotion in many psychology departments. It became untenable—and untenurable—to investigate such topics as mental imagery, fantasy, and even emotion unless they could somehow be recast in the guise of overt behaviors.

As a result, until the 1960s there was little direct research on day-dreaming and mental imagery, and both the concepts and methods of investigation stagnated. At the beginning of my research life, it never occurred to me to investigate anything as private and subjective as the daydreaming we all do in the course of our daily lives; and, besides, no satisfactory tools for researching it existed. When I finally got around to thinking about the area, I was faced with difficult questions: How could I analyze daydreams quantitatively? How could I even know systemati-cally what they are and what they are like? How do I describe them sci-entifically?

My particular journey toward research on daydreaming began with a massive failure in a quite different area. The Association of American Medical Colleges had just hired Helen Gee—a bundle of creative energy steeped in the University of Minnesota's psychological assessment tradi-tion—to improve their ability to predict which of their applicants would succeed best as medical students. College grades and Medical College Admission Test scores were helpful predictors, but there were still a good many students admitted to medical school who failed or just dropped out. Gee decided to use the best psychometric methods of the 1950s to assess applicants' personalities, including their needs for achievement and social life, as well as their interests and values, in the hope that this information would better enable medical schools to admit their best applicants.

I joined the project as a research associate and designed my doctoral dissertation as part of the larger effort. On the assumption that different kinds of personalities might fare differently in different school environ-ments, my dissertation looked for interactions between environmental and personality variables on students' performance. As it turned out, the personality variables yielded only trivial improvements in predicting students' success, and the interactions with environmental variables improved only trivially on that.

Fortunately, doctoral degrees do not depend upon whether or not dissertations come out right, but rather on whether they were reasonably well designed and executed. I received my degree, but continued to pon-der this dilemma. We had used what were then the most sophisticated measures of personality. We felt sure that we were not mistaken in our most basic hypothesis, that personality makes a difference in success as a medical student. What could have gone wrong?

I decided to look more closely at how we measured personality. Given that the dissertation had focused on personality interactions with the environment, I went back to the journal literature with a basic question: When investigators predict that personalities will interact with something, was there some way of measuring personality that enables investigators to confirm these predictions more often?

The answer seemed to be "yes," and in an unexpected direction. When investigators measured personality using fantasy-based methods, in which people had to exercise their imaginations, such as Rorschach inkblots or the picture-story Thematic Apperception Test (TAT), the results confirmed their predictions of interactions significantly more often than when they used true-false and forced-choice questionnaires. This was surprising, because by then—1961—the fantasy-based "projective" measures had begun to fall out of favor with research psychologists, and questionnaires had become their preferred tools. The next step, then, was to ask, what makes fantasy-based measures better at confirming predictions about personality interactions?

It was at this point that the trail petered out and disappeared. I had set out to review the current theories of fantasy, but found that there was no such thing, at least not in integrated, reasonably comprehensive form based on good evidence. Apart from reviews of research on inkblots and TAT stories as assessment tools, the last theories of fantasy were those of Sigmund Freud and Julien Varendonck, the latter writing in 1921. Freud thought of fantasy as unrealistic wish-fulfillment, and he characterized daydreaming as infantile and regressive. His theory of daydreaming was unsystematic and mired in ambiguities and misconceptions. Varendonck recognized the universality of daydreaming and its contributions to creativity and humor. He also anticipated more modern findings, such as the role of emotions in instigating and steering daydreams. He undertook a systematic, introspective investigation of mostly his own daydreams—excellent for its kind of work, but nonquantitative and limited. Both theories were badly dated and neither held the answer to my question.

To go on meant to construct a new-generation theory of fantasy. It would have been an utterly daunting task had it not been for two facts. First, there was a large research literature on fantasy-based personality measures whose potential for telling us about fantasy as such had hardly been tapped. Second, research methods had improved to the point that a rigorous program for investigating fantasy seemed feasible. In particular, David McClelland and his students and converts, especially John Atkinson and Heinz Heckhausen, had developed elaborate ways to quantify TAT stories and had subjected them to advanced quantitative analysis (see McClelland's Chapter 9 in this volume). Because their primary interest was in motivation, not in fantasy as such, they did not pursue the implications of their results for a theory of fantasy; but they did blaze an inviting trail into research methods on fantasy, one I intended to follow.

I decided to move on two fronts. On the empirical front, my colleagues and I launched an extensive series of experiments on TAT stories that told us a good deal about their properties and limitations as proxies for daydreaming. But it was on the other front—the theoretical front—that we made the most progress during this period. I began to assemble and reinterpret the large body of published data on fantasy. Before I had gone very far, however, Jerome Singer published his 1966 book *Daydreaming,* the first on the subject worthy of note since Varendonck's in 1921.

Upon discovering this book, I experienced conflicting emotions: excitement that Singer had broken the ice in this research area, and heartache that I had been scooped. The book had done some of what I had planned and therefore forced me to go beyond my original objective. In retrospect, this was a very good thing, because it freed me to focus on areas that I might otherwise not have attempted. I analyzed the existing evidence on every kind of individual fantasy I could find—on children's play and adult dreams as well as on daydreams, TAT stories, and inkblots. As I mulled over those findings, I began to see ways in which all of these respond to the same basic influences. With ideas drawn from Varendonck, Singer, McClelland, Hull, Mowrer, Simon, Mandler, and others, I began to see a model of how naturally occurring thoughts and dreams arise, including the waking fantasies we call daydreams.

This model, published in 1971 as *Structure and Functions of Fantasy,* begins with the proposition that our thoughts and dreams are governed by our goals. When we become committed to a goal, that fact launches an inner state about that goal, a hypothetical state that I dubbed a current concern. When you decide to sharpen your pencil, fix your bathroom sink, start a relationship, attain a college degree, make a million dollars, or win a Nobel Prize, you initiate a current concern about that goal. The concern is latent; it stays out of consciousness most of the time. But, when you encounter something that reminds you of your concern, you react with a little burst of emotion to that reminder, and if you can sensibly do something to advance yourself toward that goal, you act. If there is nothing constructive you can do about the goal at that moment, you still react, but the reaction is likely to be purely mental and probably a daydream.

For example, if your sink is plugged and you have resolved to fix it, all kinds of pipes, other bathrooms, desires to wash your hands, and similar cues will remind you of your plugged sink and your plans to unplug it. Sometimes you will have realistic thoughts about it, such as whether to use a drain cleaner or take apart the trap; other times you may fantasize inserting a stick of dynamite in it and blowing the thing up.

Furthermore, according to the theory, the mental images you have in your daydreams are not just mental ghosts, but integral parts of your brain systems at work—the same brain systems, at least in part, that you would be using if you were actually seeing and doing what you imagine seeing and doing. Our daydreams and night dreams are ourselves in action, though somewhat insulated from our actual environments.

We had come a long way theoretically, but we needed to test the new theory and to fill in the details through empirical investigation. The TAT methods we had been using were poorly suited to our new questions. I yearned for methods that would capture naturally occurring thoughts, for methods of analyzing those thoughts so that they could be related to participants' individual concerns and feelings, and for methods of assessing the concerns themselves. During the next few years, I focused on developing two kinds of methods: methods to assess naturally occurring thought and methods to assess our new motivational and volitional construct, current concerns.

Finding better ways to measure thought content was hard, at first. The 1960s marked the end of the strict behaviorist reign in American psychology, but those of us breaking out of it had to contend with our own backgrounds and training. When research participants told TAT stories, we could treat the stories as behaviors and score them. But when we tried more direct means of finding out what they were thinking, we kept coming back to asking them simply to tell us. Their reports to us were still behavior, but we hoped and actually assumed that their reports had some reasonably strong relationship to their thoughts, which we were ultimately interested in investigating. We were interested not in a science of reports but in a science of thought.

My departure from "acceptable" science made me cautious. Reports of thought *are* inevitably flawed—fragmentary and distorted. We needed a method that minimized the problems, one that did not exert a distorting influence on participants' thought flow itself and also minimized reporting errors. We tried asking participants to speak their thoughts—to think aloud—as some cognitive psychologists did to study problem-solving, but we concluded that what our participants spoke was drastically different from normal silent thought. We avoided questionnaires that asked participants to describe their thoughts long after the event, because of both memory loss and the cognitive difficulties of generalizing about themselves (as my dissertation supervisor Donald Fiske had been fond of pointing out). But in the end a set of other research traditions gave us ideas that we could integrate into a workable method.

I found much encouragement in Singer's 1966 book. Like Varendonck, he observed some of his own daydreams; but with his colleague, John Antrobus, he also devised a technique for laboratory assessment of thought. This consisted of periodically signaling participants to report whether or not they had had a thought about something other than their assigned task since the last signal. Using this method while participants were supposed to be doing assigned tasks, Singer, Antrobus, and their students found that people daydream less when tasks are more complex, when under time pressure, and when the stakes for doing well are high. The method was new and simple, and it enabled me to think more imaginatively about how better to capture the stream of consciousness.

There were also other important examples to draw upon. Dream investigators had developed a method of waking their participants at unpredictable times and asking them to describe their last dream images. Industrial psychologists had used a method of activity sampling—describing workers' behavior at various time points. And psychologist Paul Cameron was stopping people in supermarkets and in his lectures and asking them to report their latest thoughts.

It was a short step to combine these methods into the one I have dubbed thought-sampling. We trained research participants to report their latest thoughts, using a standardized reporting format, whenever we signaled them to do so. In the laboratory, we signaled them by tones at irregular intervals on audiotapes. Outside the laboratory, we had them carry "beepers." Because these signals came at sporadic intervals averaging more than half an hour, participants' thoughts were not greatly influenced by the fact that they would have to respond to the beeper. And, because they reported immediately after each signal, when their mental images were still fresh, forgetting was reduced to a minimum. In the end, we settled on thought-sampling as the most productive, least-distorting method for our purposes.

To assess current concerns, we initially engaged participants in extensive, probing interviews. For several hours, often involving two or more sessions, each participant told us what he or she was trying to accomplish at that point in life—what he or she was hoping to bring about, escape or avoid, attack, or explore. We recorded a tremendous variety of concerns, ranging from preparing for an upcoming test, moving from a noisy apartment, making up with a boyfriend, to getting closer to God. We also developed ways to quantify what people told us. Over the years we refined the interviews, supplemented them with questionnaires, and eventually developed a series of questionnaires that replaced and actually improved upon the labor-intensive interviews.

In honor of our original method, we called the most comprehensive of those questionnaires the Interview Questionnaire. In it, participants list all of their nontrivial concerns by life area and then rate each concern on a number of dimensions, such as what they would like to do about it, how committed they feel to the corresponding goal, the likelihood that they will attain it, the amount of time pressure they are under to do something about it, and how long they expect to take to reach the goal.

The point of these methods was to test aspects of the theory of fantasy described above, which was really by that time a broad theory of thought flow. In a nutshell, we were setting out to test the hypothesis that what we think about at any given moment is heavily influenced by things we encounter that remind us of our current concerns. To test this theory, we needed at least three components: A method to assess thought, a method to assess current concerns, and a method to deliver cues to participants to remind them of their concerns. We now had the first two methods and still needed the third.

Devising a cue-delivery method posed some serious problems. The cues needed to be salient enough so that participants could realistically respond to them, yet subtle enough so that they would not know that we were trying to remind them of their concerns.

Simply reading cue words for their concerns to our participants seemed too obvious. Eventually, we thought of playing tape recordings of people reading aloud from works of literature, with occasional modifications in the texts to cue participants' concerns and nonconcerns. For example, to a student trying to break into one of the helping professions, we embedded into the text short passages such as "What do they need? What can be given?" in a way that blended smoothly into the text. Then, after each of these "embedding sites" of modified text, we could stop the tape and sample thoughts.

This method had some promise, but it was still inadequate. Our "control" sites, in which we embedded cues associated with matters supposedly not of concern to that participant, still cued too many thoughts. The reason, we discovered, is that even many of those cues had remote associations with bona fide concerns. For example, the supposedly neutral cue, "gray blob," stimulated one participant to think about her roommate, who loved elephants.

My student Deb Smith remembered that cognitive psychologists had developed the method of "dichotic listening"—playing two different stimulus tapes for the participant at the same time, one channel to each ear. What if we did that with our literary narrations and embedded a cue for a concern in one channel while embedding a cue for a nonconcern in the other channel? Then, if we stopped the tape and sampled thoughts shortly after each embedding site, we could assess which of the two stimulus passages in each pair had the greatest influence on thought content. We would have a laboratory analogue of the crowded party, at which different conversations catch your attention as people all around you are saying things that interest you.

In the earlier of these experiments, participants were free to shift their attention between the two tapes—and therefore between their two

ears. By moving a toggle switch they told us which side they were listening to at each moment. An experimenter had interviewed them previously and given them questionnaires to fill out that told us about their current lives. We used this information to embed concern-related and
nonconcern-related cues into the two stimulus channels.

Passages that were designed to remind people gently of their current
concerns influenced listeners' thoughts much more reliably than did
other passages. Participants paid more attention to the concern-related
passages, they were much more likely to remember them after, and those
passages were much more likely to trigger thoughts, including daydreams.

For example, one research participant was, at the time, deeply
involved in a theater production. One stimulus passage written for her
contained the words "whether the *drama* persists or fades with the
demise of *applause,* it is yet certain to unfold in *stages*. . . ." At that point,
her thoughts shifted from a daydream about visiting a friend to imagin-
ing her role in the play, her job in the theater, and the people she worked
with.

Judging from these results, thoughts pop into our heads when we
bump into some kind of cue—a word, picture, or other representation,
either from the outside world or from within our own ongoing thought
stream—that reminds us of a current concern. At that point, we notice
the cue, store it in memory, and start thinking about it in relation to our
concerns.

We theorized that the process by which concern-related cues trigger
thought segments most likely represents a largely automatic process.
However, the results from our thought-sampling experiments with
awake participants could not rule out the possibility that they were
deliberately shifting their attention and thoughts to cues that interested
them. To get around the possibility of deliberate shifts in attention, we
decided to see whether the process works the same way with dreams. In
1979, my student Timothy Hoelscher designed a laboratory sleep experiment in which he periodically read to sleeping participants brief words
or phrases that were related either to one of their individual current concerns or to something else. A few seconds later he woke them up for a
dream report. Just as with our waking participants, the concern-related
words influenced what participants dreamed about much more reliably
than did other words.

For example, the cue we read to one sleeping participant was the
name of his girlfriend, Beth. A short while after repeating her name three
times, we woke him and he reported a dream that revealed a considerable amount about his desires and anxieties, including those associated
with being a participant, which required him to sleep in the laboratory
with EEG electrodes pasted to his scalp. He reported: "I woke up with
my girlfriend," who was "going out with somebody else. And she was

living with this guy for a week. And somehow I was on a moped and we went to her house." The dream goes through a number of strange twists and turns and ends with Beth's sister telling him "about an experiment where they hooked electrodes up to someone's head—they had girls hiccup and they measured their hiccups. So I was just going to tell him about my experiment, and I was awakened." His desire for Beth, his fear of losing her to someone else, and his bemusement with our experiment are all clearly represented in this dream, all automatically triggered during sleep by the sound of her name.

These results strongly confirmed the theory that cognitive processes, including thoughts, are governed by a nondeliberate mechanism for automatically focusing on cues related to our current concerns. When we commit ourselves to particular goals, we thereby also ordain the contents of our consciousness in the hours, days, or years to come.

I became increasingly curious about what human consciousness is like for most people in normal everyday life. My colleague Miles Cox and I undertook a series of investigations in which we sampled students' thoughts throughout the course of their normal daily lives, as well as during examinations, basketball games, studying, and filling out personality questionnaires. In all of these investigations we signaled research participants at unpredictable intervals, usually with a beeper or programmable watch. At each signal, participants filled out a thought-sampling questionnaire, which asked them first to describe, in their own words, their latest thoughts and then to rate those thoughts on a series of rating variables. They included such attributes as the detailedness, clarity, visualness, auditoriness, spontaneity, directedness, strangeness, controllability, and time frame of the thought.

We found that we daydream on average about half the time; that the three most common definitions of daydreaming (fanciful thoughts, spontaneous thoughts, and thoughts about something other than the here and now) are virtually uncorrelated with one another and hence really refer to different, independent aspects of thought; that in most of our thoughts we are talking to ourselves in more than a few words; that most of our thoughts contain some visual imagery, and nearly half contain some sound other than our own self-talk.

This means that our daydreams and other thoughts are really multimedia affairs. For example, one participant, cued by our tape, lapsed into a daydream "of a cabin in the woods surrounded by grizzly bears." She rated this daydream as pretty visual and very auditory—she could see the bears in her mind's eye and hear their grunts and growls. She periodically commented on the experience to herself as it unfolded. Much of it was spontaneous, but she also found herself directing her imagery in places, perhaps trying to make it come out all right.

Apart from these investigations, I continued to press my central questions. What are the mechanisms by which current concerns exert their influence on what we daydream and otherwise think about? What goes on inside us, both experientially and neurologically, to bring this about?

I spent much of the late 1970s and 1980s trying to understand and investigate these questions. Colleagues, students, and I performed a number of diverse research projects. We undertook some questionnaire studies of daydreaming. But because naturally occurring daydreams are hard to dissect in the laboratory, we turned to simpler cognitive processes, such as attention and memory, in order to gain a preliminary understanding of daydreaming. The results of these studies suggest that current concerns influence the stream of our consciousness through emotional activity.

For example, in two separate investigations, Jason Young and Werner Schneider asked research participants to look at a television monitor and respond as quickly as possible about what they saw— whether the string of letters in the middle of the screen was an English word or not, or whether a letter in the middle was an X or a Y. In each case, the screens contained other (distractor) words which participants were instructed to ignore. When these words bore on participants' current concerns or aroused participants' emotions, their presence on the screen slowed the performance of their main decision tasks. In other words, the distractors grabbed their attention, forcing them to process these words automatically and probably nonconsciously. This unintentional processing diverted their cognitive activity enough to interfere with their main assignment.

This interference came about, at least partly, as a result of participants' emotional reactions. It was most evident when the concerns represented by the distractor words were very important to participants. Further, participants who characteristically react with strong emotion were slowed down by the distractor words significantly more than calmer participants. These results all support the idea that emotions affect cognitive processing and, therefore, daydreams.

Given that our current concerns and our emotional reactions both affect our thoughts, the question arises as to whether they do this independently or whether one of them acts as the agent of the other. Michael Bock and I, along with our student Ulrike Bowi, investigated this by asking students to perform various tasks with words and later gave them a surprise test to see which words they could recall. They were most likely to recall words that were related to their current concerns or that were emotionally arousing, and most words were both or neither. But for the few words that were one but not the other, it was the emotionally arousing words unrelated to their concerns that these students recalled most, rather than the concern-related words that left them cold emotionally.

But most of our emotional reactions are predicated on our current concerns. Our joys, fears, angers, disappointments, and depressions are mostly reactions to how we are faring in our enjoyment and pursuit of the various goals in our lives. Our commitments to goals control a large part of our emotional life and thus our thoughts and daydreams.

Physiological evidence supports this notion. When we become emotionally aroused, or when we simply notice something new, the skin on the palms of our hands momentarily conducts electrical current more easily. This is called a skin conductance response (SCR). My student Mary Katherine Larson-Gutman and I have shown that hearing words that are related to one's current concerns evokes more SCRs than hearing other words. Reiner Nikula has shown that if you stop participants after spontaneous SCRs and ask about their most recent thoughts, participants are more likely to report thinking about a current concern than if they are stopped at other times, when they are more likely to report thinking about a past or inactive concern.

We have also begun to look at how people regard their daydreams, and have found that many consider their daydreams to be highly private. Based on research conducted with my students Michael D. Murphy, Jill Ostrem, and Kimberly Stark, most people are more reluctant to disclose their daydreams to others than they are to disclose other things about themselves. Furthermore, those who are most prepared to disclose their daydreams are people who are emotionally strongest and feel socially most confident.

This, of course, is not the end of the trail. Over the past 25 years, we have learned a great deal about daydreaming, much of it described in my 1990 book, *Daydreaming*. But, we have just scratched the surface of truly understanding daydreams. We need both to deepen our understanding of how emotions mediate our cognition, including daydreaming, and to explore further the many facets of daydreaming.

Acknowledgments

The TAT portion of our work was funded from 1964 to 1972 by Grants GS-458 and GS-2735 from the National Science Foundation. In 1973, the National Institute of Mental Health, under Grant MH24804, took over as funding agency from NSF and continued to support the project until 1980. It enabled a stream of talented students and recent graduates, coordinated for seven years by Steven G. Barta, to pour into it their energies and talent. The research was also supported at crucial points by the University of Minnesota Graduate School and the Office of Alcohol and Other Drug Abuse Prevention. Those others in the research group who made particularly important contributions to the development of the ideas and methods described in this chapter include Timothy J. Hoelscher, Sandra R. Johnson, Thomas W. Mahoney, Madeline E. Maxeiner, Michael D. Murphy, Jill Ostrem, Anthony Palmer, Rachel Froiland Quenemoen, Deborah A. Smith, Kimberly Stark, and Susan Stumm.

SUGGESTED READINGS

FARAH, M. J. (1988). Is visual imagery really visual? Overlooked evidence from neuropsychology. *Psychological Review, 95,* 307–317.

HURLBURT, R. T. (1990). *Sampling normal and schizophrenic inner experience.* New York: Plenum.

KLINGER, E. (1977). *Meaning and void: Inner experience and the incentives in people's lives.* Minneapolis: Univ. of Minnesota Press.

_____(1990). *Daydreaming: Using waking fantasy and imagery for self-knowledge and creativity.* Los Angeles: Jeremy P. Tarcher (distributed by St. Martin's Press).

SINGER, J. L. (1975). *The inner world of daydreaming.* New York: Harper & Row.

WILSON, G. (1978). *The secrets of sexual fantasy.* London: Dent.

WILSON, S. C., & BARBER, T. X. (1983). The fantasy-prone personality: Implications for understanding imagery, hypnosis, and parapsychological phenomena. In A. A. Sheikh (Ed.), *Imagery: Current theory, research, and application* (pp. 340–387). New York: Wiley.

E. JERRY PHARES *(Ph.D., Ohio State University) is currently Professor of Psychology at Kansas State University. He is a Fellow of the American Psychological Association and he has served as Head of the Psychology Department at Kansas State University. His research interests over the years have centered on locus of control and social learning theory. He is the author of numerous papers and books including* Locus of Control in Personality *and co-author of* Applications of a Social Learning Theory of Personality. *He has also authored* Clinical Psychology: Concepts, Methods and Profession *and* Introduction to Personality. *His hobbies include reading biographies of historical figures, being a basketball fan, and trying to stay alert.*

11

From Therapy to Research: A Patient's Legacy

❖

Hearing a slight cough and then a faint sound of shuffling feet, I looked up from my desk to see a young man standing outside my office door. He stood there awkwardly with his head lowered and his hat literally in his hand.

I asked him, "May I help you?"

"Uh, uhm, I was told to come here."

"You must be my one o'clock appointment—Mr. Karl Smith (not his real name)."

My first impression of Karl was that he was a young man in his early to mid-twenties, shy, awkward, and probably a loner who found it almost impossible to initiate or sustain any kind of social interaction.

There was little in these first few moments to suggest anything out of the ordinary. In fact, it had all the earmarks of a routine case. Little did I know that this case would not only change my professional life forever, but also profoundly influence the nature of social learning theory!

THE CASE BEGINS

Karl and I talked for about 30 minutes that first day, but it was hard going. He showed no conversational spontaneity whatsoever and it was next to impossible to get much out of him beyond a yes or a no. Even questions, such as "What seems to be the problem?", elicited little in return. As it turned out, he was not even sure why he was in my office. Apparently, Karl had gone to the VA Claims Office on the first floor. The clerk quickly realized that he needed more help than she could provide, so she sent him up to the Mental Hygiene Office.

It seemed, then, that the first order of business was to decide what Karl's problems were and what, if anything, we could do about them. Karl agreed to a series of four meetings on a once-a-week basis so that we might decide what would be appropriate for him. However, he entered into this agreement without much enthusiasm. Like many other veterans at that time, he was entering into the therapy relationship passively. He probably wanted to make sure that his pension claim would not be jeopardized by failing to be cooperative with me.

I decided to administer several diagnostic tests along with several background interviews in order to gain some idea of what made Karl tick. The Wechsler-Bellevue Intelligence Scale was administered to get a general idea of Karl's level of intellectual functioning. This could be important later in making specific vocational or academic plans for him. Three personality tests also were administered. First, the Rotter Incomplete Sentences Blank (ISB) was given. This test requires the patient to complete a series of 40 sentences and provides a rough idea of how the person behaves in everyday situations. The Thematic Apperception Test (TAT) consists of a series of ambiguous pictures in response to which the patient is asked to make up stories. This helps the clinician figure out what needs are motivating the patient. Finally, the Rorschach was administered. Here, the patient is shown ten inkblots and asked what they might represent. The obtained responses offer clues about the structure of the patient's personality and just how serious any problems may be.

What did all this interviewing and testing reveal about Karl? Basically, it confirmed and fleshed out my initial fleeting impressions as he stood in my doorway.

> The Wechsler suggested that Karl was of average intelligence but that his verbal skills and ability to think abstractly were rather limited. The three personality tests revealed a person who showed little spontaneity or imagination. He gave few responses and they were poorly articulated. Most were very common or simple to give. Take the following examples:

ISB	Back home:	Is where I want to be.
	At bedtime:	I go to sleep.
	A mother:	Is wonderful.
TAT	Card 13 MF:	(A man standing beside a bed, his forearm against his head. A woman is lying on the bed.) This here looks like a man sad over his sick wife.
	Card 18 BM:	(A man standing. Behind him, someone's hands are on his arm and shoulder.) I guess this guy is drunk and someone's helping him home.
	Card 8 BM:	(A young man standing in the foreground, a rifle at the side. In the background there is a surgery scene.) Maybe there was a hunting accident and they are operating on this man.

Rorschach   Card I: Looks like a Halloween mask.
                    Card V: Looks like a bat.
                    Card IX: I don't know what it could be.

Still, some questions remained. Was Karl just a young man with an impoverished approach to thinking, feeling, and acting? Or could it be possible that despite his test responses, he was really a repressed individual striving as hard as he could to keep a lid on his inner life to prevent an eruption of some frightening set of reactions? These were important questions whose answers would largely determine the course of treatment I would take with Karl.

Several interviews followed the personality testing. He continued to have great difficulty in expressing his feelings. Yes, he was unhappy. Yes, he felt a lot of discomfort. Yes, he wanted to feel better. No, he was not at the end of his rope. No, he was not afraid of any specific things, such as heights or closets. And, no, he had no urges to hurt himself or others. In short, although he was unhappy and distressed, he wanted to get his life moving and feel that he was accomplishing something. None of this suggested a classical psychotic or neurotic patient. But what was he?

Some background information might shed some light on this question. He was a 23-year-old male who was in the Army during part of the Korean War. He had dropped out of high school in the eleventh grade. His father, whom he remembered as an unemployed carpenter, left home one day and never returned. Karl was about five years old at the time. Since that time, he was raised almost exclusively by his mother. There were some relatives, but Karl could not remember any of them spending time with him. His mother did not have any friends; no one ever came to the apartment. She worked days as a cleaning woman in a downtown office building. About all Karl could remember in the way of fun with his mother were a few bus rides around town in the evening to escape the heat that so often plagued their apartment on summer nights. Mostly they ate at home, sat on the porch, and listened to the radio. It was always just Karl and his mother. And they never really seemed to communicate much.

Why did Karl join the Army? Not surprisingly, he was unsure. In a vague way, he somehow felt he owed it to his country. As hard as it was to relate to Karl, you got the feeling that there was a streak of nobility buried inside him somewhere. But he also felt that something was lacking in his life. Maybe he thought the Army would bring him closer to other people and to those things that seemed so lacking in his own life. He remembered a conversation with his mother as they were sitting on the porch one night shortly before he enlisted. It probably went something like this:

"I'm thinking of joining the Army."

"You are?"

"Yeah."

"What for?"

"Well, maybe it would be good for me?"

"Maybe."

"I guess I'll go downtown tomorrow and see about it."

Such was the decision-making process in the Smith family.

After about a month of interviews and tests, it was time to address Karl's problems, chart a course of action, and begin our therapeutic journey. The most striking feature seemed to be Karl's extremely limited repertoire of social skills. He knew next to nothing about interacting with people—any kind of people—women, employers, friends, or whomever. Save for his mother, his social contacts were virtually nil. Not only was this true today, it had always been true, even during his service in the Army. His needs for love and affection, recognition, and achievement were buried under a thick layer of poorly developed social skills. In short, Karl's problems did not seem to center around the presence of debilitating symptoms, but around the nearly complete absence of social skills.

It so happened that the consultant on this case was Dr. Julian B. Rotter, Professor of Psychology and Director of the Clinical Psychology Training Program at the Ohio State University. (Generally, whenever the pronoun *we* is used in this chapter, it acknowledges the collaborative and seminal efforts of Dr. Rotter both on this case and on subsequent research). He was a noted theorist who had recently formulated a distinctive theory of social learning. Briefly, this theory stated that when people choose to behave one way rather than another, it is because their expectations for receiving gratifications as the result of that behavior are greater than they are for other behaviors. For example, suppose I have a reasonably strong desire to achieve As and Bs in class. I will read, study, and otherwise try to prepare myself. But this is only when I expect that such behaviors will help me achieve my goal. If my expectations are low, I will choose not to study, and elect to go to a ballgame or watch TV instead.

The decision, then, was to look at Karl from the vantage point of social learning theory. What emerged from our analysis, as noted previously, was a young man with very low expectations for achieving satisfactions in life and with an equally restricted array of social behaviors. But this did not mean that Karl was without desires, goals, aspirations, or needs. He was a real person and, as such, he wanted to be liked and recognized. He wanted to be a part of life, not just a spectator. But how do you do this? Therein lay Karl's problem—he did not know. Love, affection, and recognition all demand other people. To be liked requires someone to like you. To be recognized requires another person to recognize you.

But what do you do to achieve such goals? Or, even if you have an idea about the way to go about it, how do you develop enough confidence to try such risky behaviors in the first place? Surely it is true that when we pursue affection, recognition, or other psychological needs, there is the implicit risk of failure. And failure hurts. Indeed, it can hurt so much that many of us will avoid trying to achieve important goals if there is a chance we will fail. Sometimes we decide it is better not to try at all.

THE NATURE OF THERAPY

Given these thoughts on Karl's problems, what could therapy do for him? It could do a lot, we thought, if therapy were described as follows:

- It is basically a learning process through which the therapist tries to achieve planned changes in behavior, thinking, and feelings.
- A patient's difficulties are best viewed as efforts to solve problems (often in very inadequate ways).
- The therapist attempts to guide the learning process so that inappropriate behaviors and attitudes are weakened and more appropriate ones strengthened.
- New experiences can be especially effective in bringing about changes in the person's life and, in a sense, are more important than what transpires in the course of a therapy hour.
- It is a kind of social interaction.

This view suggests a flexible approach to therapy. It will not be just the offering of unconditional positive regard. It will not be the exclusive use of hypnosis, free association, or some other therapeutic technique. It will, however, be anything that has the potential to enhance Karl's ability to solve problems. It will demand an active role on the part of the therapist. Sometimes this will mean explaining to Karl the meaning of his behaviors, his thoughts, or his feelings. Often, it will involve direct reinforcement and encouragement. Above all, it will mean guiding Karl into the kind of real-life settings that will help induce change in his life.

THERAPY IS UNDERWAY

Karl was especially troubled in two very critical areas: social-sexual and education-employment. With the aforementioned general social-learning principles in mind, we began our efforts to increase his prospects for success in these two broad life areas. Therapy became an educational process through which Karl would learn to seek and achieve gratification. This success would, in turn, increase his confidence that additional success was possible. Specifically, therapy could be described as an attempt to teach Karl how to find a job and keep it, talk to women, make dates with them, and the like. Typically, the process involved making suggestions to Karl during a session. For example, he would be advised specifically on how to initiate a conversation with an acquaintance or how to ask a clerk about an item he could not find in a store. In the next meeting, he would report on his attempts to carry out these suggestions and then the two of us would discuss those attempts in great detail. Just how slow and painstaking, as well as revealing, this would all turn out to be, we could not even guess.

What follows is a rather standard series of interchanges with Karl.

"Look, Karl, we have been talking now for several sessions about your interest in watch-repair school. I know the VA will pay for it. So, when are you going to decide?"

"I guess I would like it. But I don't know . . ."

"I know you would, too. I think maybe you are putting it off because you're afraid of screwing up," I suggested.

Karl, after a long pause, replied, "It would be nice to have a skill."

"Okay, then," I resumed. "Let's go through the routine again. You call the school—I gave you the number—when the receptionist answers, tell her what you want. You want to make an appointment to talk about enrolling; you're a veteran and so on. Got it?"

Karl did not respond.

I pushed again. "You will call, won't you? I think it's the best thing you could possibly do right now. Do it and we'll talk again on Thursday."

Four days later, Karl returned. I knew him well enough by now to tell that he was bursting to report something to me. But he was not going to begin until I prompted him. Again, I would have to drag it out of him.

"Well, how did the appointment go, Karl?"

Looking down at his shoes, he replied, "It was okay. I made the appointment and they were expecting me. We talked some and I start classes next week."

I was so excited I nearly leaped out of my chair. This was the first real movement in weeks. He was finally doing something to take charge of his life. I smiled and shook his hand. He barely looked up, betraying not the least bit of an emotion. So much for those great moments in therapy!

Seeking to reinforce his success and bolster what I thought must be his growing self-confidence, I plunged ahead.

"I guess you feel pretty good then. I told you that you could do it, right?"

Karl was noncommittal.

"Karl, what are you thinking?

"I think they had several openings, so they let me in."

"What?"

"I mean, it wasn't competitive or anything like that. I just was there when there was an opening. Besides, I'm a veteran."

Not ready to argue with our first small success, I let it go. But this would not be the last time this theme arose.

There now began a series of meetings in which Karl was repeatedly urged to try new activities, meet new people, and explore new situations. I worked on his day-to-day interactions with students at the vocational school. I encouraged him to extend his conversations with bus drivers, lunch-counter personnel, store clerks, and the like. We wanted to build up his terribly limited repertoire of social-interaction behaviors in any way we could.

One day, as Karl and I were talking about eating in restaurants, that typical veil of indifference descended over his face. This was a recognizable signal by now that something was going on behind his facade. But gleaning information from Karl was sometimes like playing twenty questions. Nevertheless, after several questions, I finally elicited the information that he was interested in a waitress in the restaurant where he often ate. So I began asking about her; "What's she like?" "Do you talk with her?" and so on. Since we had had some limited success in the vocational area (even though Karl was still not ready to take credit for it), this little episode seemed to offer another opportunity to move into the social-sexual arena.

Once again we undertook the task of increasing Karl's social skills and confidence—this time with a woman! Our major fear was that by the time Karl became geared up to make his move, the waitress would have moved on to a new job. In any case, therapy school was in session again so that each meeting became a lesson. Role-playing techniques would have been a logical choice to help expand his skills. Unfortunately, Karl was so self-conscious that I could not get him to participate. Therefore, talk, suggestions, gentle persuasion, and encouragement became my tools. I began with the most basic levels: his tone of voice, his manner, his facial expressions. For Karl, the questions were: "Do I look at her? Do I say thank you? Do I leave a tip (and how much)? Do I come back every day or do I skip a few meals? What do I do if she says something to me? I can't talk to her first; she might not like it. What if she laughs at me? What do I do if she acts interested; no, she wouldn't do that."

This phase lasted for what seemed an endless number of sessions.

Each hour was detailed, repetitive, and usually dull. But each time I began to settle into the gloom of my own boredom, I roused myself by thinking how potentially important all of this was to Karl. Sure, this was not incest, or Oedipal conflicts, or repression, or hot-blooded emotions. But it was therapy and it was, I believed, beginning to have an impact on this man's life and attitudes. My own mid-therapy crisis, then, was short-lived.

Finally, one day the breakthrough came. The waitress had begun to talk to Karl. And miracle of all miracles, he talked back; not much, but enough. They even exchanged names and discussed where they had gone to high school. Later that same week, they inadvertently met on a bus and realized that they lived in the same general neighborhood. They had a nice chat and parted with each suggesting that they would probably meet on that same bus line the next day.

Since his behavior in both the employment and social areas was beginning to pick up, we decided to back off a bit and consolidate our gains. I continued to encourage his efforts in these two areas but did not pressure him to move into any new territory. Like a military commander who had captured some high ground, my intent now was to occupy it, make it my own, and prepare for the next engagement by trying to fully understand the reasons for our victory. In therapy, the goal was similar. Karl and I had achieved some success. It was important that he understand the reasons for that success so he could turn it to his advantage in the future. The behaviors were beginning to fall into place; now came the work of making sure that his confidence and expectation for future success were likewise in place.

This brought us face-to-face with our next major set of problems.

THERAPY BEGINS TO STALL

Human behavior has always been thought by psychologists to be governed by certain principles, such as the *law of effect*. What this means is that rewarding a behavior will increase the likelihood of its occurrence and punishing it will decrease that same likelihood. We were depending on this simple notion to guide our efforts with Karl. We taught him to make certain responses, watched them lead to success, then sat back and observed how they increased in their potential for occurrence. Eventually, there would grow in Karl the belief that he could achieve success in employment and in social relationships. Confidence and an increased level of personal adjustment would be the final product. This is what we believed and, for a while, this is what seemed to be happening. Karl was, in many small ways, more successful. But, as he and I discussed these little triumphs, a growing feeling of uneasiness began to envelop me. There just was not the degree of behavioral change, nor indeed, the change in personal beliefs that had been anticipated. In many ways, Karl seemed no more self-confident than when he started therapy. Successful, yes, but confident, no. And this made no sense.

Dr. Rotter and I discussed these matters at length. What could be responsible for this apparent stalemate in progress? We recalled some of Karl's remarks. When he was accepted into watch-repair school, he attributed his good fortune to the fact that there were several openings, that there was no competition, and that he was a veteran. Then we went back through the case notes on his discussions about his waitress friend. He had said that she did not have any friends either, that they just happened to meet on the bus that day, that he really was a lucky person sometimes. He even noted that his luck seemed to have taken a real turn for the better. Most people may, from time to time, make the same remark—but it is really just a remark. For Karl it seemed to mean much, much more.

Now here was an interesting thought. What if Karl really did believe in luck, chance, or whatever one chooses to call it? What if he believed that in the most pervasive sense? That would explain Karl's attitudes and responses toward me. From the very beginning, he regarded me as an authority figure. What's more, he endowed me with a kind of wisdom and knowledge that was very gratifying, but hardly accurate. But its importance was underlined in the remarks he occasionally made after we discussed some of his adventures. For example, after discovering that his appointment at watch-repair school was in order and that they were expecting him, he said, "You were right about what you told me to do; just what you said really happened." About a friend at school, he observed, "That was really smart of you; you told me to laugh at his jokes; I did, and he really liked it." In a subtle way he seemed to be saying, "The reason *my* efforts worked was due to *you*; you are making good fortune for me."

AN IDEA PRESENTS ITSELF

Dr. Rotter and I continued to discuss the impasse with Karl at great length. We tried enumerating some of Karl's behavioral characteristics. This, we thought, might help illuminate matters. For example:

- Karl made few attempts to acquire information. This greatly impeded his efforts to achieve any kind of goals. He did not seem tuned in to important cues in his world.
- Karl was, in many ways, singularly susceptible to social influence, particularly when he felt the influence was coming from someone

with status. Thus, at my urging, he would try any number of new behaviors.

- Karl seemed to be a curious mix of calmness and anxiety. At times, his limited arsenal of coping behaviors seemed to panic him. But more often than not, he adopted a sort of fatalistic outlook that exclaimed, "Why worry, you can't change things anyway."

We thought a lot about all of this and what it could mean. And then someone made a remark about a dissertation completed by Alvin Lasko at Ohio State University a few years earlier. He had discovered that just knowing that a person had failed on a task 10 times in a row did not necessarily enable you to conclude that this person's confidence was now very low. Perhaps this person had earlier been correct 12 times and, as a result, now feels that after all these failures it is about time to be correct again. In short, a critical factor in understanding how expectation for success or confidence develops is not the absolute number of successes and failures but their pattern. In explaining this, Lasko also suggested that perhaps in some learning situations the important thing is not just that a given response is correct but who controls the outcomes following the response.

Suddenly, the lights came on. The reason behind Karl's peculiar responses seemed obvious. He did not regard his own efforts as influential. He believed that the outcomes following his behaviors were outside his personal control. When his efforts were successful at the watch-repair school or with the waitress, his expectations for future success did not increase. But why, then, should they? When you are not in control of a situation, successes and failures do not convey any meaningful information about the future. This is like playing a slot machine when everything is controlled by luck. Hitting the jackpot is nice but it should not lead you to increase your expectations for hitting the jackpot again. After all, you are not in control, so what can that success possibly teach you?

If Karl really believed that his own actions were unrelated to achieving success, then his behavior made sense. Why try to acquire information or prepare yourself if rewards and punishments occur independently of your behavior? Why not rely on other people, such as a therapist? They are knowledgeable and their efforts are what really count. And why get terribly upset over things you cannot control? Maybe, then, Karl's reactions were not so odd after all. Karl was not responding in defiance of learning theory. Rather, it was our conceptualization of learning theory that must be incomplete. The important elements are not just behavior and reinforcement but one's *belief* about who controls the occurrence of reinforcements. Formulating these ideas was very exciting. But the next step was critical. We must test our hypothesis instead of depending upon sheer speculation.

*T*HE RESEARCH BEGINS

Our work with Karl raised some very important questions about how reinforcement works. To find the answers to those questions it was important to proceed slowly and carefully. To learn specifically how reinforcement works in relation to personal control, we needed to contrive a situation where exact control could be exerted by the experimenter. In a sense, we wanted to construct a laboratory replica of Karl's experience. We believed that Karl had failed to increase his expectancies for success following reinforcement because he did not feel in control of the situation. If we could develop two situations, one where subjects felt in control and one where they did not, we could reinforce their behavior and then observe its effects on their expectancies. If all went according to plan, subjects who felt in control should change their expectancies for future success in response to success or failure. However, subjects who did not feel in control should exhibit fewer changes in expectancies following success and failure. If such an experiment worked out, we could later pursue the idea that people exhibit generalized beliefs about the extent of their personal control and that these beliefs vary from one person to another. But first, the laboratory research.

The first study we devised consisted of two perceptual tasks. Subjects were asked to look at lines and then decide whether or not they were the same length. They also looked at colors and then decided whether or not they were the same hue. Half the subjects were told that these tasks were so difficult that success was largely a matter of chance. The other half of the subjects were instructed that success and failure were totally determined by skill or ability. Over a series of trials they made their perceptual judgments about color and length. But prior to each trial, they were asked to state an expectancy for success or what could be called a confidence level. For example, "How many chips are you willing to bet that you will be correct on the next trial?" This betting behavior was our measure of expectancy.

To make a long story short, two major findings emerged. First, fluctuations in expectancies from trial to trial were greater in the skill condition than in the chance condition. Second, the frequency of changes in expectancy was greater in the skill than in the chance condition.

How did we interpret these findings? Well, the likely explanation seemed to be that skill conditions offer a greater basis for generalizing from the past to the future than do chance conditions. When success and failure are attributed to one's own efforts or personal control, the past is viewed as entirely relevant to the future. But in chance situations or in ones where the individual is not really in control, the past becomes irrelevant to the future. Basically, then, learning is different when skill as opposed to chance is involved. And this is exactly what we had hypothesized was happening with Karl.

Now, finally, we were getting a handle on these matters. This research, born out of our ruminations about the inexplicable behavior of one patient, would eventually lead us considerably beyond that one patient. What was at stake now was not merely helping a single patient, but probing the nature of learning and the role of personal control in human behavior. Suddenly, the arena had grown much larger and the implications still larger yet.

RESEARCH CONTINUES AND EXPANDS

Over the next several years, research continued at a furious pace. At first, the focus was on control as a characteristic of specific situations. A number of very interesting findings emerged that helped give shape and substance to our earlier ideas about Karl. For example, it was determined that when escape from a painful electric shock is possible as a result of a subject's efforts, greater learning will occur in that situation as compared to situations in which escape is outside the subject's control. Again, when personal control exists, it is important to pay attention and learn. But when personal control does not exist, why pay attention to cues that seem to bear no relationship to avoidance of the painful stimulus? Interestingly, this latter study predated by several years research on what has come to be called "learned helplessness." This refers to a tendency in both animals and humans who have been exposed to inescapable painful stimuli to later fail to attempt to escape even when given the opportunity to do so. All of this is reminiscent of the extreme sense of personal helplessness and apathy that enveloped prisoners in Nazi concentration camps during World War II. Many of them succumbed to death because they saw their environment as totally uncontrollable. There was no point in paying attention to life when only death can occur. The conclusion from this and other research seemed clear. Learning and performance are reduced and anxiety and stress are increased whenever aversive stimuli are either unpredictable or uncontrollable.

But this was not all that was going on. We had come to believe that Karl possessed a general belief system that he carried about with him from situation to situation. He did not just wait until he got himself into a situation before deciding that it did or did not offer the opportunity for control. He actively construed most situations that way from the very beginning. His belief that luck, fate, chance, or other forces controlled his life was like a pair of eyeglasses that he wore everywhere and through which he gained very personal images of the world.

Dr. Rotter and several of his colleagues went about constructing a questionnaire that would tap into such a belief system and allow us to decide how much a person saw events as personally controlled. An example of an item on this questionnaire is the following:

I more strongly believe that (select either a or b):

a.   Many people can be described as victims of circumstances.
b.   What happens to people is pretty much their own doing.

When a person predominantly chooses items that cast people as the products of luck, chance, fate, as under the control of powerful others or unpredictable events, the person is said to be *externally* oriented. When a person typically perceives events or outcomes as the result of his or her own behavior or relatively permanent characteristics, then we say that person is *internally* oriented.

With the development of this questionnaire and the subsequent establishment of its reliability and validity, a veritable flood of research activity occurred. Since 1966 a truly amazing volume of research has been published on what has come to be called *internal versus external control of reinforcement (I-E)* or *locus of control.* The studies now number in the thousands! Between the years 1970 and 1974 alone, Rotter's research on I-E was the second most frequently cited work in the *Journal of Consulting and Clinical Psychology*, a major outlet for research in clinical psychology.

*U*NDERSTANDING GROWS

Consider the following scenes:

- A four-year-old struggles to open his box of candy. You lean down to help him but he howls in anger and cries, "I can do it myself!"
- A seventy-five-year-old widow, frail and at times confused, cannot, realistically, continue to care for herself. You explain to her as lovingly as you can that she must move to a nursing home. She sobs uncontrollably and begs to be allowed to remain at home.
- You are riding in the passenger seat of your friend's car. Each time he approaches a car, you tense up and press your foot against the floorboard. You silently berate yourself for not insisting that you drive.

Now we understand the importance of the foregoing examples and many other similar slices of life as well. But, in a sense, everything goes back to Karl. Our struggle to understand him gave rise to a simple hypothesis about the manner in which expectancies change following reinforcement in skill and chance situations. This, in turn, led to studies about the effects of a broad personality dimension involving personal control.

Over the years, research on perceived control from scores of other investigators and other laboratories has taught us more and more. We now realize that maintaining a sense of personal control is a central goal for all people. And the frustration of one's sense of personal control can lead to severe distress and even death, as noted earlier in the case of the Nazi prison camps. Only now do we realize that so often the physical and mental decline we see in aging individuals is affected by their inability to exercise control over their own lives. Recent research also shows that involving patients in their own health-care maintenance can facilitate their recovery from illness. People who believe they possess personal control are more sensitive to health messages and are more likely to try to improve their health status. Such people are also more likely to be better adjusted and less anxious than those who do not feel in control of their lives. On the other hand, those individuals who do not feel in control are less active in acquiring information about their surroundings, are more susceptible to being influenced by other people, and are less likely to become actively involved in affecting their own little corner of the world.

*E*PILOGUE

What happened to Karl? During a six-month period, I gradually decreased the frequency of his visits to the clinic and eventually he discontinued therapy altogether.

It seems evident that therapy did a number of good things for Karl. First, it significantly enlarged his repertory of interpersonal skills. This, in turn, led to some notable successes in work and in social relationships. Ultimately, too, his willingness to attribute responsibility to himself for his successes was strengthened. With that came increased confidence that he could achieve things on his own. His realization of this was slow, halting, and never really complete. But it was light years from where he had begun.

Follow-up information was sketchy. However, by putting bits and pieces of information together, this much emerged. He broke off his relationship with the waitress. Subsequently, he secured a permanent job as an inventory clerk in an appliance warehouse. He met another woman there and, after a brief courtship, they were married. Several months later he called the clinic and informed a social worker that everything in his life was "going fine" and he no longer needed to keep in touch. Beyond that, nothing is known—he made no further contacts with the clinic.

All in all, this was an enormously gratifying case. Karl was helped and his eventual independence dimmed any likelihood that he would become a burden to society rather than a contributing member. But, in a larger sense, we all benefitted from this case. Our knowledge of learning theory, the importance of internal attributions, and the relationship of all this to the therapy process were greatly enhanced.

The topic of personal control is still one of the major research thrusts in psychology. What we have learned is the result of the efforts of many researchers throughout the world. In the case of our own contributions (and maybe many others as well), however, there remains Karl. Perhaps the best way, then, to end this chapter is simply by saying, "Thank you, Karl. Thank you for what you taught us. For it was out of your unhappiness that we were better able to understand and take those first simplistic research steps. Many patients pass through therapy and leave only the faintest of footprints. But yours are still there. And at least one psychologist will never forget."

SUGGESTED READINGS

PHARES, E. J. (1976). *Locus of control in personality*. Morristown, NJ: General Learning.

————(1991). *Introduction to personality* (3rd ed.). New York: Harper Collins.

ROTTER, J. B. (1982). *The development and application of social learning theory: Selected papers*. New York: Praeger.

————(1990). Internal versus external control of reinforcement: A case history of a variable. *American Psychologist, 45,* 489–493.

————CHANCE, J. E., & PHARES, E. J. (Eds.) (1972). *Applications of a social learning theory of personality*. New York: Holt, Rinehart, and Winston.

STRICKLAND, B. R. (1989). Internal-external control expectancies: From contingency to creativity. *American Psychologist, 44,* 1–12.

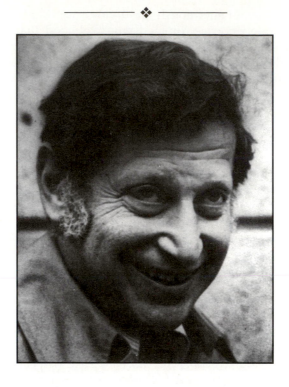

*E*RIC *SCHOPLER* (Ph.D., University of Chicago) is Professor of Psychology and Psychiatry, and Director, Division for Treatment and Education of Autistic and related Communication handicapped Children (TEACCH) at the University of North Carolina School of Medicine, Chapel Hill. Dr. Schopler is the author of numerous texts, chapters in texts, and articles in the field. He is Editor of the Journal of Autism and Developmental Disorders and is editorially involved with six other related professional journals. Among his advisory activities is his involvement with the Work Group to revise the Diagnostic and Statistical Manual of Mental Disorders. Recently, the American Psychological Association honored Dr. Schopler with the Distinguished Professional Contributions to Public Service Award, and he received the only statewide honor awarded by his university for greatest contribution to human welfare. Dr. Schopler also enjoys raising catfish and cows on his farm.

12

The Anatomy of a Negative Role Model

❖

Today the majority of people have heard of autism, especially if they have seen the 1990 Academy Award–winning film *Rainman,* in which Dustin Hoffman portrayed the autistic Raymond with extraordinary clinical accuracy and insight. Raymond would be diagnosed as higher functioning autistic, meaning that his language and IQ were in the near normal range. However, his social interactions were impaired and peculiar. In addition, he had some special savant skills such as a highly developed rote-memory capacity that enabled him to remember and keep track of numbers, dates, and playing cards.

It is important to note that the high level of functioning represented by *Rainman* occurs only in 15 percent of the autistic population. The remainder show varying degrees of mental retardation. They all share the following three primary features of autism:

1. *Impaired Reciprocal Social Interaction:* A child may exhibit this feature as a lack of awareness of others. For example, a young child may not seek comfort in times of distress. He or she may fail to imitate the actions or behaviors of others or exhibit impairments in social play, consistently preferring solitary play to interactions with other children. These youngsters are not able to form peer friendships requiring an awareness of others and of social conventions.

2. *Impaired Reciprocal Communication and Language:* A child might exhibit language impairments such as repeating certain words and phrases without any functional intent or using speech that is abnormal in pitch, rate, rhythm, and intonation. Such a child characteristically is unable to converse with others despite an adequate capacity for speech. Some children even have limited resources for nonverbal communication and are not able to make their wants known with appropriate gestures. For example, instead of signaling that he wants a drink by opening the refrigerator door and getting the juice carton off the shelf, an autistic child may take his mother's hand and pull her toward the

173

refrigerator. The child may also lack appropriate eye movements, pointing responses, and other simple communicative gestures.

3. *Marked Restriction of Activity and Interests:* At the lower level of developmental functioning, a child may perform odd repetitive body movements such as hand-flicking, twisting, spinning, or rocking. A child may also display an excessive need for repetition, insisting on always following the same route to familiar places, dressing in the exact same sequence every day, or lining up toys instead of playing with them. At a higher level of functioning, an autistic person might amass facts about a particular subject such as astronomy, calendars, or, as in *Rainman,* numbers translated into an extraordinary ability to play "Black Jack." If any interruptions in the repetitive activities occur, the autistic individual is likely to become markedly distressed.

The main purpose of this chapter is not so much to review the current status of autism research, but to give the reader an idea of the renowned Bruno Bettelheim as a role model, and to offer the optimistic possibility that even a controversial teacher can become a constructive force in a student's education.

I first met Bruno Bettelheim when he was a professor at the University of Chicago during the post–World War II period. He was a popular teacher, especially among undergraduates, with a reputation for dramatic lecturing—being highly articulate and facile with Freudian concepts. He used these freely for personal interpretations of students' questions and comments, and his analytic responses were animated by wit, sarcasm, and derision—anything for his argument to prevail. Some thought him to be brutally authoritarian, while others credited him with the original insights of a great and brilliant psychoanalyst. Arriving at the university, I had become more interested in disturbed children from a previous summer job and was curious to find out what made Bettelheim so controversial, as well as what I could learn from him.

Looking back on my student days from the perspective of a senior research psychologist with a career committed to the understanding and treatment of autism and similar childhood disorders, I recognize that it is difficult to identify the educational events shaping a career. If specific techniques and special skills are involved, these offer clear guidelines to the mentor first demonstrating them. But in clinical psychology, concerned with interpersonal relations shaped by complex factors of thought and feeling, the impact of clinical teachers is more global and harder to specify.

I should admit that at the beginning of my career I was not always undaunted. In my case, uncertainty was at a peak as an undergraduate. Having been born in pre–World War II Germany, I had not resolved my own relationship to the violence and dislocation which I had experienced, both geographically and psychologically. By the time I had entered the University of Chicago, it was difficult for me to distinguish the confusion and uncertainty originating in me from that rooted in the outside social and political world. Practitioners of psychoanalysis staked their careers on locating the turmoil inside. Their method of free association was no help in distinguishing internal from external sources of stress. The field of clinical psychology, with a growing branch rooted in empirical research, seemed to offer the most promising directions for answers to problems of living and adaptation.

Although a number of immigrant teachers had come to the faculty of the University, I was especially drawn to Bettelheim's classes. He, after all, came from Germany, as had my family. Unlike us, he had actually been in a Nazi concentration camp and then started the Orthogenic School on the campus of the university for children he described as victimized by families with extreme stress not unlike that suffered by concentration camp victims.

THEORY VS. EMPIRICISM

Bettelheim was intriguing to anyone interested in autism and related disturbances of childhood. He was said to practice an original form of teaching in which he shared brilliant psychoanalytic insights into students' personalities from their class contributions, insights supposedly applicable to the understanding of severe psychopathology. One of the first examples of these teaching methods to make the rounds happened in his class on personality theory. It was a large lecture group of some 75 students with little time for questions. Midway through the lecture, he noticed a woman in the second row knitting as he expounded the Freudian stages of psycho-sexual development. She was a few years older than the others, as she had served in the Women's Army Corps. Although she remained quiet, Dr. Bettelheim appeared visibly disturbed by the body language of her knitting. He interrupted his lecture to inquire, in his heavy German accent, whether she understood the meaning of her behavior. She shook her head, eyes wide with puzzled astonishment. He told the class and her that she was expressing unconscious hostility toward her father from unresolved Oedipal feelings, and she now felt compelled to transfer her frustrated sexual feelings into disrespect toward authority figures like him.

Our present generation of students might find it hard to understand or empathize with the respect and even reverence felt by the undergraduates back then in the presence of a professor with authority and reputation. This aura emanating from her silent classmates magnified the student's confused surprise and embarrassment as she dropped the knitting to her lap.

At the next meeting of the class. Bettelheim was warming to his description of the phallic phases of development. The ex-WAC was there in the same seat as before, and out came her knitting again. This time Bettelheim interrupted his lecture at once. Looking up her name in the assigned seating chart, he addressed her in furious exasperation. If she still didn't have the insight into her own behavior, perhaps he had better spell it out in more graphic detail. "Your knitting is a sublimated form of masturbation carried out before the entire class."

Propelled by her adrenaline, the young woman sat bolt upright. Her response was refracted from the cutting edge of emerging sexual liberation and was to echo through the lecture halls long after graduation: "Dr. Bettelheim, when I knit, I knit, and when I masturbate, I masturbate."

It was difficult to identify the educational meaning of this interaction or what it taught us about personality theory, the subject of the course. One thing seemed clear. Bettelheim's theoretical explanation of the student's knitting behavior was shown to be ludicrous by her cryptic response, possibly a dramatic illustration of empiricism. Perhaps it was Bettelheim's real intent to evoke original thinking in his students by caricaturing the theories he was teaching with overstated application to personal interaction. Since less dramatic though similar interactions characterized almost every lecture, could this be a brilliant and original teaching approach?

I was soon to have the opportunity to examine these questions from my own interactions with this unique and overbearing teacher. The occasion was an evening lecture sponsored by the members of the Hillel House, a kind of home away from home for Jewish students. Dr. Bettelheim was the invited speaker. His topic was "Anti-Semitism Today." The student turnout was unusually large, with many sitting on the floor or standing out into the hallways. Most of them were there expecting understanding and empathy for their anticipated barriers of prejudice to admission for medical or law schools. You can imagine the group's surprise when Bettelheim's lecture theme was identified with his opening rhetorical question: "Anti-semitism, whose fault is it?" He paused as if expecting every student to volunteer his own thoughts to this emotionally burdened question. Finally, the silence was pierced by Bettelheim's pointed finger drawing an arc, encompassing all of us. "Yours!" he shouted. "Because you don't assimilate, it is your fault. If you assimilated, there would be no anti-Semitism. Why don't you assimilate?"

He answered his own rhetorical question with a passionate monologue bent on having us give up and reform this hopeless vice of Jewish identity. I will not try to recreate this remarkable lecture here, but you can believe that he tried every trick of persuasion in his Germanic repertoire of sarcasm, guilt, and shame. He implied knowledge of our shabby spiritual secrets. "How many of you are Jewish for religious reasons?"

He regarded the absence of any answers with a triumphant smirk, then shifted to sarcasm. "If it is for cultural reasons, what is this Jewish culture? Who are the great Jewish composers? Who are the timeless artists? Who are the great writers? Shalom Asch?" This Yiddish writer, popular at the turn of the century, often wrote about the common spiritual heritage of Christians and Jews. He might have been used as support for the assimilating argument, but instead, Bettelheim dismissed Asch with a retching "Yech," indicating a writer not worthy of a tile in the shabby mosaic of Jewish culture.

By the end of his lecture, Bettelheim had told us about his experiences in a Nazi concentration camp, where he had been incarcerated during the coldest winter months. He developed a severe case of frost-bite in his hand, which subsequently became infected. He requested medication and bandages from the Nazi guards, whose lack of sympathy or responsiveness inspired Bettelheim to assume his notion of the Nazi value system. "If you won't give me the bandages, then give me a knife, so I can cut off my hand." Responding to this request with respect, the guard gave him the bandages. Bettelheim attributed his success to a conscious "identification with the aggressor." This experience seemed to persuade him that he had become an expert at avoiding Nazi persecution.

Maybe under the life-threatening pressure of the Nazi concentration camp, identifying with the aggressor is one of the accessible survival tactics, but in this lecture, he laid upon our group of students the burden of his concentration-camp insight—guilt for the chronic and lethal injustice of anti-Semitism—simply for our presence here at Hillel House instead of being at the Congregational Church across the street.

We came to the question period in the stunned silence of embarrassed confusion. By now, I had come to the recognition that Dr. Bettelheim was a master at evoking this mental state in his students. Still inspired by the knitting student in the personality-theory lecture, I raised my hand for clarification.

I understood that he had told us we could cure anti-Semitism if we got rid of our Jewish religious and ethnic interests, and if we had our identifying noses altered. If this was a correct summary of his position, I asked, "What's the difference between you and the anti-Semite?"

In red-faced anger, Bettelheim shouted, "I am only the doctor prescribing the cure."

I followed up, "You mean by identifying with the disease?"

"Yes, by identifying with the disease," he shouted.

At this point, other students seemed relieved by a straightforward interpretation of his rather misplaced theory for explaining anti-Semitism. He had a knack for taking a plausible theory and pushing it to an exaggerated caricature, defiantly personalized against his audience. This seemed like a heavy didactic burden for a group of students, even at a place like the University of Chicago, proud of convening an enthusiastic and creative teaching faculty. Perhaps he was trying through an emotional discourse to develop student acceptance of his favorite theories.

He did attract many students with his unique teaching style. Did they select his lectures because he taught his theories at a personalized emotional level, or was it that they hoped to deflate his autocratic bullying as I and my knitting colleague had done?

I had many opportunities to examine these questions during the rest of my undergraduate career and later as a graduate student.

Postgraduate influence

After college graduation I tried several lines of career development, but eventually returned to my interest in severely troubled children. I accepted a position at the Emma P. Bradley Hospital for such youngsters in Providence, Rhode Island. While I was at Bradley, the director, Maurice Laufer, wanted to sponsor a symposium on childhood psychosis. He asked us to suggest possible speakers. Seeing an opportunity to learn more about Bettelheim's understanding and treatment of autistic children and, perhaps, to bridge the yawning gap between academic knowledge and the real world left by my past university experience, I suggested his name for the symposium.

Dr. Laufer declined the suggestion. He thought Bettelheim had an offensive manner of teaching that tended to undermine staff morale. Disappointed by being denied the opportunity to learn directly about Bettelheim's treatment techniques and feeling foolish for not having anticipated the unpopularity of my eminent, former teacher, I decided to write him a letter sharing my disappointment with him. I told him that, in spite of my recommendation, they did not want to invite him because of his reputation for having a negative effect on students' morale. I expressed my regrets that his effectiveness as a teacher was so curtailed by his manner.

In a few days, he replied. If I was really interested in what he had to teach, I should not go by what people said about him, but should visit the Orthogenic School for a few weeks and see for myself.

This invitation came as quite a surprise, especially since up to that time, he had not permitted any student observers at his school. I had been thinking about reentering graduate school in the Ph.D. program for clinical child-development. A few weeks observing at the Orthogenic School would serve as a good transition back to the academic life. What I learned about autistic children during this period was to help shape my later research and treatment efforts.

The Orthogenic School was in an old church with surrounding buildings, creatively redesigned as a residential school by Bettelheim. The interior decoration was beautiful and striking, bold colors and patterns in unusual coexistence. One side of the stairway leading to the dormitory was covered with an engaging mural of hand-painted tiles depicting the

Paul Bunyon legend. Large stuffed animals donated by the Marshall Field department store stood in the classrooms. In the courtyard was a large modern statue resembling a reclining woman with smooth voluptuous curves, but no other details. This cement sculpture represented the cold, stone mother, so deeply implanted in the school's mythology. She bore the responsibility for the children's difficulties and their presence in the school. The children were permitted to crawl all over the statue as a therapeutic experience to help them work through presumed feelings about their own mothers. One of the halls contained a toy closet filled with candy, readily accessible to staff and children as a nonspecific positive reinforcer, perhaps a compensation like the high course grades for the excessively forceful demands of the director.

The food served during meals was well above average for institutional cooking. Fresh fruit was readily available in the staff room. Overall, the place gave an impression of the affluent and colorful home of an eccentric and creative patriarch. I was reminded that Bettelheim's own formal education had been in art history.

While the physical plant and the high caliber of the counselor staff led me to conclude that if I had a seriously disturbed child, I might want to send him here, the process of understanding the children, treatment methods, and professional training were another matter altogether.

Diagnostic formulations were created, in part, from a detailed family history questionnaire. A surprisingly large number of questions dealt with sexual experiences and attitudes, making Freudian explanations for the child's problems easy and all but inevitable. I wondered how diagnostic evaluation of such children, based on their coping skills, behaviors, and deficits would compare with an evaluation based on psychoanalytic theoretical assumptions. Such a comparison would be demonstrated in the assessment series I developed later in my career, as discussed below.

In staff meetings, Bettelheim consistently discounted intervention suggestions against the destructive effects he ascribed to the absent parents. Not until I had more direct experience with parents of autistic children did I recognize what an exaggerated caricature he had made of parental struggles with the stresses of their autistic children.

Bettelheim used staff meetings to reinforce Freudian concepts. He rotated the discussions of individual children. As in his college-class lectures, he dominated these meetings, and with only a minimum of information, he would soar off into unexpected and aggressive interpretations, often with the effect of strengthening counselor-child ties. His dramatic ability to involve counselors emotionally with him promoted their compliance toward him and their bonding with the children.

In spite of my doubts regarding his approach, I decided to pursue my interest in severely disturbed children and to find out what I could learn through an empirical research program. I would develop a proposal, not only to meet the requirements of my Ph.D. dissertation, but also to have the opportunity to discuss some important clinical issues from a scientific perspective with Dr. Bettelheim.

In my work with autistic and schizophrenic children, I had noticed that they tended to touch and lick their toys and other objects rather frequently, and that they seemed relatively less interested in auditory or visual stimuli. In other words, they seemed to prefer using their near receptors of touch, smell, and taste over the distance receptors mediating visual and auditory information. No one had studied receptor preferences empirically, though William Goldfarb had published his observations of the phenomenon. If this intriguing observation characterized that group of children, then an exciting alternative explanation for the causes of the condition might be found. Rather than showing social withdrawal from the unconscious hostility of parents, here was an opportunity to identify perceptual problems rooted in the children's neurobiology.

I immersed myself in developing procedures comparing tactual interests with visual interests, to be used on a sample of autistic, mentally retarded, and normal children. Eventually, I came up with a set of interesting procedures that included such comparisons as same-colored blocks with different textures and same-textured blocks with different colors, and figures rotating on a visual display and the same figures in a container to be explored only tactually. I had tried these procedures on my own offspring, and they loved them. I had rewritten my research proposal until it was approved by my exacting dissertation committee. I was now ready to submit my proposal to Dr. Bettelheim and to request permission to study the children at his Orthogenic School.

At the appointed time, I came to his office at the School. The light in the room was quite dim; his desk lamp spot-lighting only his face; my dissertation proposal there before him. I was not prepared for his abrupt response.

"Very interesting," he said. "But why is it that you scientists always try to prove with research what we have known clinically all along? Of course I will not expose my children to such an undertaking."

I had no ready answer for his unexpected question. Of course, I should not have been surprised that he had refused to have his children used for such a frivolous task. Dejected, I left his office. Why had I selected a clinically obvious problem and spent months working out the research details?

By the time I reached home, the answer occurred to me with lucid clarity. Of course, I had developed such an empirical research project because it was a university requirement for obtaining a Ph.D. in psychology. Bruno Bettelheim was a professor in this department who shared in the responsibility for setting out scientific dissertation requirements. How dare he address me as "you scientists." Equally important, I wondered whether he saw the study of perceptual and cognitive problems as a threat to the unverified psychoanalytic explanations he seemed to cherish. Though I had been denied the most obvious source of research subjects, I swore to search out the needed sample of children.

With the aid of several midwestern treatment facilities, the experiment was conducted. I compared children's preferences for visual and tactual stimuli in four standardized situations:

1. Children could choose to view color slides (e.g., animals, scenery), which changed automatically every 20 seconds, or receive moderate hand vibrations by pushing the appropriate lever.
2. Children could choose to play with a kaleidoscope or a piece of dark-hued putty, which resisted the formation of shapes but could be explored tactually.
3. Children could choose to play with blocks that were either of uniform texture with varied colors and pictures, or uniform in color, but with different textures (e.g., fur, sandpaper).
4. Children could choose to observe toy animals rotating on a disc or feel toy animals in compartments covered by cloth sleeves.

I found that the proportion of visual and tactual preferences (in terms of time spent with the stimuli) was significantly lower in the autistic group than in control groups of retarded and nonhandicapped subjects. It supported Bernard Rimland's scholarly critique of psychoanalytic formulations and provided one of the building blocks of data for a theory of autism that stresses neurological and biological factors.

Although our subsequent studies showed that the relationship between visual and tactual preferences did not have the most far-reaching treatment implications, the experiment did lay the groundwork for identifying the important perceptual and cognitive processes summarized below.

*I*MPLICATIONS FOR MY WORK

Bettelheim drew a parallel between his own terrifying and extreme experiences in a Nazi concentration camp and the extreme stresses experienced by autistic children inside their families. He brought these children together in the Orthogenic School where he tried to rehabilitate them, and maybe himself, with a "good" residential school (camp) experience. Even more impressive, he was able to persuade many students and mental-health professionals that his residential program was the best possible treatment.

His contribution was as an artist, often through literary metaphor, not as a social scientist. He did not seem to have the observational detachment with which social scientists seek empirical evidence for the interpretation of their own observations. He was less interested in the rules of evidence than he was in dominating interpersonal debate with the convictions and rhetoric informed by his subjective muse. Moreover, the effects of literary metaphors are usually general, shaping the reader's feelings and aesthetic intuitions. This is a different process from using objective observation and data for making probability predictions for realizing educational or treatment goals.

Bettelheim had a lasting, though antithetical influence on my thinking and research on causation, diagnosis, and treatment of autism. While parents were still regarded as the primary causal agents for the autism disorder, I argued that they were being scapegoated by mental-health professionals. If parents sometimes acted confused in seeking help, we must first consider the effects of guilt generated by inappropriate psychoanalytic blame of parents. Instead of targeting parents for producing autistic behaviors in their children, various biological mechanisms could be identified. Research has shown that autism can be produced by genetics, viral infections, biochemical differences, and neurological and brain abnormalities as in the cerebellum.

Under the psychoanalytic influence, autistic children were often considered "untestable," and it was accepted that only the more experienced psychoanalysts were qualified to diagnose this esoteric condition. To counteract this mythology, my colleagues and I developed a 15-item rating scale, the Childhood Autism Rating Scales (CARS) (see Figure 12–1) with good psychometric properties, usable by any reasonably well-trained tester.

The behaviors assessed were drawn from the criteria widely used for diagnosing autism. For example, the severely abnormal behavior of autistic children often includes unresponsiveness to others (I—Relationships with People); strange finger movements, peculiar body posturing, rocking, or spinning (IV—Use of Body); preoccupation with smelling, tasting, or feeling objects (IX—Near-Receptor Responsiveness); and underresponsiveness to sounds (VIII—Auditory Responsiveness) and/or sights (VII—Visual Responsiveness); and infantile or unusual vocalizations (XI—Verbal Communication).

More important, the psychometric approach to diagnostic assessment enabled us to learn the characteristics of autism (described in the beginning of this chapter) that were not included in the behavioral definition or always attended to by behaviorists. This process enabled us to distinguish *relative* strengths and weaknesses essential for providing these children with an appropriate education. These autism deficits include difficulties with organization and change, problems with memory (especially in areas not involving special interests), generalization or abstraction, and auditory processing. On the side of strengths are rote memory skills for special interests, and processing visual information.

I. Relationships with People

II. Imitation

III. Affect

IV. Use of Body

V. Relation to Nonhuman Objects

VI. Adaptation to Environmental Change

VII. Visual Responsiveness

VIII. Auditory Responsiveness

IX. Near-Receptor Responsiveness

X. Anxiety Reaction

XI. Verbal Communication

XII. Nonverbal Communication

XIII. Activity Level

XIV. Intellectual Scatter

XV. General Impression

Scoring: 1 = Normal
2 = Mildly abnormal
3 = Moderately abnormal
4 = Severely abnormal

FIGURE 12.1
The Childhood Autism Rating Scales (CARS).

These cognitive concepts are useful not only for special educational intervention, but also for research identifying the neurological correlates in particular locations of the central nervous system.

For the purpose of identifying characteristics not necessarily part of the autism definition but essential to any individualized program, we developed the Psychoeducational Profile, which also overcame some of the misunderstanding from the claims that these children were untestable. Figure 12–2 shows the test profile of a boy 4 years 10 months of age in the seven function areas across the top. It shows that this boy has peak skills in gross motor areas at about his chronological age. On the other hand, his receptive and expressive language skills are at approximately the 2-year level of development. This means that, for example, he can be taught to use a tricycle, but with simpler language than would be used with a 4-year-old, nonhandicapped child. The Psychoeducational Profile was extended by Gary Mesibov and colleagues to the adolescent and adult populations to help identify appropriate living situations and job placements.

Perhaps the major difference in my approach from the Bettelheim model can be seen in the statewide North Carolina service/research program that I initiated. This program for the Treatment and Education of Autistic and Communications Handicapped Children (TEACCH) was based on working with parents as co-therapists instead of viewing them as the cause of the disorder. The purpose was to enable such children to

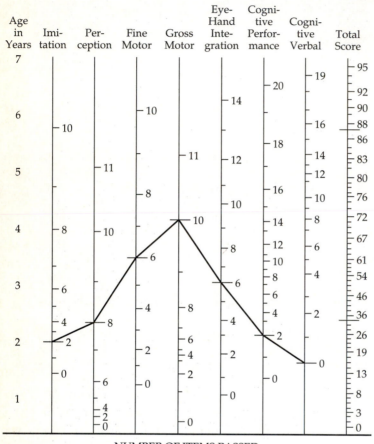

NAME   JOHN Q.

C.A.   4 years, 10 months

PSYCHOEDUCATIONAL PROFILE DEVELOPMENTAL FUNCTION SCORES

FIGURE 12. 2

Psychoeducational profile developmental function scores.

remain in the community and to attend public school instead of being removed to a residential treatment program. Our educational system is based on formal and informal assessments in which each child's skills and special interests are distinguished from his or her deficits. An educational program is then designed using environmental accommodations for the deficits of autism mentioned above. Individual programs building on existing and emerging skills are implemented. For example, the deficits of autism in auditory processing are overcome by compensating with the relative strengths in visual processing. Visual cues, schedules, and learning systems that can be carried over into adult vocational place-ments are used to increase adaptive functioning. Such teaching struc-tures provide accommodation to the autism deficits and foster indepen-dent functioning and skill development.

The TEACCH Program, located in the University of North Carolina School of Medicine, was committed to clinical service, relevant research, and multidisciplinary training. TEACCH was decentralized into six regional centers instead of being under the top-to-bottom control of one director. Collaboration between parents and clinic staff was extended to parents and teachers during years of public-school attendance and to supported employment and job coaches during the adult years. Outcome of treatment effectiveness was demonstrated by numerous empirical studies, and this program has now been implemented in many foreign countries.

CONCLUSION

For me and perhaps for the parents of autistic children, Bettelheim did play a useful role. When he blamed parents for their children's autism without evidence and with less ambiguity than any other psychoanalytic writer, his position was much easier to recognize as extreme. He enabled us to work with greater clarity toward correcting existing social neglect and misunderstanding of autism than would have been possible without him. For me, he demonstrated both the viability and positive contribu-tion potential of a negative role model.

SUGGESTED READINGS

BETTELHEIM, B. (1959). Feral children and autistic children. *American Journal of Sociology, 64,* 455.

_____(1967). *The empty fortress.* New York: Free Press.

GOLDFARB, W. (1956). Receptor preferences in schizophrenic children. *AMA Archives of Neurology and Psychiatry, 76,* 643–652.

KANNER, L. (1943). Autistic disturbance of affect contact. *Nervous Child, 2,* 217–230.

MESIBOV, G., SCHOPLER, E., SCHAFFER, B., & LANDRUS, R. (1988). *Individualized assessment and treatment for autistic and developmentally disabled children: Volume 4. Adolescent and adult psychoeducational profile (AAPEP).* Austin, TX: Pro-Ed.

RIMLAND, B. (1964). *Infantile autism.* New York: Appleton-Century-Crofts.

SCHOPLER, E. (1965). Early infantile autism and receptor processes. *Archives of General Psychiatry, 4,* 327–335.

_____(1971). Parents of psychotic children as scapegoats. *Journal of Contemporary Psychotherapy, 4,* 17–22.

————(1989). Principles for directing both educational treatment and research. In C. Gillberg (Ed.), *Diagnosis and treatment of autism* (pp. 167–183). New York: Plenum.

————BREHM, S., KINSBOURNE, M., & REICHLER, R.J. (1971). Effects of treatment structure on development in autistic children. *Archives of General Psychiatry, 24,* 415–421.

————& LOFTIN, J. (1969). Thought disorders in parents of psychotic children: A function of test anxiety. *Archives of General Psychiatry, 120,* 174–181.

————& MESIBOV, G. (1987). Introduction to neurobiological issues in autism. In E. Schopler & G. Mesibov (Eds.), *Neurobiological issues in autism* (pp. 3–11). New York: Plenum.

————, ————& BAKER, A. (1982). Evaluation of treatment for autistic children and their parents. *Journal of the American Academy of Child Psychiatry, 21,* 262–267.

————, ————SHIGLEY, R.H., BASHFORD, A.H. (1984). Helping autistic children through their parents: The TEACCH model. In E. Schopler & G.B. Mesibov (Eds.), *The effects of autism on the family* (pp. 65–81). New York: Plenum.

————& REICHLER, R.J. (1971). Parents as cotherapists in the treatment of psychotic children. *Journal of Autism and Childhood Schizophrenia, 1,* 87–102.

————, ————BASHFORD, A., LANSING, M., & MARCUS, L. (1990). *Individualized assessment and treatment for autistic and developmentally disabled children: Volume 1. Psychoeducational Profile revised (PEP-R).* Austin, TX: Pro-Ed.

————, ————& LANSING, M. (1980). *Individualized assessment and treatment for autistic and developmentally disabled children: Vol. 2. Teaching strategies for parents and professionals* (2d ed.). Austin, TX: Pro-Ed.

————, ————& RENNER, B.R. (1988). *The Childhood Autism Rating Scale (CARS),* Los Angeles, CA: Western Psychological Services.

SHORT, A. (1984). Short-term treatment outcome using parents as cotherapists for their own autistic children. *Journal of Child Psychology and Psychiatry and Allied Disciplines, 25,* 443–458.

DONALD MEICHENBAUM *(Ph.D., University of Illinois) is one of the founders of Cognitive Behavior Modification. He has written numerous articles and books, including* Cognitive Behavior Modification: An Integrative Approach, Coping With Stress, *and* Stress Inoculation Training. *He co-authored* Pain and Behavioral Medicine, Facilitating Treatment Adherence: A Practitioner's Guidebook, Stress Reduction and Prevention, *and* The Unconscious Reconsidered. *He is Associate Editor of* Cognitive Therapy and Research *and is on the editorial boards of a dozen journals. Editor of the Plenum Press series on Stress and Coping and currently Professor of Psychology at the University of Waterloo, Ontario, Canada, he is also a clinical psychologist in private practice. He has been a consultant for such groups as business organizations, psychiatric and medical hospitals, educational institutions, and institutions for adolescent offenders, and mental retardates. He is the father of four children which helps explain his continuing interest in the topics of stress and coping.*

13

The Personal Journey of a Psychotherapist and His Mother

❖

M y mother, who lives in New York City, recently came to Canada to visit. Here in Ontario I conduct research, teach clinical psychology, and see clients in psychotherapy. In her mid-seventies, she is still a vibrant person who continues to commute to work in mid-Manhattan. Whenever she visits she is full of stories about her daily adventures in the "Big Apple." Invariably, these anecdotal accounts cover incidents involving her work. On a recent occasion she related a common and somewhat prototypic account of a coworker who asked her to help move some files. As the story unfolded, my mother not only conveyed what had happened to her, but she also commented on how she felt and thought in complying with this request.

> "So, what should I say? I did what she asked. I'm a nice person. Who would know that the files would be so heavy and I could hurt my back?"
> "You lifted boxes?" I asked.
> "But that's not the worst," she responded. "I came back into the office and I found that Sadie, who asked me to help her, was gone. Now, I start getting angry—not with Sadie, but getting down on myself."

Interestingly, my mother's stories never seem to include mere descriptive accounts of what transpired. She also provides a running commentary evaluating her accompanying thoughts, feelings, and behaviors.

> "You know it's bad enough I lifted something that I shouldn't have. I decided I shouldn't get upset too. I noticed that I was working myself up. I caught myself and thought, look you've got choices. You don't have to get yourself down because you made a mistake."

189

As she was telling me her story, I realized that I had listened to such tales throughout my entire childhood and adolescence. I recalled that each evening at dinner we shared stories of what had happened to each of us and how we had handled these events. Our thoughts and feelings were part of the dinner menu. In addition, free of charge, my mother provided commentary about her thoughts as well as about those of others. She conveyed how we could "notice," "catch," "interrupt," "choose," different thoughts and behaviors. She was the indefatigable problem-solver.

In a moment of insight, I realized that my entire research career, which has been spent trying to understand and measure how adults and children think and how their thoughts influence their feelings and behavior, had its origins at my family's dinner table. My mother was an "undaunted psychologist," coping and teaching us to cope with the normal and not so normal perturbations of life. Perhaps this style was not unique to my mother and such procedures could be applied to those who are not coping well.

Such acts of talking to oneself come naturally to anyone from New York City. Given the common dangers of living in a large urban crime area, with high risks behind each corner, you quickly learn to talk to yourself. For example, when leaving a subway station or a bus station at night you are prone to talk to yourself (*covertly*, so you do not attract undue attention).

> "It's okay, I can make it to my apartment without getting mugged. Only two more blocks. Look at those guys on the corner. Hold on, I'll cross the street. I'll walk by those people. There is more light over there. . . . See, I made it!"

In order to further appreciate the pervasiveness of the phenomenon of talking to oneself, consider that I grew up close to where Woody Allen was raised. Anyone who has seen such Allen films as *Annie Hall, Hannah and Her Sisters,* and *Crimes and Misdemeanors* will recognize the frequent occurrence of his characters talking to themselves. In fact, I am convinced that somewhere along the way Woody Allen must have had dinner with my mother.

Each of us tends to talk to ourselves at times. Consider for instance someone who is learning to drive a car. At first, the novice driver goes through a mental checklist producing conscious, deliberate, intentional thoughts—"Adjust the seat, check the mirrors, buckle up, check oncoming traffic, pull out slowly," and so forth. With practice and with the development of proficiency the driving act becomes automated and the covert verbalizations (or inner dialogue) drop out of the repertoire. But, when the automaticity of the driving act is interrupted or blocked in some way (e.g., icy road conditions, the presence of a police car, etc.), the driver is once again likely to talk to himself or herself. Moreover, the content of one's thoughts can influence one's performance of the task.

Let us consider another example of when individuals may talk to themselves. Envision high- vs. low-test-anxiety students taking an examination. Halfway through the exam other students begin to hand in their exam papers. What do you think the "inner dialogue" of the high- and low-test-anxiety students is likely to be?

Research indicates that high-anxiety students are prone to view such an event as a personal threat, leading them to question their ability, to become self-preoccupied about possible failure, and to worry about future negative consequences. In contrast, the low-anxiety students are more likely to appraise the other students' handing in their exam papers early as a reflection that they don't know the material.

Similarly, when high and low socially anxious college students were asked to keep diaries of their thoughts during social interactions, very different patterns of "inner dialogue" emerged. The high socially anxious students were much more self-preoccupied, self-deprecatory, and negative in their internal dialogue than were the low socially anxious students.

In collaboration with my graduate students, I have spent the last twenty years struggling to understand how to measure and conceptualize such thought processes and their relationship to feelings on the one hand, and to behavior on the other hand. Moreover, could we develop psychotherapeutic procedures to help clients function more adaptively instead of being incapacitated by their anxiety, depression, anger, or general stress? Could we teach clients not only to talk to themselves differently, but also to behave and feel in a more adaptive fashion?

This personal-research journey began in a Veteran's Administration (VA) hospital in a small rural Illinois community. Leaving the confines of New York, I attended graduate school at the University of Illinois, in Champaign, Illinois, and I had a clinical internship at the nearby VA hospital. There I became very interested in the thinking processes of psychiatric patients who were diagnosed schizophrenic. I was interested in the schizophrenics' thinking and language patterns, in particular, their wandering attention, their literal interpretation of requests, and their loose associative thinking. For instance, when a schizophrenic is asked to interpret proverbs such as "Don't cry over spilled milk," he may respond in a literal fashion, by saying, "Don't drink milk, you may spill it!" When asked to interpret the proverb, "The grass is always greener on the other side of the fence," the schizophrenic may provide a personalized response such as, "Grass, I am allergic to grass," and then provide clang associations such as "Grass, ass, mass, . . . like at church where the grass is greener." I became fascinated with what contributed to such "cognitive slippage," as it is colloquially called, and moreover, what could be done to help schizophrenics change their behavior.

Some suggestions of what could be done to help schizophrenics were offered by the research on social communication conducted by Bertram Cohen and his colleagues. They found that schizophrenics evidence a deficit in their ability to notice, monitor, and edit their thought processes. Under most conditions, when we notice that our attention is waning, when our thoughts are drifting, when our speech is becoming too literal, too idiosyncratic, or too tangential so that others cannot follow what we are saying, we catch ourselves and engage in "repair operations." We might say to others (or to ourselves), "Hold on, I lost my train of thought for a moment," or "Oh, let me explain that again." Moreover, we also have the ability to plan and edit what we will say before we say it, and monitor our own and others' comprehension as we speak. Cohen's research suggested that schizophrenics were less likely to engage in such cognitive self-regulatory processes.

My initial research efforts in graduate school were designed to determine if schizophrenics could be taught how to monitor, control, and edit their thoughts and language. The training involved direct instruction, modeling, encouragement, and social reinforcement. The training, indeed, proved successful in fostering such self-control skills in schizophrenics. This was evident when several schizophrenics were observed to spontaneously talk to themselves, instructing themselves to "give healthy talk," "pay attention," "make sense," and the like. Somehow the schizophrenics had taken the interpersonal instructions and turned them into private speech to guide and control their behaviors.

As a follow-up study, in collaboration with Roy Cameron, we decided to try to explicitly teach schizophrenics to "talk to themselves" in a self-controlling fashion. By means of direct instruction, modeling, and rehearsal with feedback, we taught schizophrenics how to notice, catch, and interrupt episodes of "cognitive slippage," and how to monitor and edit what they said to others. What we were trying to achieve in training paralleled what the psychiatrist John Strauss had reported for some schizophrenic patients. When interviewed by Strauss, schizophrenic patients reported that they could often notice, at least a week ahead of time, that they might be having a psychotic episode coming on (or what is technically called, "noticing prodromal cues"). Moreover, they also reported that they would often engage in a number of coping efforts such as withdrawing from demanding situations or they would talk to themselves in a self-controlling coping fashion. Thus, the techniques that we included in our training paradigm simulated what some schizophrenic patients were doing naturally.

However, when I left Illinois for a teaching position at the University of Waterloo in Ontario, Canada, I did not have immediate access to a population of adult psychiatric patients. Instead, I was confronted with the clinical challenge of working with impulsive and hyperactive children. These children have difficulties with self-control. As the Canadian psychologist Virginia Douglas observed, these hyperactive children lack the ability to "stop, look, and listen," or as another psychologist Russell Barkley later observed, they evidence a "self-regulatory deficit," a difficulty following instructions, especially when those instructions must sustain their behavior over a period of time, and when there is little or no continual feedback. For instance, in school, where these children have the most difficulty, teachers frequently give instructions to the class that are supposed to guide and control the students' behaviors over a prolonged period of time. "Okay class, now let's get out our workbooks and work quietly." Such teacher instructions have less guiding and controlling influence for hyperactive children. Moreover, research findings indicate that such impulsive children infrequently plan, monitor, self-interrogate, or constructively self-evaluate (learn from failures).

Perhaps such impulsive children could also benefit from self-instructional training, learning to talk to themselves in a self-controlling fashion. But how should such a training program be conducted? Some suggestions came from two Russian psychologists, Lev Vygotsky and his student A. R. Luria. They both had proposed that children become socialized and develop higher mental functioning as a result of social interactions. They proposed that children respond initially to the directives of others, and that in turn, in an abbreviated and transformed manner, they "internalize" interpersonal speech in the form of self-speech. With practice the child's speech, to use Vygotsky's term, "goes underground" and becomes private speech.

An example from one of my children conveys the developmental sequence that Vygotsky had in mind. My two-year-old son, David, had a yen for eating apples, which my wife and I readily satisfied. The only problem was that he disliked apple skins and he was given to spitting them onto the floor. In fact, when I came home from the office I felt like the woodsmen in Hansel and Gretel following the path of . . . apple skins. So I said, "See David, apple skins, dirty. I pick up the skins and throw them into the garbage can and not on the floor."

At this point David would usually applaud my nightly performance. An interesting event occurred, however, one day when my wife took David to the beauty parlor with her. In order to keep David busy she brought along some apples for him. As expected, once again David began to spit the skins on the floor, at which point my wife said, "David, no, dirty. See, the skins go in the ashtray."

Note, my wife was more influenced by my cognitive modeling than was my young son. What happened next is the reason for this anecdote.

David once again took a bite of the apple, chewed on it, and then dropped the skin on the floor. But this time he looked down at the skin and said, "Bappy . . . door . . . all done"; then retrieved the skin and put it in the ashtray (one that you had to press a button to open). Once again, "Bappy . . . door . . . all done," followed by a second retrieval.

In order to understand this statement you need to know that "Bappy" was David's word for anything that was dirty; "door" was his word for the concept open, as in the case of opening the top of the ashtray; and "all done" was "all done." Thus, David took a complex interpersonal instruction: "Now, David dear, we don't drop things on the floor, that is dirty. Instead, we bend down, retrieve what we have dropped, find an appropriate receptacle, place it there, and even congratulate ourselves for having done so." Now, if you were going to send a telegram and you wished to conserve words, what you might say is, "Bappy . . . door . . . all done."

In this case, David was able to extract the meaning of the interpersonal instructions, and then transform the message into his own abbreviated private speech. In turn, these verbalizations came to guide and control his behavior. With repeated trials the private speech dropped out of the repertoire and his apple skin dropping behavior stopped.

This process is similar to a parent warning a young child, by saying, "No, don't touch, hot!" In turn, one can see the child later admonishing himself, "Hot, hot!" and then restrain himself.

It is exactly this process of internalization that Vygotsky had in mind. This developmental sequence suggested a possible training paradigm to help impulsive, hyperactive children develop self-control. Consistent with Vygotsky's and Luria's model, we developed an intervention program that included a trainer working on a one-on-one basis with an impulsive child. The trainer would perform a task (e.g., a puzzle task) while talking out loud to himself:

> What am I supposed to do? Okay, go slowly. Think ahead, what do I have to do first? . . . Good, that's it. . . . No, don't go too fast. . . . Good, I did it.

Following such cognitive modeling the child was given the opportunity to do the same task while given instructions by the trainer; then while talking aloud to him or herself; then while whispering to him or herself; and then without overt speech. With practice, the child's speech, to use Vygotsky's term, "went underground."

In our first study, impulsive children were successfully taught to talk to themselves in a self-controlling fashion. Since our initial study, there have been more than 5,000 self-instructional training studies reported in the literature with a wide variety of child, adolescent, and adult populations—including retarded and learning-disabled children, adolescents who have problems controlling their temper, and adults who are phobic, anxious, or schizophrenic. The results of these studies indicated that individuals can be taught cognitive strategies (e.g., how to specify goals, plan, monitor, check) and that such training can affect their performance.

The cognitive skills that my mother had shared at the dinner table could be applied to a variety of diverse clinical populations.

*D*EVELOPING COGNITIVE-ASSESSMENT PROCEDURES

The research challenge was not only to develop such training programs, but to more adequately *assess individuals' cognitions* and to determine how such "inner speech" is related both to an individual's feelings and to his or her behavior. We next employed a number of different assessment approaches to determine what people say to themselves. Let us briefly consider the variety of tools available to tap your "internal dialogue."

Not everyone is as public with his or her internal dialogue as is my mother. Since cognitions are not directly observable, we have employed a variety of ways to assess an individual's internal dialogue, or what are called automatic thoughts. The following list of assessment procedures conveys some of the ways psychologists tap an individual's inner dialogue.

- Interviews—in an open-ended interview, subjects are asked explicitly what they were thinking when doing a particular task.
- Thought listing—subjects are asked to list specific thoughts they may have had while performing a specific task.
- Videotape reconstruction—subjects are asked to watch themselves on a videotape following their performing a specific task or behaving in a certain situation. The videotape is used as a cue reminder to help subjects reconstruct what they were thinking. This assessment procedure can also use imagery reconstruction procedures, where subjects visualize a specific recent incident and report on their accompanying thoughts and feelings.
- Questionnaires—subjects are asked to fill out questionnaires that list various thoughts they might have had, indicating whether they had had each thought and noting how frequently.
- Think aloud—while doing a specific task, subjects are asked to think out loud, verbalizing each and every thought they have.
- Thought sampling—subjects are asked to carry a beeper with them; during the day, when the beeper goes off, they record their immediate thoughts.
- Verbal discourse to either oneself or to others—observers record and analyze what people, especially children, spontaneously say to themselves, in the form of private speech, as in the case of my son David. Although, one should not equate speech with thought, both social and self-discourse provide a "window" to infer the nature of

an individual's mental processes (e.g., planning, monitoring, evaluating, elaborating).

- Infer cognitive processes from performance on tasks such as those
based on an analysis of the errors that are made. For example, if a
child makes specific repetitive errors in math, then one can infer
what cognitive features are absent.

In short, there are a number of diverse ways to tap the nature of an
individual's "inner dialogue." We have used these assessment procedures to study a variety of diverse populations, such as high- and low-
anxious individuals, depressed and nondepressed clients, subjects who
can and cannot cope with physical pain, novices and experts while performing various tasks, impulsive and nonimpulsive children, and others.

Illustrative of this work are the findings on high- and low-anxiety
individuals in evaluative situations. The cognitions of high-anxiety
individuals, using various assessment procedures, indicate that they
tend to have self-preoccupying thoughts, which result in lowered levels
of performance. Their inner dialogue or automatic thoughts are
marked by a sense of inadequacy and self-deprecation, an anticipation
and expectation of failures, and a marked concern about the possible loss
of regard by others. Task-irrelevant intrusive thoughts that focus attention on themselves, rather than on the task, characterize high-anxiety
individuals.

We discovered, however, that all individuals have some negative
thoughts at some time. It was not the mere presence or absence of negative ideation per se, but rather the ratio of negative to positive thoughts
that characterizes those individuals who have difficulty coping. For
example, Robert Schwartz reported that highly anxious individuals have
a 2 to 1 ratio of negative to positive ideation, as compared to the opposite
ratio for those who are low-anxious.

But our research indicated that the relationship between thoughts
and feelings is complex. Feelings can affect thoughts just as readily as
thoughts can influence feelings. For instance, when individuals feel anxious or depressed, this influences what they attend to concerning their
past and future, as well as the present. When we feel anxious, we tend to
become preoccupied with concerns about the loss of personal control
and possible bodily harm. When we are depressed, we tend to focus on
other negative events, namely failures, disappointments, and the like.
Our "emotional antennae" are out and this colors how we see things and
how we appraise our ability to cope. In short, our research highlighted
the fact that thoughts and feelings are two sides of the same coin, bidi-
rectionally influencing each other.

Putting aside for the moment my laboratory-research hat and
putting on my clinical hat, a case study illustrates the complex interrela-
tionship between thoughts, feelings, and behaviors. Consider a patient, a

lawyer, I treated for several months for severe problems with anxiety, as well as anger and depression. This gentleman reported innumerable examples of when he felt people had tried to "take advantage of him" (e.g., a waiter who gave him the wrong change or his children's lack of appreciation for what he had done for them). These events triggered his anger and when his "fuse" was lit, it was very difficult for him to interrupt and reduce his anger and accompanying negative feelings. His personal concerns about fairness, equity, and justice were pervasive and this led not only to anger, but on some occasions they led to verbal and physical aggression.

A bit of background may help explain how this client's emotional problems developed. He was the only child of an immigrant father whom he felt was "taken advantage of" by others. As he observed, "no one, but no one was going to take advantage of him like they had done to his father." As a result of these past experiences, this patient had a tendency to perceive injustices, even in ambiguous and uncertain situations. He would rarely entertain any other explanations for what had transpired. For example, a simple error such as receiving the wrong change from a waiter could trigger anger since it was viewed as an intentional effort to "try and take advantage of him." He had a prepotent tendency, a set of "perceptual blinders," that colored the ways in which he viewed his world, his past, and his future.

Moreover, his aggressive, distrusting behavior toward others "pulled" reactive aggressive responses from others. Thus, his aggressive interpersonal style inadvertently helped to create the counteraggressive reactions in others that he complained about. His thoughts and fears became self-fulfilling prophecies. As a result, he could continually point to others' reactions that invariably confirmed his views of himself and the world (evidence to confirm his beliefs). He also tended to interpret ambiguous events as fitting his view that others were out "to take advantage of him." He failed to appreciate, however, how his thoughts, feelings, and interpersonal style contributed, inadvertently, to the very concerns that he complained about.

Interestingly, his developmental concerns about fairness, equity, and justice not only contributed to him having a "shorter fuse" than most, and to more-frequent explosive episodes, but they also contributed to his engaging in "altruistic behaviors." For instance, he was very active in working for Amnesty International (a worldwide organization that fights for freedom and justice). He also took on legal cases of principle that other lawyers would not touch. Thus, while his preoccupation with fairness, equity, and justice contributed to his anger and aggression problems, it also led to his altruistic behaviors.

We each may have similar concerns about justice, fairness, and equity, but they do *not* result in our developing problems with anger and aggression. What is different about this lawyer? For him, these issues

became a predominant life theme or personal prejudice that totally colored the way in which he viewed himself and the world. As a result of
carrying this conceptual and perceptual prism, the client paid a very
high price interpersonally (loss of friends, broken marriage), intraperson-
ally (constant feelings of anger and often accompanying feelings of anxiety and depression), and physiologically (hypertension and headaches).
Thus, the client's beliefs and developmental concerns about fairness,
equity, and justice influenced how he appraised events, how he felt, and
how he behaved. Moreover, how he felt (e.g., vulnerable, helpless, and
hopeless) accentuated his primary "core concerns." This, in turn, contributed to his behaving in a more aggressive fashion that "pulled" coun-
teraggression from others. In turn, such reactions from others provided
data to (re)confirm his beliefs about both the world and his perceived
dismal future. In this way, a "vicious cycle" became self-perpetuating
and self-debilitating.

We have spent the last twenty years of research trying to accurately
describe these interactive processes and to develop treatment programs
that can reverse this pattern. We have worked on the development of a
set of psychotherapeutic procedures called *cognitive behavior modification*
that are designed to help people recognize, interrupt, and understand
how such patterns developed and are maintained. We work collabora-
tively with clients to help them develop and practice producing different, more adaptive, behavioral patterns.

TOWARD THE DEVELOPMENT OF PSYCHOTHERAPEUTIC PROCEDURES

Psychiatry and psychology have made great strides in helping clients
break self-perpetuating maladaptive cycles, whether they involve problems with anxiety, anger, or depression. In our clinic we have been working on a series of cognitive-behavioral-therapy procedures designed to
help patients to:

- Become aware of the complex interrelationships between their
  thoughts, feelings, and behavior.
- Appreciate the intrapersonal and interpersonal impact of their
  thoughts (beliefs, expectations, attributions, thinking style) on their
  feelings and behavior and vice versa, as well as on others.
- Recognize that how they behave may inadvertently exacerbate
  their problems.
- Break presenting problems into smaller, manageable problems.
- Notice, interrupt, and change the ways they think, feel, and
  behave.

- Personally experiment in behaving differently, starting off slowly and then undertaking more demanding challenges.
- Anticipate possible failures along the way and to view such failures, if they should occur, as learning occasions (as in the case of someone who learns to ride a bike and who occasionally falls).
- Take credit for personal successes.
- Accept the results of their personal experiments (i.e., the data) as evidence to "unfreeze" the beliefs they hold.
- Understand how such concerns or issues developed and the intrapersonal and interpersonal price they pay for holding such beliefs.
- Begin to entertain and to exercise incompatible beliefs, or views of themselves and the world, and to have the courage to perform personal experiments in order to try out these new beliefs (e.g., that the world is not against them).
- Learn to talk to themselves differently before, during, and after situations that previously elicited negative stressful reactions.
- Have these more-adaptive coping styles become habitual in nature, or automatic, so they don't even have to think about their coping efforts.

The following clinical case example illustrates how these psychotherapeutic procedures are employed. A major clinical population that receives psychiatric treatment includes those individuals who report problems with anxiety. In fact, anxiety disorders are the largest single group of mental disorders. One particular form of anxiety problem is called panic disorders, and it affects some 12-million individuals in the United States. Recent research has indicated that the cognitive-behavioral procedures that we have been working on are particularly effective with individuals who experience panic attacks. Consider the case of Cindy, a 35-year-old secretary who reported a history of panic attacks. As she observed, "My heart races. I can't catch my breath. I feel like I am going to faint. I get hot and cold flashes. I sweat and shiver all over. I feel I am going crazy or as if I am going to die."

Medical tests indicated that there were no physical reasons for Cindy's condition. She was experiencing panic attacks, a form of anxiety disorder. David Barlow, a psychologist at the State University of New York at Albany and his colleagues, as well as the psychiatrist Aaron Beck, who is at the Center of Cognitive Therapy in Philadelphia, have been pioneers in developing effective cognitive-behavioral psychotherapeutic procedures to help patients like Cindy. Following their lead I worked with Cindy to help her to better understand the nature of her anxiety and panic. In a collaborative fashion, we worked on Cindy's collecting information (data) about herself, in the form of self-monitoring.

She was asked to keep track of her feelings of anxiety and any accompanying thoughts, as well as noting the specific situations in which such anxious feelings arose. In this way she could discover that her thoughts (e.g., "I'm going to panic. I can't handle this, I'll fall apart. I'm losing control."), her accompanying hyperventilation (i.e., heavy, deep, rapid breathing), and her accompanying feelings (e.g., apprehension, loss of control, anxiety, depression), all contributed to and exacerbated her panic attacks. As we traced the situations in which she experienced panic attacks, we identified common triggering events (e.g., situations in which she might be evaluated). She also became aware of how her tendency to "stuff down her feelings," as she described it, and not express them contributed to her vulnerability to panic attacks. Moreover, she came to recognize that she tended to focus her attention on her bodily cues, and that she often misinterpreted these feelings, viewing her so-called stuffed feelings as a sign that she was about to lose control and to have a panic attack. This self-appraisal would further contribute to her hyperventilating, which in fact, contributed to some of the bodily changes she reported (e.g., dizziness, hot and cold flashes, and the like). As she described it, she would then "catastrophize" (blow things out of proportion), which in turn would cause her to hyperventilate more, and thus, the "vicious cycle" of thoughts, feelings, hyperventilation, would escalate into a panic attack.

In therapy, Cindy learned how to relax as she practiced breathing control in order to manage her hyperventilation. She also developed coping self-statements that she could say to herself to control her thoughts when she noticed the onset of panic episodes. She was able to practice these coping skills both within the therapy sessions (e.g., while doing strenuous exercises that simulated panic symptoms) and in her everyday experiences (e.g., while shopping in crowded stores, while giving a public speech).

In addition, cognitive restructuring procedures were used whereby Cindy learned to question herself about the conclusions she was prone to draw about herself. She learned how to question how she appraised events. As a result of therapy, Cindy was more likely to ask herself, "Are my views of myself accurate? Let me check them out. If I share my feelings and tell others how I feel instead of stuffing them down will I be rejected?"

She also learned to consider alternative explanations for events that happened to her. For instance, she learned to ask herself, "How else can I explain his reactions, instead of taking them so personally? What other possible explanations are there for what happened?"

In addition to *considering the evidence* that did and that did not fit her views of herself, as well as considering *possible alternative explanations* for what happens to her, Cindy also learned to *reconsider the implications* that she would draw from events. Cindy came to ask herself, "Even if the events are true, does it necessarily imply everything that it first seemed to imply? Is it as bad as I am making it out to be?" As Cindy learned and practiced these behavioral and cognitive skills, she no longer had panic attacks and she became a more open and secure person.

THE RESEARCH AGENDA

In the last decade, a number of cognitive-behavioral therapists have demonstrated that employing such psychotherapeutic procedures can help people who are not only anxious, but also those who are depressed, angry, indecisive, stressed, as well as those who experience both marital and familial conflict. In some instances, these cognitive-behavioral procedures need to be supplemented by medication, or by the involvement of significant others (spouses, teachers, peers), or by environmental changes (e.g., how an organization can be changed in order to reduce stress).

The initial results from this psychotherapeutic research have been quite encouraging, but *not* yet fully proven. There are no "quick" fixes to the complex problems of living that clients bring to psychotherapy. As psychotherapists, we remain undaunted by the research challenges that lie ahead. We are confronted by such questions as: How can we better understand the nature of the distress that our clients present? How can we make our treatments more effective so they lead to longer lasting and generalized improvement?

In our attempt to answer these questions we are likely to talk to ourselves. But my mother would have expected no less.

SUGGESTED READINGS

BARLOW, D., & CERNY, J. (1988). *Psychological treatment of panic.* New York: Guilford.

BECK, A. T., RUSH, A. J., SHAW, B. F., & EMERY, G. (1979). *Cognitive therapy of depression.* New York: Guilford.

DODGE, K. (1986). A social information processing model of social competence in children. In M. Perlmutter (Ed.), *Cognitive perspectives on children's social and behavioral development* (pp. 77–125). Hillsdale, NJ: Erlbaum.

MEICHENBAUM, D. (1977). *Cognitive behavior modification: An integrative approach.* New York: Plenum.

———(1985). *Stress inoculation training: A practitioner's guidebook.* New York: Pergamon.

PATTERSON, G. R., REID, J. B., JONES, R. R., & CONGER, R. E. (1975). *A social learning approach to family intervention, Vol. 1.* Eugene, OR: Castalia.

ROBERT **A.** **B**ARON *(Ph.D., University of Iowa) is currently Professor and Chair of the Department of Managerial Policy and Organization and Professor of Psychology at Rensselaer Polytechnic Institute. He is a Fellow of the American Psychological Association and has received numerous awards for teaching excellence. Professor Baron has published more than eighty articles in professional journals and twenty invited chapters. He has served on the editorial boards of numerous journals and is currently an associate editor for* Aggressive Behavior *and* The International Journal of Conflict Management. *He is the author or co-author of twenty-one books, including* Social Psychology, Organizational Behavior, Understanding Human Relations, *and* Human Aggression. *At present, Professor Baron's major research interests focus on applying the principles and findings of psychology to behavior in work settings. Professor Baron has long been a runner; his hobbies include woodworking, enjoying fine food, and music.*

14

Reducing Aggression and Conflict

The Incompatible Response Approach, or, Why People Who Feel Good Usually Won't Be Bad

❖

*I*t was 1967, and I was hard at work on my doctoral dissertation when I first heard about the *aggression machine* developed by Arnold Buss. I had always found the topic of human aggression fascinating, so my first thought was: "Wow, imagine that—a device for measuring aggression! Why didn't someone tell me about this sooner?" So, I knew right away that I had found my niche. I wanted to study human aggression. I couldn't wait to finish my dissertation so that I could get started.

When I received my degree and found my first job at the University of South Carolina, I set about building an aggression machine. It wasn't easy. I knew a little electronics, but not much. And this was 1968—a time when, by today's standards, available equipment was quite primitive. But soon I found the help I needed when an undergraduate electrical-engineering student agreed to assist me. So, in a matter of a few months, there it sat: my own device for measuring aggression. It wasn't very complex, just two boxes, and yet it seemed pretty effective. One box consisted of a row of switches with a light above each one (see Figure 14–1). The second box, which would be placed in another room, had lights corresponding to each of the buttons on the first box. Subjects were told that they were participating in a study concerned with the effects of punishment on learning. Each time the learner (actually my assistant) made an error on a simple learning task, they would deliver an electric shock to this individual by pushing one of the buttons. The higher the button, the stronger the shock; and the longer they held it down, the longer the shock would last. Of course, the supposed "vic-

FIGURE 14.1
The aggression machine.

tim" never received *any* shocks. But as long as subjects believed this story, it seemed reasonable to argue that whenever they used shocks above the weakest one or two, they were engaging in aggression: they were actively choosing to harm another person when, in fact, such behavior was not necessary. The higher the buttons they pushed, and the longer they held them depressed, the greater their overall level of aggression.

Now that I had an aggression machine, I wasted no time in getting started. I began by conducting studies on the effects of exposure to aggressive and nonaggressive models. Would subjects' aggression be influenced by the actions of another person who pushed uniformly high or low buttons? The answer was quickly apparent: they would. Those who watched another person (an assistant) push uniformly high buttons chose higher ones themselves, and pushed them for longer periods of time, than subjects who saw no model. And those who watched another person push uniformly low buttons chose lower ones than subjects in a control group who saw no model prior to their own opportunity to aggress. So, modeling did appear to work where aggression was concerned.

Then I turned my attention to environmental conditions. Would people exposed to high temperatures be more aggressive than those exposed to comfortable ones? Here, results were surprising: at first, aggression *did* increase as temperature rose (e.g., from the 70s to the 80s Fahrenheit). But then, as temperature increased still farther (into the 90s), aggression actually decreased. Why? Further studies suggested one possible answer: when temperatures were extremely high (in the mid-90s), subjects were so uncomfortable that they concentrated on getting out of the study, and out of my overheated laboratory. Thus, they chose to act in a noncontroversial manner, by directing weak shocks against the victim.

While conducting these and other studies, I soon became quite adept at making people angry. After all, to study aggression it's necessary to make people angry. In the absence of such feelings, choosing high buttons on the aggression machine might be explained by subjects' desire to help the assistant learn, *not* by any motive to hurt him in some manner. So, I devised several techniques for angering my subjects. In one of these procedures, subjects overheard the assistant making derogatory remarks about them. In another, they received evaluations of essays they had written that were either favorable (the no-anger condition) or harsh and sarcastic (the anger condition). Whatever technique I used, subjects who had been angered generally pushed higher buttons on the aggression machine, and for longer periods of time, than those who had not been angered. Here, in short, was further evidence that the machine was indeed measuring something akin to anger and the desire to hurt another person.

As I carried out these initial research projects, however, my attention was drawn repeatedly to a basic question: What techniques and procedures would prove useful in reducing aggression? Certainly, we knew very well how to provoke aggression; this proved to be a fairly easy task. But how could such behavior be reduced or deterred? Psychology offered only two major answers. Aggression, it was maintained, could be deterred through punishment or through catharsis. Punishment referred to instances in which perpetrators of aggression received negative consequences for their aggressive acts. Catharsis referred to the idea that permitting angry persons to "release" their anger in safe, nonharmful ways would drain the motivation behind aggression, and so reduce such behavior. While both techniques were supported by some evidence, it was clear that neither was highly effective.

Growing evidence suggested that in order for punishment to succeed in deterring aggression, certain conditions must be met. To be effective, punishment should be swift, certain, and intense. It is precisely these conditions that are missing from the legal systems of most nations. When individuals commit violent crimes they are not always apprehended, and if they are, they are not always punished for their crimes. Finally, even if they are, such punishment may occur months or even years after the crime, because of the slowness with which our criminal justice system often operates. So, punishment, it appeared, had important limitations as a means of deterring violence. It could, in theory, work, but conditions in the real world seemed to operate against its being very effective.

Catharsis, too, seemed to suffer some important drawbacks. Yes, it seemed that when angry individuals engage in vigorous nonaggressive actions (e.g., strenuous exercise), they feel less angry and experience reductions in the tendency to aggress. But how long do such reductions last? Existing evidence provided a discouraging answer: only for relatively short periods of time. Human beings have long memories, and they are highly accomplished at bringing unpleasant, anger-provoking scenes to mind. Faced with vivid images of real or imagined wrongs at the hands of others, anger is quickly re-established, and the probability of aggression rises once again. Further, findings indicated that after being angered by others, individuals often dwell on "evening the score." This can only be accomplished through some harm to the person who annoyed them. Attacks against punching bags, inflated toys, or other inanimate objects may cause them to feel better (less tense or irritated) temporarily, but they do not produce lasting reductions in the desire to repay the original targets of anger.

So, while punishment and catharsis are both effective in deterring aggression in some instances, they do not, on close scrutiny, appear to be the all-powerful and all-effective means of accomplishing this goal that existing texts and popular opinion suggest. This conclusion set me to thinking about what other techniques might be more effective in reducing aggression. One possibility gradually began to emerge. As a graduate student, I had taken several courses in which the notion of response incompatibility had been considered. One of these courses was concerned with internal conflicts, and focused on the fact that often individuals find themselves in situations where they have competing tendencies to perform—or avoid—different behaviors. For example, a rat that receives electric shocks at the place where it finds food will develop a strong tendency to approach and avoid the same spot (after all, it has received painful jolts in this place). Animals faced with this predicament can sometimes be observed running toward the food cup, screeching to a halt, reversing their direction, and then, when far enough away from the source of food, reversing direction once again. Human beings often find themselves in situations that are similar in structure if not specific content. Should they reach for that piece of chocolate cake? It's enticing, but they *are* on a diet! Should they go to the movies instead of studying? The movie will be fun, but there is that test in two days. . . .

I also learned about incompatible responses, and their effects, in a course on clinical psychology. Here, I read that in order to treat certain kinds of phobias (intense irrational fears), some clinicians trained individuals in techniques for inducing feelings of relaxation—for example, procedures for relaxing their own muscles. Once these techniques were mastered, clients were asked to imagine scenes or events that made them fearful and then put their relaxation techniques into effect. The result: feelings of relaxation were incompatible with feelings of fear, so their fears were weakened.

I began to formulate an interesting working hypothesis: perhaps aggression, too, could be reduced by incompatible responses. I wondered whether feelings of anger and overt tendencies to aggress against others could be reduced by exposing individuals to stimuli or events that induced feelings incompatible with anger and aggression. While this was an intriguing idea, little did I suspect that I would spend the next twenty years investigating it, and its implications, in various ways!

THE INCOMPATIBLE RESPONSE HYPOTHESIS: INITIAL TESTS

What feelings, precisely, might prove incompatible with anger and aggression? Several possibilities were suggested by existing evidence about aggression and my own personal experience. Among these, two seemed most promising: empathy and humor.

Empathy: Responses to the Pain and Suffering of Others

When human beings aggress against others, they often witness pain and suffering on the part of their victims. When aggression is successful in reaching its intended goal (inflicting some form of pain), those on the receiving end of such assaults demonstrate their discomfort in a variety of ways, including groans and facial contortions. What reactions will aggressors have to such responses? Two contrasting patterns seemed likely. First, when aggressors are extremely angry and believe that their aggression is justified, exposure to such *pain cues* might be reinforcing. After all, the suffering of my enemy *is* sometimes pleasant to behold! In such cases, witnessing the discomfort of others would probably fail to deter subsequent aggression and might, at least initially, increase it.

In contrast, when aggressors are not very angry, or when they perceive that the scales have been balanced, a different reaction might occur. In fact, under such circumstances, aggressors might actually experience empathy toward their victims, sharing, vicariously, the discomfort experienced by these persons. And even if full-scale empathy did not occur, aggressors might well experience sympathy for their victims. They might, in short, feel sorry for these persons. Such reactions—empathy or sympathy—might serve to deter aggression; feeling sorry for a victim or sharing her or his pain vicariously would be incompatible with anger and acts of aggression. So, it seemed possible that signs of pain or suffering on the part of a victim would reduce aggression when aggressors had not been strongly provoked, but would actually increase it when they had been strongly angered.

How could this prediction be tested by means of the aggression machine? One approach would involve exposing subjects to signs of pain on the part of the supposed victim. Since this person was not actually receiving any shocks, however, these reactions would necessarily be "faked" ones. When I tried to train persons working with me on my research to demonstrate such cues in a consistent manner, I quickly discovered that this was difficult. They were not, after all, trained actors! The wide variability in their "performances" was unacceptable in experimental research.

I puzzled over this issue for a while and then, one day, it hit me: if we already had an aggression machine, why not invent a pain meter—a device that would show—by readings on a meter—the amount of pain experienced by the victim? Such a meter is, of course, impossible; pain is a subjective reaction, and even today, psychologists do not have probes that can detect, and accurately read, such states. But this didn't stop me: I simply constructed the device shown in Figure 14–2. Through a series of buttons, I could control the readings shown on the pain meter. In this way, subjects could be exposed to any level of supposed pain on the part of the assistant that I wished.

Now it was a relatively simple task to investigate the impact of pain cues on subsequent aggression. In a series of studies, I exposed some subjects to very high pain cues; whatever buttons they pushed on the aggression machine, the pain meter reported that the victim was experiencing intense pain. Other subjects, in contrast, were exposed to weak pain cues. Even when they pushed highly numbered buttons on the aggression machine, the victim seemed to experience only fairly mild pain.

To test the hypothesis that individuals who had been strongly angered would react to pain cues with increased aggression while those who had not been angered would respond with reduced aggression, I conducted a study in which half the participants were angered (through verbal insults) and half were not angered. Within each of these conditions, half received pain cues indicating the victim's discomfort each time they delivered a shock to this person. The remainder did not receive such information. Subjects who had not been angered responded to pain cues with reduced aggression. Those who had been strongly angered actually responded to such information with increased aggression. Moreover, further evidence indicated that these contrasting reactions were indeed mediated by subjects' emotional states. Those who had been angered reported feeling happier and more relaxed in the presence of

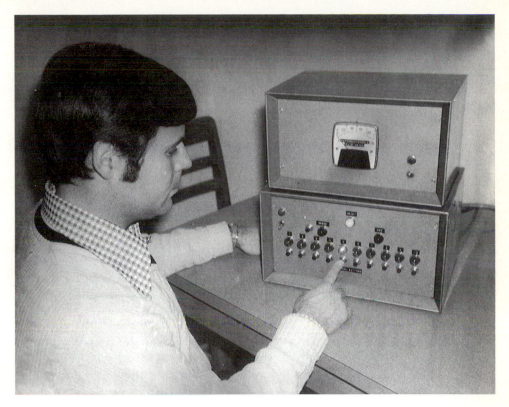

FIGURE 14.2
The pain meter.

pain cues than in their absence. Those who had not been angered reported feeling less happy and more tense in response to such stimuli.

Humor: Where Aggression Is Concerned, Laughter May Indeed Be Good Medicine

Have you ever had the following experience? You feel annoyed or irritated with someone. Then, unexpectedly, they do or say something that
makes you smile. When that happens, your annoyance—or at least a substantial part of it—seems to vanish. My own experience has led me to
conclude that humor may be another reaction that is incompatible with
feelings of anger or aggression. This seemed like such a reasonable
notion that I turned to the existing literature on humor, fully expecting to
find that this idea had been tested before. Much to my surprise, however,
I found that it had never been tested. Instead, most investigations of

humor had focused on very different aspects of this uniquely human reaction. I decided to conduct a series of studies designed to determine whether exposure to humor could indeed reduce the intensity of aggression on the part of previously angered persons.

The first of these studies was quite straightforward. Participants were either angered or not angered and then, before having an opportunity to aggress against another person by means of the aggression machine, were asked to examine either humorous cartoons (e.g.: Two roaches are shown walking along a library shelf. One turns and remarks to the other: "I've always found Freud a little tough to swallow.") or neutral pictures of scenery, furniture, and abstract art. As predicted, angry subjects who examined the humorous cartoons showed lower aggression against the assistant than those who examined the neutral (nonhumorous) pictures.

Around the time that I conducted this experiment, however, other research was being published that seemed, at first glance, to demonstrate opposite results. In these investigations, Leonard Berkowitz found that subjects exposed to humorous materials actually showed higher levels of aggression than those exposed to neutral materials. What could account for this discrepancy? The answer seemed clear: in his studies, the humor contained hostile or aggressive themes, such as one person "putting down" another. In my study the humor was just plain silly; little or no hostility was present. So, it seemed that hostile humor might actually increase aggression.

To test this hypothesis, I conducted several additional studies in which subjects were exposed to different types of humor. Subjects viewed either hostile humor (cartoons with an aggressive edge), nonhostile humor (cartoons that were merely silly in nature), or sexual humor (cartoons with sexual content). Results were fairly clear: hostile humor did indeed increase aggression relative to conditions in which subjects viewed neutral materials. However, both nonhostile humor and sexual humor reduced aggression. Interestingly, an additional type of humor—sexual humor with an exploitative sexual theme (humor in which one person is shown taking sexual advantage of another)—did *not* reduce aggression. Together, the results of all these studies seem to indicate that humor is indeed an effective means of reducing aggression, provided it does not contain an underlying theme of hostility.

Mild Sexual Arousal: Titillation and the Promotion of Restraint

If the proverbial "being from Mars" were to visit the United States or many other nations in the 1990s, it might quickly reach the conclusion that, as a species, we are obsessed with sex. Everywhere our Martian turned, it would see sexually oriented stimuli, on billboards, magazines, the television screen, and a hundred other sources. And this is the key point: for many persons, such stimuli *are* attractive. Moreover, exposure to them induces feelings of titillation that, again, many persons describe as pleasant. To the extent this is true, it seems possible that exposure to such stimuli, too, might induce feelings incompatible with anger and overt aggression.

To determine if this is indeed the case, I again turned to a straightforward laboratory experiment. In an initial study, male subjects were either angered or not angered, and then, before aggressing against a supposed victim (once more, an experimental assistant), were exposed to one of two types of stimuli: photos of highly attractive female nudes, or the same neutral photos of scenery, furniture, and abstract act described previously. I predicted that angry subjects exposed to the nudes would experience positive feelings incompatible with anger and so would demonstrate lower levels of aggression against the victim. In fact, this was true. Moreover, subjects exposed to the nudes did report more positive feelings than those exposed to the neutral photos.

So far, so good. But then, just a couple of months before my article describing this research was scheduled to appear in a major journal, the *same journal* published another paper, by Yoram Jaffe and his colleagues, with precisely opposite results. In this experiment, exposure to sexual materials *increased* rather than reduced aggression. At first, I was stunned. How could sexual stimuli both reduce and increase aggression? As I read and reread this article, however, one possibility quickly came to mind. In my research, subjects had been exposed to relatively mild sexual stimuli—nudes from current issues of *Playboy* and similar magazines. (Remember, this was 1972; the photos in such magazines were considerably less explicit than the ones included today.) In Jaffe's study, subjects read torrid erotic passages—ones that were very graphic and vivid in detail. It seemed possible to me that these stimuli had induced stronger levels of arousal among subjects than the photos of nudes I had used. Further, it seemed clear that while most people find mild levels of sexual arousal pleasant, many find stronger levels—especially when they can do nothing to reduce them—somewhat frustrating. Further, it also seemed possible that the explicit stimuli used by Jaffe and his colleagues may have induced negative as well as positive reactions in some subjects. After all, not everyone likes graphic descriptions of sexual behavior. And even if they do not find such materials objectionable, they may view some aspects of the behavior described as distasteful or unappealing. So, it seemed possible that mild levels of sexual arousal would indeed reduce aggression by inducing positive feelings incompatible with anger. However, stronger levels of arousal, induced by more-explicit stimuli, might induce stronger arousal and negative reactions which would *not* reduce aggression and might, in fact, increase it.

To test this possibility, Paul Bell and I conducted an experiment in which male subjects were angered or not angered, and then, before aggressing by means of the aggression machine, were exposed to one of several types of stimuli. One group saw the same neutral photos of scenery and furniture used in my previous studies. Another saw attractive females in bathing suits and similar outfits. A third saw the same nudes used previously, while those in two additional groups saw photos of explicit sexual acts or read explicit sexual passages. We predicted that aggression would at first decline as sexual arousal increased from near zero to mild or moderate levels, but would then increase at very high levels of arousal. Our findings confirmed this prediction. We then speculated about whether the same findings would occur among females. To find out, we conducted a parallel study with female subjects, but this time we used photos of attractive young men in varying states of undress. The same sexual acts and erotic passages were also employed, since these depicted sexual activity by both sexes. Again, results supported the hypothesis. Aggression decreased as sexual arousal moved from low to mild levels, but then increased as higher levels of arousal were induced among subjects.

INCOMPATIBLE RESPONSES AND AGGRESSION: SUMMING UP

In sum, evidence gathered in many different studies, conducted over almost a 10-year period, provided fairly consistent support for the incompatible response hypothesis. Whether such reactions were induced through exposure to signs of pain and suffering on the part of another person, through humorous cartoons, or through mildly arousing sexual stimuli, results were much the same: aggression was reduced as a function of the presence of such stimuli. It appeared, therefore, that we had uncovered another potentially useful technique for reducing aggression.

But there was one sizable fly in the ointment, so to speak. All of these findings were obtained in laboratory studies employing the aggression machine. There was no direct indication that the incompatible-response approach would work in real-life situations. How could we obtain such evidence? After wrestling with this issue for quite a while, I finally hit upon a possible solution. As you probably know from your own experience, many persons who are mild and reserved in daily life seem to lose their restraint when they get behind the wheel of a vehicle. They may shout at other drivers, make obscene gestures at them, and honk their horns to express their anger or irritation. These observations led me to consider traffic situations as a context in which to conduct field research on the incompatible response hypothesis.

The location for this investigation was a moderately busy intersection near a major university. An automobile driven by one of my assistants would simply pull up to the red traffic signal and stop. If several cars had pulled up behind him, he proceeded as soon as the light turned green, and no data were collected. If only one car was behind, however, he failed to move. In fact, he remained stopped at the light for fully 15 seconds. This is a very long period of time and one during which many drivers demonstrated their irritation by honking their horns, rolling down windows and shouting, or making gestures at the assistant. Needless to say, we recorded all this information, from concealed locations, on a tape recorder and on special rating sheets. In a control (no incompatible response) condition, this is all that happened. In three other conditions, however, we attempted to induce incompatible responses among the frustrated motorists. In one of these conditions (empathy), a female accomplice hobbled across the street on crutches, with a bandage on her leg. In a second (humor) condition, she crossed wearing a humorous clown mask and waved at the waiting motorist as she passed. In a third group (mild sexual arousal), she crossed while wearing a very brief and revealing outfit. In an additional control (the distraction group), a female accomplice merely crossed the street between the assistant's car and the motorist's car. Please note that in all four conditions, the accomplice crossed while the light was still red; which was the only safe way to proceed.

The incompatible-response hypothesis predicts that motorists would be less likely to honk their horns, or take longer to honk, in the empathy, humor, and mild-sexual-arousal conditions than in either the control or distraction group. Results offered clear support for this hypothesis. While fully 90 and 89 percent of the motorists honked in the control condition and distraction groups, only 57, 50, and 47 percent honked in the empathy, humor, and sexual-arousal conditions. Similarly, motorists honked much more quickly in the two control groups than in the three incompatible-response conditions. This study provided evidence that the incompatible-response effect could—and did—occur in realistic contexts as well as within the confines of the research laboratory. To say that I was pleased is an understatement. Everyone likes to be right and to make accurate predictions, and psychologists are no exception to this basic rule. Moreover—and this is far more important—I was (and am) convinced that the incompatible-response approach is a valid and potentially useful means for reducing human aggression. Given the violent nature of the world in which we live, I feel that this is a contribution of more than trivial importance, and one in which I take a bit of pride.

*I*NCOMPATIBLE RESPONSES AND ORGANIZATIONAL CONFLICT: THE ADVENTURE CONTINUES

And that, I thought, was that. As the 1980s dawned, I was convinced that I had done all the research I wished to do with respect to the incompatible-response hypothesis. It was now on its own, and would have to survive—or perish—under the careful scrutiny of other researchers. My career was moving into other areas. I spent two years in Washington, D.C., serving as a program officer at the National Science Foundation. During that time, I decided that I was ready for a change. I was interested, more and more, in applying my knowledge of social psychology to understanding behavior in organizations, especially in work settings. In other words, I was becoming an industrial/organizational psychologist. The topics I chose to study were closely related to my earlier work on aggression. One line of research I decided to pursue was what I now term the interpersonal causes of organizational conflict. I wanted to find out what social factors lay behind the costly conflicts that erupted, all too often, in many large companies.

Within this context, I focused on many different factors: the role of destructive (excessively harsh and inconsiderate) criticism; personality characteristics such as the Type A behavior pattern; and attributions—individuals' conclusions concerning the reasons behind confrontational actions by others. Much to my surprise, however, I found myself drawn again to the incompatible-response hypothesis.

Conflict is a serious problem for many organizations. Managers report that they spend from 15 to 25 percent of their time dealing with some aspect of this problem. Given this fact, it seemed only reasonable to consider various techniques for reducing the frequency or intensity of such conflict. And here is where the incompatible-response hypothesis reemerged in my thinking. As I worked with a growing number of organizations, and observed an increasing sample of conflicts, it became clear that many of these conflicts did not stem from clashes of interest, the traditional explanation for their occurrence. Instead, they seemed to derive from social factors such as anger, grudges, and real or imagined loss of face by the participants. To the extent this was the case, I thought the incompatible-response approach might be just as effective in resolving organizational conflict as it had been in reducing overt aggression. To explore this possibility, I conducted several related experiments.

In the first of these experiments, male and female subjects played the role of an executive in a large organization, and discussed two issues currently facing their company: should it relocate to the Sunbelt and should it invest heavily in the manufacture of a new product (a telephone that could be used while airplanes were in flight). One of the persons present was actually an assistant, specially trained to disagree with whatever views the real subject happened to adopt. The style in which the assistant disagreed, however, was systematically varied. In one condition, the assistant disagreed in a calm and reasonable fashion (e.g., "I can see why you feel that way, but I guess I disagree."). In another the assistant disagreed in an irritating and condescending manner (e.g., "Oh come on, how could anyone possibly feel that way?"). A second aspect of the study took place after the discussion of both issues was complete. At this time, the experimenter left the room for a few moments, presumably to get some needed forms. During this period, the assistant either sat quietly or engaged in one of three actions designed to induce positive feelings, incompatible with anger, among subjects. He either offered them some candy (a cherry Lifesaver), explained that he was very tense because of several important exams, or asked them to help him choose the funniest of several cartoons for use in a class project. When the experimenter returned, participants completed a questionnaire on which they rated the assistant on several dimensions (e.g., likability, pleasantness) and indicated how they would respond to future conflicts with him. They did this by rating their likelihood of using five different modes of conflict resolution: avoidance of the problem, direct competition with the assistant, surrender to his demands (accommodation), compromise, and collaboration—working together in a "win-win" approach to maximize joint outcomes. These had been shown, in previous research, to represent basic modes of conflict resolution.

Results indicated that subjects assigned lower ratings to the accomplice and reported a stronger likelihood of reacting negatively to him in future conflicts when he had behaved in a condescending manner than in a reasonable one. Second, and of greater importance, they reported more willingness to collaborate with him when they had been exposed to the incompatible-response-generating procedures than when they had not. In other words, those given a small gift, exposed to humorous cartoons, or induced to feel sorry for the assistant (to experience sympathy for him), reported being more likely to adopt a collaboration strategy than those in the control condition.

These findings were extended in follow-up studies in which different procedures were used to induce incompatible responses among angry subjects. My colleagues and I found that small gifts and self-deprecating remarks by one's opponent (e.g., "I really have no experience in these things, so I don't know whether I'm making the right offers or not") both significantly increased tendencies to make concessions to one's opponent and to report preferences for collaborating with this person, during simulated negotiations. Mild flattery by the opponent (e.g.,

"You're really doing a good job representing your department") pro-duced similar but weaker effects. In contrast, excessive flattery (e.g., "Gee, my opponent . . . is one of the sharpest people I've met recent-ly. . . .") did not produce these effects.

Taken together, the results of these studies indicate that the intensity or persistence of conflict may sometimes be reduced through the induc-tion of positive-affective responses, incompatible with anger or irritation. Moreover, such procedures seem to be effective when performed during confrontations or negotiations, as well as when performed before indi-viduals have an opportunity to express their anger in overt terms.

Does this mean that negotiators should rush out and purchase sup-plies of candy or other small gifts, begin collecting cartoons and jokes, or start practicing their delivery of flattering remarks? Not necessarily. All of these techniques for inducing incompatible responses can—and sometimes do—backfire. If individuals perceive that gifts, humor, or flattery are being used to "soften them up," then they may react with anger, and subsequent conflicts may be intensified rather than reduced. Clearly efforts to reduce organizational conflict through the induction of incompatible responses must be undertaken with consid-erable caution.

It should be noted that professional negotiators often use such tactics in an effort to enhance the likelihood of reaching mutually beneficial agreements, especially in instances where negative emotions, such as anger, threaten to interfere with the overall process. In a sense, therefore, such persons have been using the incompatible-response strategy all along. My research over the past two decades has begun to indicate how such tactics operate—what psychological mechanisms they involve—and has helped identify specific procedures that may be useful in inducing responses incompatible with anger and aggression among recipients. What remains to be done is to determine precisely when such proce-dures will be helpful and when they may fail. Answering these questions will undoubtedly involve tying the incompatible-response strategy more closely to recent advances in our understanding of the complex interplay between affect and cognition—how feelings shape thoughts and thoughts shape feelings. I look forward to helping to forge such links in the years ahead, as I continue what now appears to be a career-long affair with the idea that, usually, it is difficult (if not impossible) to feel good and act aggressively at the same time.

SUGGESTED READINGS

BARON, R. A. (1983). The control of human aggression: A strategy based on incompatible responses. In R. G. Geen & E. I. Donnerstein (Eds.),

Aggression: Theoretical and empirical reviews (pp. 173–190). New York: Academic.

_____ & RICHARDSON, D. R. (1992). *Human aggression* (2nd ed). New York: Plenum.

RAHIM , M. A. (Ed.) (1990). *Theory and research in conflict management.* New York: Praeger.

*E*LIZABETH RICE ALLGEIER *(Ph.D., Purdue University) is currently Professor of Psychology and Director of the Social Psychology Program at Bowling Green State University, where she was awarded the Alumni Association's Master Teacher Award in 1988. The author of numerous books, chapters, articles, and papers, she and her husband A. R. "Rick" Allgeier published the third edition of their text,* Sexual Interactions, *in 1991. She was named by the American Psychological Association as a G. Stanley Hall Lecturer on sexuality in 1986. Actively involved with The Society for the Scientific Study of Sex, Dr. Allgeier has been a Fellow of that organization since 1983, and served as its 1985–86 President. Dr. Allgeier has served on the editorial boards of four professional journals and is Editor-Elect of* The Journal of Sex Research. *She loves traveling and watching college basketball, and she is an avid reader of mystery and espionage novels.*

15

So-So Sexuality: Field Research on Gender Roles With a Preliterate Polygynous African Tribe

❖

Many of us who lived in the San Francisco Bay area during the 1960s attempted to live out a number of utopian fantasies. During that period communes flourished, the latest movements toward gender equality began to take root, young people were politically active in their attempts to bring the Vietnam War to an end, and some tried to engage in so-called free speech and free love. We were called Flower Children, and some of us thought that by renouncing materialism, private ownership, gender role restrictions, and sexual exclusivity, we could provide a model for a better world.

Toward the end of that period, anthropologist Charles Laughlin received a National Science Foundation grant to study economic redistribution during times of scarcity among a preliterate, polygynous tribe in Northeastern Uganda called the So. Laughlin (my former spouse), our three young daughters, and I flew from the United States to Uganda. Although Laughlin was interested in the So's economic system, I wanted to study their beliefs and behaviors regarding gender roles and how those related to their reproductive and sexual relationships. By virtue of being polygynous (literal meaning: many women; connotation: a relationship form in which it is acceptable for men to have more than one spouse), the male members of the So had the opportunity to engage in multiple sexual relationships and marriages. I was curious to see how that worked for them because despite the protestations of my fellow flower children that if you loved someone, you ought to be happy if they were happy involving themselves sexually with others, many of these relationships foundered when jealousy reared its ugly head. The intensity of the jealous feelings was such that those experiencing them thought that they were somehow "natural." Thus, I was interested to see if the So had found a mechanism by which wives were not jealous of one another when their husbands had multiple partners. If true, the claim that jealousy is a "natural" condition for humans who share mates would not be supported.

Prior to going to Uganda, I had been involved in a seminar on the year 2000 at the University of Oregon. Since the issue of overpopulation was a major concern of the seminar, I was also interested in the family-size desires of the So and how their norms about reproduction might interact with gender-role expectations and with sexual practices.

When we left for Africa, all that we knew about the So was that they herded cattle and were polygynous. Because the So were relatively untouched by 20th-century civilization, I had some rather naive Rousseauian expectations that they would exemplify open, uninhibited sexual expression.

First we went to Kampala, the capital of Uganda, to gather the sparse information that was available on the So provided by missionaries' records and government documents and to purchase supplies (tents, kerosene refrigerator, medicines, and food). We bought a Land Rover and painted it with red designs (peace symbols and other abstract designs) to make it clear that it wasn't a government vehicle. Traveling northeast into the hotter and drier climate, we noticed that the Ugandans wore less clothing. As we neared Moroto, the village at the base of Mt. Moroto where we were to live for the next nine months, the men were totally nude, or, in some cases, dressed in nothing but a cape slung over one shoulder. I was fascinated because I had only seen one penis at a time and, all of a sudden, here were all kinds of penises in different shapes and sizes in open view. At no time, however, were the women totally nude in public. They always wore an abbreviated piece of cloth or leather that covered their pubic hair but left their buttocks bare.

After a few weeks in the village of Moroto, we were surprised to hear that the So were cannibals. We felt more than a bit anxious about our well-being. Although there had been no other indications that we might be in danger of providing dinner, it was with some trepidation that we drove as far up the mountain as we could. That wasn't far, as there were no roads. We left the Land Rover and trudged farther up the slopes of Mt. Moroto. Within 15 minutes, we were greeted by an elderly woman, followed by a number of other So. The woman and I smiled at each other, and she reached out to take our two-year-old daughter, Katy, from my arms. Although the earlier claims that the So were cannibals turned out to be unfounded, I was nonetheless reluctant to hand over our youngest daughter, partly because of the brownish liquid oozing from a hole in the woman's lower lip. The lip holes were considered attractive and were usually filled with some sort of metal plug; a practice similar to ours in North America except that we make holes in our ear lobes and dangle objects from them. The woman wasn't wearing a plug that day, and I later discovered that the liquid that had formed a narrow stream down her chin onto one dusty breast and down to her stomach was a mixture of saliva and tobacco that the So liked to chew. I did hold Katy out to her, and Nate (her name, as we later discovered) took her and tried to cuddle her, but Katy began to wail loudly, so Nate shook her head back and forth, and we smiled at each other as she handed Katy back to me. That was our initial contact with the So.

ENVIRONMENTAL, ECONOMIC, AND SOCIAL BACKGROUND

Before I describe how I studied the So's gender-role beliefs and their sexual attitudes and behaviors, I want to tell you about the general environmental, economic, and social context in which the So lived. Mount Moroto is arid and desertlike with no standing water: the concept of a lake or river was unknown to the So.

The So lived in huts within fenced compounds. There were 51 compounds on Mt. Moroto, containing an average of about 10 huts each. An average of 31 (range = 2 to 89) people lived in each compound. It was very hot, frequently over 100° during the day, but because of the very low humidity, I found the heat far more bearable than an 80° summer day in Ohio.

The So were organized into 15 different clans. Cattle and goats provided the basis of a clan's (and a man's) wealth and status. The livestock were owned by men (not women) and often loaned to other members of their clan when needed to pay for wives. The cows and goats were slaughtered, roasted, and eaten only for such ceremonial or ritual purposes as funerals or weddings; they were not eaten on a daily basis even during periods of famine due to crop failure. They milked the cows and goats, drank some of the milk, and made butter out of the rest. Occasionally they made a small incision in the jugular vein of a cow and drank a small amount of blood.

Their main source of food was from their gardens and from gathering wild edible plants and roots. They also raised a few chickens, and shortly after we arrived, one of the women brought us an egg—a major gift. The gardens were owned and tended primarily by women, although there were a few old bachelors who maintained their own gardens. They had two growing seasons a year during which they cultivated sorghum and maize. They also had frequent droughts and no means of irrigating their crops. During our first growing season, there was plenty of rain, but the second growing season failed and a number of very old and very young So died from a combination of malnutrition, dehydration, and the endemic diseases of the area: hepatitis, malaria, and dysentery.

The So governed themselves (although the word "governed" suggests a more formal structure than was accurate) by a council of elderly male representatives of each of the 15 clans. The council made decisions for the tribe on a variety of issues ranging from how to retaliate against neighboring tribes to the appropriate punishment for an adulterous woman. In most cases, nonmembers of the council could observe their deliberations, but decisions were made only by the council members, and women could not become members. This practice of governance only by men is similar to what exists in many of the major religious organizations in Western industrialized countries. The principal difference is that many members of Western cultures question the exclusion of women from religious policy-making bodies, whereas among the So, the exclusion of women was taken for granted. I will point out that there were a few elderly and highly respected So women who were able to exert indirect power on council decisions. For example, the husband of one elderly couple was a council member. He was also frequently drunk on the native beer that the So made. His eldest wife was viewed as wise and she frequently instructed him on what positions she thought he should take on various issues, not unlike the perception the American public had of the relationship between Ronald and Nancy Reagan (the parallel that I draw here is not to drinking, of course, but to a wife's influence over a powerful husband's policy positions).

Beyond the issue of governance, there were many other sharp differentiations between the roles and acceptable behaviors for males versus females. Women were of value for two major purposes: their capacity to have babies and their diligence as gardeners. In all formal respects, men had more status, power, leisure, and sexual freedom than did women. Women prepared meals for their families, but the men were served their meals separately from the women and young children. Men's lives were also at far greater risk, because only males participated in livestock raids on neighboring tribes or in the defense of their own cattle. The gender differentiation was expressed in both significant and relatively trivial ways. Only males could make decisions affecting the tribe and have multiple wives and sexual partners. Only males could sit on the three-legged stools they whittled, as I discovered after sitting on one shortly after we arrived only to be told politely and apologetically that women do not sit on them. When a cow or goat was slaughtered for ritual purposes, the most edible portions of the meat were distributed to the men who gathered near the roasting animal; women sat on the periphery of the group with their children, and were given such delicacies as goat jaw for their portion. As a function of being a woman, of course, I sat with the So women during such ceremonies and found the loss of the status that I enjoyed in my own culture (and the chewing of the tough goat jaw) difficult at times.

We spent the first few weeks on Mt. Moroto setting up camp, which consisted of two small tents covered by a thatch roof and surrounded by a fence that the So built for us so that we, too, would be protected from the raids of neighboring tribes. Actually, although we got into the Land Rover to avoid being hit by stray arrows and spears during the frequent raids, we were in no danger because we didn't own any livestock.

RESEARCH METHODS

Our first active research endeavor was to conduct a census of the entire group on Mt. Moroto, partially so that we could draw a random sample of families for the series of interviews we had planned. We went to every compound and collected genealogies for the 1,649 people living on Mt. Moroto. The gender ratio was 88 males for every 100 females. Using a table of random numbers, we selected a sample of 20 families. This was a time-consuming process. It would have been easier, of course, to conduct interviews with those members of the So who had approached us initially, but the more gregarious members of the tribe might not have been representative of the tribe as a whole, and we wanted to be able to generalize our findings to the entire group. Thus, a random sample of families was necessary.

A family was headed by a wife and included her preadolescent children and her husband, although he only lived in her hut full-time if he had no other wives. Such monogamous marriages comprised 45 percent of our sample. The first wife of a man with more than one wife was referred to as the "big" wife; subsequent wives were referred to as "little" wives. If a man had two wives (as 30 percent of the men did), three wives (20 percent), or four wives (5 percent), he divided his time equally among his wives. For example, a man with four wives (four was the largest number of wives any So male had at the time we were there) lived with each for a week before beginning the cycle again. This "equal time" policy appeared to be affected only by how much food a woman could provide during times of famine and her menstrual cycle. Husbands generally did not sleep in the hut of a wife while she was menstruating because they believed that to do so would be to risk disease. The sole exception to this involved a man who was unusually taken with his "little" wife; and he made it clear that although he would sleep in her hut while she was menstruating, they did not engage in sexual intercourse during her menstrual period.

After selecting the sample, we approached each family and

explained that we would like them to teach us about the So, and that we would pay them to meet with us for interviews once every two weeks. Using a portable typewriter, I constructed the interview schedule involving sets of semi-structured items and altered the items for subsequent interviewing sessions based on the results of previous interviews. During the first few interviews we collected relatively innocuous background information. After that, I began to ask questions relevant to their gender-role and sexual norms, beliefs, and behaviors. I conducted the interviews separately with wives and husbands, going as far at each session as I could, given the constraints of time and sensitivity of the questions.

The only difficulty I had with the women came during the initial interviews while I was still trying to learn the language. In the dirt I drew pictures of bodies, including genital anatomy, and asked the women to tell me the So words for the different body parts. It turned out that there was no word for clitoris nor any concept of such an organ. There was also no word for masturbation or female orgasm. There was a word for the excitement of ejaculation, but that was seen as a word, and an experience, applicable only to males.

Because of So norms regarding discussion between males and females about sexuality, I initially had more difficulty obtaining the cooperation of the men. With each of the men, I explained that the only way that I could learn about them was for them to tell me about the So and their lives. They would agree, but each time I asked a sensitive question during the early interviews, they politely explained to me that men weren't supposed to talk to women about such things, just as they had politely pointed out my faux pas in sitting on one of the three-legged stools. I would reiterate the necessity of their talking to me if I were to learn, and after a few interviews, they appeared to accept my norm- and role-violations.

Rather than describe what I learned in the order in which I learned it, I will report So lifestyles in a rough developmental sequence. My information on the gender-role and sexual socialization and behavior of children came from direct observation, memories of adults in the sample, as well as their observations and expectations of their children and reports by our daughters.

GENDER-ROLE AND SEXUAL REHEARSAL AND EDUCATION

Infants were initially cared for and breastfed by their mothers, but because women of child-bearing age were at their prime in terms of

being able to care for gardens and hunt for edible wild foods, the daily
care of infants was taken over by elderly women and older sisters, within
two or three months following birth. Depending upon the distance
between the compound and a woman's garden, the infant would either
remain in the compound most of the day and be carried by a five- or six-
year-old sister to her mother's garden for breastfeeding, or the older sister would accompany her mother to the garden with the infant and
watch the infant under a thatched wall-less roof while her mother
worked. Infants were also comforted by human pacifiers—that is, elderly
women would "dry" nurse irritable babies. As the girls grew older they
spent increasing amounts of time helping their mothers tend their gardens, gather plants and berries, and prepare foods.

Meanwhile, boys were expected to help their fathers in herding the
cows and goats from the compounds in which they were kept to grazing
areas. This division of labor by gender was affected to some extent by the
gender composition of children in the family. That is, a woman who had
only sons would be helped with the care of younger children by an older
son; in a family with only daughters, an older daughter would help with
goat herding. The So women, however, tended to have close relationships with one another and would lend their children to one another to
engage in gender-appropriate roles, so that cross-gender-role behavior
was the exception rather than the rule.

From the age of nine or ten for boys and somewhat younger for girls,
children engaged in various forms of sexual rehearsal. It was common to
observe a boy running at full speed toward the back of a girl and thrust-
ing his pelvis forward at her buttocks as he collided with her. This
was done in public with no apparent embarrassment, and onlookers,
including the adults, laughed. I, too, laughed when our two older
daughters first received this kind of attention, although it did inspire me
to initiate discussion with them about "appropriate" and "inappropriate" physical contact at a younger age than I would have done had we
been in the United States. More privately, boys and girls stood or laid
against one another and rubbed their bodies together, but as far as we
could discover, vaginal penetration didn't occur among prepubescent
children.

Until they reached the age of about nine, children lived in their
mothers' huts, and thus had the opportunity to observe parental intercourse. They also reported watching postpubescent couples having intercourse in the bush, although this "voyeurism" was neither invited, nor
permitted if discovered. Such observations, along with their own experimentation, comprised their sex education. Parents did not provide information about sexuality to either their same- or other-gender offspring.
The few women who received any information from their mothers
reported that they were told that intercourse was something they had to

do to get children, but there was no indication that sexual interaction might be enjoyable in its own right, and most children were told nothing at all.

MASTURBATION

Young boys engaged in the same kind of casual genital manipulation that can be observed in American children. I did not, however, see any young boys stimulating their penises when they were erect, nor did I see young girls touch their vulvas. I was told by adults that men didn't masturbate except maybe if they were off by themselves on a long trip, but that to do so otherwise would be evidence of possession by a witch or hyena (a critter believed to invade people with its spirit, making them crazy). A normal man wouldn't waste his seed that way. It was not conceivable to any man or woman with whom I talked that a woman could or would masturbate.

Evidence that adolescent males masturbated was provided by our six-year-old daughter. She had developed a friendship with a pubescent boy, and one day she came home and asked me what the white sticky stuff was that came out of the penis. I said that it was probably semen, and asked her to tell me more about it. It seems that when she and the young man had stopped to talk while on their walk, he leaned up against a large boulder, and began rubbing his penis with his hands, and this "stuff" came out.

MENSTRUATION AND PUBERTY

Most of the women in our sample were not told about menstruation by their mothers, nor did they subsequently discuss it with their daughters. A few women were told about menstruation by older sisters or other older girls, but most were unaware of menstruation until their menarche, and when they first saw their own menstrual discharge, they assumed that they were sick or had injured themselves. This conclusion is not unlike that reported by a few of my American college students when asked about their menarche.

When menstruation began, older sisters or female friends taught pubescent girls the proper procedures to follow. They oiled their thighs and pubic area and lined their vulva with leaves that they tied on under their aprons. The leaves with the menstrual discharge were later buried.

The onset of reproductive maturity was officially recognized by parents. If the family had enough resources, a ceremony—*asapan*—was held for boys. The beaded G-string for girls was replaced by an elaborate skin apron that took their mothers months to make. Again, if resources permitted, a feast was held. Neither circumcision nor clitorectomy (removal of the clitoral hood or clitoris) was performed.

PUBESCENT SEXUALITY AND COURTSHIP

There is no discernible phase among the So that corresponds to our concept of adolescence. After puberty, interest in sexual activity turns to the choice of a marriage partner.

Evening dancing was a frequent activity among the So, involving all ages and ranging from rhythmic jumping up and down in place to very explicit sexual dancing. In the latter, a man faced a woman with a hand on either side of her waist while she held her arms out at an angle on each side of his. They engaged in a series of distinctly sexual hip thrusts in the center of a group of people who produced a beat with rhythmic clapping. At times a man rhythmically moved his hands up and down a woman's body from above her waist down to her hips.

When asked about the characteristics that make a person sexually attractive, So responses made me think that they were hearing me ask, "On what basis would you choose a spouse or coworker." In my attempts at clarification, I asked specifically about body types, facial characteristics, and so forth. Facially, a pleasant expression was described as desirable by So males, apparently because it was seen as an index to temperament, rather than as a source of attraction per se. One young woman who closely fit American ideals of sexual attractiveness (slender, relatively narrow hips, high firm breasts, and rounded pretty face) was not seen as attractive or desirable as a wife by So males because she was "disobedient," "lazy," and generally uppity. I was told that another young woman with a harelip would have a hard time finding a husband, not because of the harelip, but because she was not a good worker. Characteristics deemed important by men, then, were industriousness, fertility, and something that might be labeled "non-bitchiness." Women of the So evaluated the courtship behavior of men as an indication of their behavior during marriage, and the evaluation seemed to be primarily in terms of avoiding negative attributes: I was told that, "If he talks rudely, or if he beats you, he will do it more when you marry him." A number of women, however, indicated that they had, in fact, married men they didn't like at first, because they *did* want the status of marriage. One woman who hadn't liked her husband when he was courting her said, "Some men you don't like, some men you do, but when you marry them, you will like them later on." The general pattern was for men to visit the compound of women they wished to court; but after a woman had chosen one, the others "went away."

ATTRACTION AND FANTASY

Among Western adolescents and adults, fantasy and mental sexual rehearsals are very common and often quite elaborate. While doing chores, driving, or sometimes while listening to boring lectures, we imagine extended conversations and interactions with those to whom we feel attracted. To explore the fantasy-lives of the So, I constructed a series of questions to ask several So people with whom I had developed friendships and who were not members of our sample. This process, known as conducting a "pilot test," allows a researcher to determine if questions are reasonable and to refine or replace those questions that are confusing or inappropriate. One of our friends, Auca, had stopped by to see me on his way to visit a woman in whom he was interested. I asked what he thought would happen if they were able to be alone together. He said that he didn't know, nor had he thought about it. After further probing, he indicated that there was no way to know, so why would you think about it? The same pattern of responses emerged from another young man I saw flirting with a young woman. We talked about her, and he indicated that he liked her and that she was nice. But he, too, had no idea what would happen, and also could see no point in thinking about it.

In this regard, it was interesting that Napaluk, my *daquath* (sister) when I was initiated into the tribe, was a specialist in dream divination. That is, she could "tell the future" with her dreams, and frequently used her skill to warn people that they were going to get sick or be injured. She was seen as having a special talent and people took her advice seriously, but no one else paid much attention to their sleeping or waking "dreams" (fantasies). Further, like my male friends, Napaluk did not recall having waking thoughts or fantasies of what might happen in the future, and she interpreted her dreams as messages from her ancestors or *akuc* (God) about problems that might arise.

HETEROSEXUAL BONDING AND MARRIAGE

There were no age restrictions on heterosexual relations providing that the couple was neither closely related nor members of the same clan, and the female was not married to someone else. Marriage, intercourse, and pregnancy for a female (not necessarily in that order) were seen as normal within a few years following puberty. When a woman agreed to marry a man, she told her father; and if he and his lineage agreed, the man told his father, who discussed it with his clan. Most So were quite poor, and if the family of a young man didn't have the livestock needed to buy the young woman he wanted, it was still acceptable for them to *apudori*—copulate. If partial brideprice was paid, they were partially married. However, any children that they conceived belonged to her clan until he paid the appropriate number of cows for her. The price was determined during negotiations between their fathers or other older male members of the two clans. These negotiations took place on the day of the wedding in the groom's compound, and the haggling could be quite lengthy. On the average, the cost of a wife was about 23 cows, 6 bulls, and 11 goats, with the price varying as a function of the size and wealth of the man's lineage (clan), the bargaining skill of the fathers, the personality and status of the groom, and the availability and liquidity of lineage resources. Both women and children were viewed as property.

After brideprice was paid and a couple married, the man had sole sexual access to the woman until he died or they separated. The latter was very rare, because it entailed repayment of cows from her clan to his, ownership of their offspring by her clan rather than his, etc. Thus, a woman was strongly counseled by her relatives to maintain the relationship. Married men, on the other hand, could legitimately have sexual access to anyone providing that the woman was not married to someone else.

SEXUAL AND REPRODUCTIVE ATTITUDES AND EXPERIENCES

Women unanimously described their first experience with intercourse as painful, unpleasant, and a responsibility to be endured. Napaluk's report was typical: There was a sharp burning sensation when she was penetrated and she said that she told herself over and over while it was going on that, "I have to do this to get babies, I have to get babies to get cows, I have to do this to get babies," and so on. While telling me, she rocked back and forth, with her teeth and hands clenched. Over the years, it became less painful, but was still unpleasant, and she bemoaned the fact that her husband didn't have enough cows to buy a little wife who would share marital duties with her.

Male descriptions of first and current feelings about intercourse were very different. They smiled, at times, even grinned, when talking about the enjoyment of it, and one man said that one of the bad things about the droughts and subsequent famines was that when he was very hungry, there wasn't as much "blood" (passion).

Women were abstinent during menstruation, throughout the second half of pregnancy ("because there is already someone in there"), for six months to a year after childbirth, and after menopause. The prime importance attached to women's reproductive role was shown in the fact that if a woman's husband died before the end of her capacity to conceive, she would be married to one of her husband's brothers or other relatives. If she became a widow following menopause, however, she would not be remarried. Women's feelings about sex and their ready acceptance of periods of abstinence made more sense to me after they described their coital positions and stimulation techniques (or lack thereof).

The So sexual repertoire was not extensive. Using pencils that I described as a man and a woman, with the erasers representing the heads, I asked if they had had sex like this (male pencil on top of female pencil, erasers at same end). The men smiled, and said yes. The women did not smile, but said yes. I then asked if they had had sex like this (female pencil on top of male pencil) and almost all members of the sample said no. One young man—rather atypical in some other ways, too—indicated that he and his little wife (not a member of our sample) had had woman-above coitus once or twice. Finally, I reversed the position of one of the pencils (eraser of man to lead point of woman, trying to suggest oral-genital stimulation), and asked if they had had sex like this. Although a few people simply said no, most members of the sample looked at me as if I were crazy, asking things like, "How can that be?" At first I thought there might be a problem with my pencil figures and that perhaps they thought I was suggesting oral-foot stimulation, but after probing, it became clear that it was the noncoital qualities of the representation that were foreign to them. I asked very specifically about oral stimulation of the genitals and was told that this was not done, and that to do so would be evidence that one had been possessed by a hyena. One man, who didn't invoke the hyena explanation, said that there would be no point because conception couldn't occur, and anyway, it would be too smelly down there.

After inquiring about coital positions, I asked a series of questions about noncoital stimulation—kissing, manual stimulation of breasts and nipples, massage, and manual stimulation of the genitals. None of these behaviors are part of their repertoire, and, in fact, it is considered wrong to touch the genitals except for incidental brushing of the labia while inserting the penis.

Women sometimes received treatment by a healer, not for sexual dysfunction, but for infertility. The treatment, however, included many of the practices associated with Western sex therapy: systematic desensitization, relaxation training, massage, and forbidding intercourse for a period of time. The only practice not yet reported in the literature on contemporary sex therapy but used by So healers was to anoint the woman with the entrails of a goat. Treatment for infertility was not provided for men, as it was assumed that women were the source of any difficulties with conception. Further, it was considered legitimate for a man to divorce his wife if they (she) did not conceive within a few years.

Further evidence of the importance attached to women's primary roles as "baby factories" was the assumption that if a woman didn't produce children every two or three years, there must be something wrong with her. As time went on, I received increasingly blunt questions about when I was going to have another child (our youngest was two and a half when we began living with the So), and by the time I began to receive inquiries regarding whether something was wrong, I understood enough of their values to know that it would be pointless to explain that there were other things I wanted to do—other roles that were important to me—besides making babies. I did not tell them about my diaphragm, but their reactions to my questions about what they could do if they wanted to postpone or avoid pregnancy indicated as much astonishment as my inquiries about oral sex. It was inconceivable to them that a woman would try to avoid pregnancy, and when asked how many babies they would like to have ideally (another nonsensical question from their standpoint), the universal answer was "as many as possible." *The* purpose, then, of being a woman, was to be a mother.

Thinking back to my interest in the problem of overpopulation that we had discussed in our seminar on the year 2000 at the University of Oregon, I thought that it was possible that the provision of alternate and valued roles for women might be one solution to the problem of overpopulation in underdeveloped nations. I subsequently tested the relationship between gender-role identification and family-size desires when I returned to the United States. I asked Purdue University students who held traditional gender identities versus androgynous identities (incorporating both masculine and feminine characteristics and behaviors in their self-descriptions) to indicate the number of children they would like to have. As I expected, the androgynous women wanted smaller families than did the traditionally feminine women. I should note that overpopulation was not a problem among the So because although a woman might have 12 or more children, many of them died during infancy. I vividly remember holding one young woman who had lost four of her five children during infancy or early childhood and who was crying because her one remaining child was quite ill.

In addition to expressing concern about my apparent "infertility," the So tried to be helpful by suggesting that my husband buy some little wives so that he could sire more offspring. From their standpoint, if not from ours, we were very wealthy, and they could not understand his disinclination to accept their advice (or my utter lack of enthusiasm for the idea!).

EXTRAMARITAL SEX

During the time that we lived with the So, one of the women in our sample was charged with adultery. Specifically, she went down the mountain to Nakapeliman, a small village near Moroto, drank a lot of beer, and was later found off a path on the way back up the mountain lying with a So man who had also had a lot of beer. Although she told me that they had both simply passed out on the way home, she was accused of adultery and the council of elders met to decide what to do. Following their deliberations, she was surrounded by many members of the tribe who beat her and threw stones at her. After the stoning, she came to see me with her head held high but pretty banged up. I cleaned her wounds and applied iodine and bandages. In our conversation, there was not a hint of guilt. The events had happened to her, she had been punished, and as far as I could tell, that was that. Her husband was not happy about the situation, but demonstrated similar acceptance of it: "These things happen." An illustration of the difference in their beliefs about gender roles was shown in the penalty paid by the man with whom she had been found. He was ordered by the council to pay cows to her husband's clan, but was not beaten or punished in any other way. That is, essentially, he was guilty of theft of the husband's property, and so had to pay restitution. That was the only reported case of adultery and beating/stoning that occurred during the time that we lived with the So, and I was told that it was very rare.

FRIENDSHIP

I will conclude my description of the So by talking about their friendship patterns. It was very common during the course of a day to see two males, or two females, walking arm in arm or holding hands. Among the close friendships were a number of co-wives. They sometimes lived in the same compound and would help one another with a variety of tasks, including nursing each other's babies, gardening, and making beer. These affectionate contacts between men or between women were not erotic in nature; the So were unusual among the world's cultures in that they reported no homosexuality. When I asked about homosexuality, most members of the sample were puzzled: Why would (and how could) a man have sex with a man or a woman with a woman? They patiently explained to me that two men or two women couldn't have a baby, but if two people of the same gender were to try to have sex with each other, it would be one more instance of possession by a hyena or witch.

Affectionate contact between men and women as friends or as spouses was not seen. In fact, the So gathered around our compound one day laughed with embarrassment when my husband patted me casually on the bottom as I was making coffee; their reaction was similar to what might be expected from North American students if their instructor or another student were to break wind loudly during a course lecture.

It is probably clear by now that sexual jealousy was not a common experience for the So. Some of their myths recounted horrible fates for jealous women and their offspring, but I suspect that their aversion to sex and the relative absence of close emotional bonds between marital partners, compared to those existing between same-gender friends, reduced the likelihood of jealousy. Given the high child-mortality rate of 28 percent (21 percent for birth to five years), deaths among young men from the constant intertribal warfare, and the unequal gender ratio (.88 to 1), it was understandable that they would value women having as many children as possible during their reproductive years. From that standpoint, male-female love (a concept for which the So had no word) may be seen as a luxurious by-product of affluent civilizations.

A PERSONAL CONCLUDING NOTE

The opportunity to live with the So for a year was invaluable in providing me with a perspective on gender and gender roles that is difficult to obtain when one stays within the confines of one's own culture. Our perceptions of what is natural or right are always colored by our own socialization and experiences, and I am no exception. I was a 28-year-old American mother of three daughters at the time that we went to Uganda I assumed that it was my responsibility to take the major role in parenting and house maintenance; and although I had aspirations that extended beyond my house, I believed that I could work toward those goals only *after* finishing the dishes, laundry, and other household responsibilities. The problem with dishes and other house-maintenance activities, of course, is that they are never truly completed, but it took me a while to learn to leave some of these chores undone without feeling guilty about neglecting my "real" responsibilities in favor of completing my education, or conducting research.

In that sense, the So women may be seen as blessed. Despite their relatively subordinate status in their society, they were highly valued for their ability to perform the wife/mother role and valued themselves in carrying out that role. They did not imagine themselves as members of the council of elders, for example, making decisions affecting others beyond their own children, nor did they aspire to such roles. The notion that sexual intimacy could be a source of great physical and emotional pleasure was also foreign to them. The idea that there might be something unfair about stoning and beating a woman "convicted" of adultery, but merely fining her "lover" simply didn't occur to them.

In contrast, I am part of the transitional generation in North America which has vastly increased the range of opportunities available to people regardless of their gender. Women like myself who were socialized to believe that it was acceptable to attempt roles and accomplishments beyond our roles as wives and mothers have had to contend with internal arguments with themselves about neglecting their "primary" purpose even as they have intellectually accepted and politically supported "liberation" for women—that is, access to the same opportunities that men experience to contribute more broadly to society. I strongly support that movement, but I have a favorite quote from sociologist Alice Rossi (1978):

> Modern society is a mere second in our evolutionary history, and it is naive to assume that our audacious little experiments in communal living, birth control, sexual liberation and sex-role equality can overturn in a century, let alone a decade, millennia of custom and adaptation. [p. 72]

As I sit here at the word-processor, Rick, my husband of 17 years, has just returned from a trip to the grocery store and is folding laundry from the dryer. He and our 12-year-old son are about to play basketball in our front yard, and the nicest thing for me is that I no longer feel guilty that I choose right now to engage in professional activity. In the last few decades, educated North American men and women have begun to enjoy the opportunity of experiencing a range of options based on their interests and talents rather than exclusively on their gender. But these increased opportunities are generally limited to highly educated and affluent members of our society—the opportunity for men to take a more active role in caring for their offspring physically and emotionally, and the opportunity for women to develop meaningful nonfamilial roles—as well as enjoying the creation and nurturance of a family if that is what they choose. The movement toward gender equality has not yet been completed, but I believe that to complete it, we must focus more on education and the provision of equal opportunities for blacks, Hispanics, and other groups. I agree with Alice Rossi that it was audacious to assume that we could overturn millennia of custom and adaptation in freeing people from rigidly prescribed roles based on gender. But our audaciousness has paid off, and we need to help our more constricted brothers and sisters to be able to realize their potential.

SUGGESTED READINGS

ALLGEIER, E. R. (1975). Beyond sowing and growing: The relationship of sex-typing to socialization, family plans, and future orientation. *Journal of Applied Social Psychology, 5,* 217–226.

_____ & ALLGEIER, A. R. (1991). *Sexual interactions* (3rd ed.). Lexington, MA: D. C. Heath.

_____ & McCORMICK, N. B. (1983). *Changing boundaries: Gender roles and sexual behavior.* Palo Alto, CA: Mayfield.

HEILBRUN, C. G. (1989). *Writing a woman's life.* New York: Ballantine.

LAUGHLIN, C. D., JR., & ALLGEIER, E. R. (1979). *Ethnography of the So of Northeastern Uganda.* New Haven, CT: Human Relations Area Files.

ROSSI, A. S. (1978). The biosocial side of parenthood. *Human Nature, 1,* 72–79.

Epilogue

---- ❖ ----

We hope you've come to see that psychological research is a dynamic and captivating process. Through the personal accounts of fifteen researchers, you have seen how science really happens. Research generally progresses in small steps, as a result of well-planned experiments, perseverance, and, at times, a bit of luck. Research is exacting but rewarding.

We spent a great deal of time researching and preparing this book. Input was gathered from many sources. To further develop and improve our work, we would appreciate your feedback on *The Undaunted Psychologist: Adventures in Research*. Please pass along your thoughts to us at the Department of Psychology, State University of New York— Plattsburgh, Plattsburgh, New York 12901.

Thank you.

Gary G. Brannigan
Matthew R. Merrens